praise for
MICHAEL NEWTON'S
work

Journey ...

A m ...

exr ... ied.—Dr. Hanz Holzer,
author of *Life Beyond*

This remarkable, fast-moving book uncovers some of the
mysteries of life in the spirit world.—*NAPRA Trade Journal*

Journey of Souls and *Destiny of Souls* are two of the most
fascinating books I have ever read.—Shirley MacLaine,
actress and author

Destiny of Souls

A rich volume, chock-full of interviews and fascinating
first-person narratives ... —*Publishers Weekly*

Metaphysical research at its most excellent.
—*NAPRA ReView*

Newton's offering is among the handful that deserve
to be called not just books of the year but germinal,
true culture changers ... —*The Monthly Aspectarian*

Life Between Lives

Newton's explanations are outstanding. For aspiring
spiritual regressionists, the detailed step-by-step format
of this lucid book will be tremendously helpful.
—*New Age Retailer*

Life-Between-Lives
Stories of Personal Transformation

MICHAEL DUFF NEWTON, PhD, is the founder of the Michael Newton Institute for Life Between Lives Hypnotherapy. He is one of the primary editors of this collection of thirty-two stories written by members of the institute. These authors all practice the art of helping people access their memories of the afterlife, an experience of personal transformation that, through this book, may now benefit both the original clients and you, the reader.

Dr. Newton has been a hypnotherapist for over forty-five years and a LBL therapist for over thirty years. He is considered a pioneer in uncovering the mysteries about life after death through the use of spiritual regression. His own books have sold nearly a million copies and have been translated into over thirty languages.

Dr. Newton has appeared on numerous radio and television shows and is an active speaker on the lecture circuit, explaining his discoveries and beliefs about our immortal life in the spirit world. He is now retired from active counseling practice and devotes his time to lecturing and training.

MEMORIES
of the
AFTERLIFE

Life-Between-Lives
Stories of Personal Transformation

Edited by

MICHAEL
NEWTON, PH.D.
with case studies by members of the
NEWTON INSTITUTE

LLEWELLYN PUBLICATIONS
Woodbury, Minnesota

FIRST EDITION
Second Printing, 2009

Book design by Rebecca Zins
Cover design by Lisa Novak
Cover nature scene © Westend61/PunchStock;
cover and interior floral element © Dave Smith/iStockphoto

Llewellyn is a registered trademark of Llewellyn Worldwide, Ltd.

Library of Congress Cataloging-in-Publication Data
Memories of the afterlife : life-between-lives stories of personal transformation / edited by Michael Newton, with contributions from the Michael Newton Institute. —1st ed.
    p. cm.
ISBN 978-0-7387-1527-8
    1. Spiritualism. 2. Reincarnation—Case studies. I. Newton, Michael, 1931–
II. Michael Newton Institute.
BF1261.2.M46 2009
133.901′35—dc22

                                                      2009020619

Llewellyn Publications
A Division of Llewellyn Worldwide, Ltd.
2143 Wooddale Drive, Dept. 978-0-7387-1527-8
Woodbury, MN 55125-2989
www.llewellyn.com

Printed in the United States of America

Dedication

This book is dedicated to its thirty-two authors, practitioners of a difficult craft within the Newton Institute, for the expressive and heartfelt manner in which each of their stories is presented. A special acknowledgment also goes to those generous clients of these LBL facilitators who gave us permission to use their personal stories for the benefit of the public.

Acknowledgments

With sincere appreciation to the two exceptional co-editors of these cases, Angela Noon (international) and Trish Casimira (American), for their ability, tenacity, and commitment in this worthwhile endeavor. Without them, this book would never have seen the light of day.

Finally, I would like to express deep appreciation to my publisher, Llewellyn Worldwide, and its staff for the unfailing support they have given my work over many years. As the largest metaphysical/New Age book publisher in the world, Llewellyn's influence has been inspiring in terms of fostering public awareness about soul discovery and the afterlife through hypnotherapy. The owners of this publishing house, Carl and Sandra Weschcke, have been my steadfast partners from the beginning, and without their insight and effort, it is likely that readers around the world might never have known about the spiritual message I wanted to convey with my books. They have my enduring gratitude.

And, as always, to my wife, Peggy, whose assistance, love, and understanding made it all possible.

I hold that when a person dies
  His soul returns again to earth;
  Arrayed in some new flesh-disguise
  Another mother gives him birth.
  With sturdier limbs and brighter brain
  The old soul takes the roads again.

—John Masefield

Contents

INTRODUCTION

EARLY IN THE fourth century AD, the Greek philosopher Iamblichus wrote: "A man who can unlock his soul is set free."

As a result of the forces of reincarnation, we are all products of our past physical lives on Earth as well as our spiritual soul experiences between lives. The soul of every person on this planet retains all former karmic influences of cause and effect from many sources, and these forces impact our current feelings and behavior. Thus, while people may appear to be functioning normally on the outside, we can have deep-seated metaphysical provocations of distress that are masked from traditional medical doctors, mental health professionals, and even from ourselves. There are difficult episodes in our current lives when we don't comprehend what is driving us in ways that seem irrational. The underlying reasons for these strange sensations are typically obscure, lying far below the surface of our consciousness. Most people will do anything to expose their internal demons, but where should they look?

This book is about the self-discovery of hidden knowledge contained within the unconscious mind and what unlocking this sacred information through hypnosis has meant for people therapeutically. From the hypnosis subjects whose cases are detailed here, we will see how revelations from past incarnations and the afterlife have positively affected their conscious minds, providing keys of understanding to a variety of psychological problems. These recovered spiritual memories have brought greater meaning and empowerment into their lives. This book is meant to inspire and bring new hope to people everywhere who wish to see design and order in their existence.

The cases offered in *Memories of the Afterlife* involve clients who came to a specialized group of life-between-lives (LBL) hypnotherapists for spiritual regression. Quite often, the typical client schedules an appointment simply to explore matters relating to their soul purpose in life. However, the stories in this book involve more disturbing core conflicts requiring specific resolution. The authors of these poignant stories have employed a unique hypnotherapy process with their hypnosis subjects that involves a deep trance state generally lasting from three to four hours. The scope of this book is distinctive in the approach that has been taken to document the follow-up studies devoted to the life-transforming benefits of LBL hypnotherapy. It should also be mentioned that the stories in this book are just a small sample from the large number of cases reported and reviewed online each year by the Newton Institute's general membership.

Each of our authors has presented an actual client case history. Pseudonyms are used to preserve client anonymity, with the client's permission. These stories begin by presenting the client's stated problem and how that issue was uncovered and then resolved through spiritual regression. They end with post-session communications with the client about the benefits of their LBL experience.

The guidance by LBL facilitators in these individual cases is extremely comprehensive, although condensed here by our requirements of limited story length. Therapeutic inquiry is conducted with a view to the history of relevant incarnations by the soul and particularly the soul's existence between lives in the spirit world. It is here where karmic lessons are formulated for the next life. Thus, current problems the client may be having on Earth are analyzed within the perspective of both a physical (human) and spiritual (soul) element.

For effective progression into the spirit world, it is of prime importance that potential clients find a highly trained LBL hypnotherapist to work with them. While there are a multitude of reasons where facilitator experience with the spirit realm will prove invaluable to the client, I would like to cite one area of concern as an example. On very rare occasions, a client could report a spirit world visualization that might initially seem threatening to them. Typically, such a disturbing report will mean one of two things to the skilled and properly trained LBL facilitator. Conscious interference caused by preconditioning, such as a religious belief in hell and evil spirits that do not actually exist in the afterlife, is one aspect. This involves earthly superstitions. All of our research with thousands of cases clearly shows the afterlife to be a realm of love, compassion, forgiveness, and justice.

A more customary and subtle challenge are visualizations that symbolize karmic forms of cosmic accountancy significant to the client's soul self. Here, the experienced, well-trained practitioner will recognize metaphoric scenarios that might well be designed as teaching lessons, often by the subject's spirit guide and master teachers on the spiritual plane. The client, however, may become confused and not be able to interpret such teaching manifestations for what they actually are at first. Conscious interference here by the subject could be attempts to cope with new revelations that they have not yet processed in the session. While the LBL hypnotherapist may have his or her own diagnosis in such cases, this is not allowed to interfere with client self-discovery.

To be sure, the proper measure of comfort is always offered with reports confusing to the client, but subjects are encouraged to make the effort to answer their own questions based upon spiritual messages that come to them during the deeper trance states. Given time and moving at their own pace, most clients ultimately see that their existence is truly a rite of passage—a transition to eventual enlightenment as souls. This process is both emotional and draining work for both facilitator and client, but the rewards of even one LBL session are enormous in terms of acquired self-knowledge and personal revelations of a divine plan.

The authors are all certified members of the Michael Newton Institute for Life Between Lives Hypnotherapy (TNI). Besides the Americas, they practice their craft in Europe, Asia, South Africa, and Australia. The training model for our school was an outgrowth of a methodology system developed in my Los Angeles practice during many years from an extensive volume of cases, over a hundred of which have been detailed in my previously published books. There are numerous schools for traditional hypnosis and some for past life (PL) regression. Our organization was the first to exclusively offer a weeklong, intensive life-between-lives training agenda, and it is the only hypnosis training program we give to professionals. Students come from all over the world to learn hands-on techniques from skilled LBL facilitators. The course practicum involves learning how to mentally regress each other into past lives and to a former existence in the spirit world *between* these lives. The work is both demanding and uplifting to the LBL student, because they are exposed to their own spiritual insights during training.

Since the authors in this book were already trained hypnotherapists with experience in their own right before I met them in the classroom, it is understandable that after graduation and certification, they have gone on to utilize their own talents and techniques in practicing spiritual regression. While they all use our LBL methodology model, each regression therapist featured in this book is different from one another in the way they assist people in uncovering memories about life after death. In my view, TNI graduates who consistently replicate the findings of those who have gone before them, while adding new truths to our spiritual paradigm, bring validity to the whole process. Thus, you will see a commonality of memory recall about the afterlife that is woven through all the LBL cases presented here. Some background PL information relevant to the case will also be included in these stories. These authors and many other certified LBL practitioners within the international network of our organization can be reached through our referral website at www.newtoninstitute.org.

While people seek us out from basic curiosity about their spiritual life, many others have acutely personal reasons—trying to understand the loss of a child, emotional or behavioral concerns, relationship issues, or a fear of dying—that they cannot resolve through traditional therapeutic means. People come to us from all walks of life, with many belief systems, ranging from atheism to a fundamentalist religious persuasion, and yet, once in deep hypnosis, they all recount memories of an afterlife that is strangely uniform in concept and perception. The grandeur of this transcendental design is what brings meaning to our work, because it demonstrates order and purpose in the universe.

It has been my impression over many years of public appearances that increasingly larger groups of people in all cultures are searching for a new kind of spirituality that is more personal to them. Spiritual discoveries that come from the inner mind allow for the exposure of personal truths that no outside religious intermediary or institutional affiliation can duplicate. People who have this kind of spiritual experience see a universal conscious-ness that is not indifferent to the actions and fates of human beings. Recog-nizing their own personal spirit guide specifically assigned to them, as well as interacting with soul mates and companions in their soul group during the LBL experience, adds to this conviction. The knowledge gained from such an internal revelation often leads to life-changing alterations that ease the troubled minds of the average person struggling to understand reasons for their existence on Earth. This is what the cases presented here reflect.

I believe the forces of intelligent creation go far beyond the religious concept of an anthropomorphic god. These spiritual forces, encountered by people in a deep trance state, indicate that creation of intelligent energy is so vast in our universe as to be incomprehensible to the human mind. However, the eternal soul mind sees connections to a series of higher beings in the afterlife who are not gods but rather more advanced souls who have completed their own physical incarnations and are available to serve others who have not finished their karmic work. These evolved teachers are part of the link of a higher consciousness that brings elements of a grand design into the human brain from the soul mind. I call those facilitators who assist in the art of uniting a conscious human brain with the unconscious immor-tal soul "spiritual integrationists." Each of us has this mental dualism in our nature, which may be confusing to people in a fully conscious state. This potential problem is what LBL hypnotherapy endeavors to resolve with people who come to us for help. Through the integration of mind and spirit, we seek to assist them with self-revelations concerning the age-old ques-tions of who am I, where do I come from, why am I here, and where am I going? The LBL practitioner facilitates their hypnosis subject on a spiri-tual journey to unravel these personal mysteries and bring greater aware-ness and meaning to their life by fostering understanding about who they really are as a person. Learning how one's immortal soul character unites with a temporary human brain to produce one personality for one lifetime is rather like a cosmic experience for people. Once this unconscious duality of self is uncovered and the true identity of the soul is exposed, it becomes so liberating that often clients emerge from an LBL session with new serenity and spiritual transcendence.

In my lectures, writings, and radio shows, I have often explained to the public that I was originally resistant to the New Age movement. By training, I was a traditional therapist who specialized in hypnotherapy. Initially, I was not even particularly metaphysical in my approach to client difficulties involving the need for behavior modification. This outlook began to change after my initial past-life discovery, followed some time later by my first life-between-life case in 1968, which is described below. However, it would take years of research before I had enough data to properly map the spirit world and develop a sequential methodology for asking questions. By 1980, I realized I should prepare to write a book on my findings, and therefore I kept more detailed records; thus, many of the cases in my books stem from the 1980s and 1990s. Also, my skill level as an LBL hypnotherapist and my knowledge of the spirit world was much greater in these decades than in the earlier years.

As with so many other significant events over the years, my early revelations about an afterlife in the spirit world seemed to arrive on my doorstep rather by accident. I now realize there are no accidents in the scheme of things, especially for major events; this is what the people whose cases are discussed in this book have come to know as well. My small case contribution is not as complex as many of the cases you are about to read. Because it was my first LBL case, it will always be embedded in my memory as the beginning of fulfilling my purpose in this life: to offer a new, very personal spiritual belief system without the need for institutions or intermediaries. I would title the following condensed story "the missing friends."

A middle-aged woman whose name was Una came to me with problems that centered around her feelings of isolation and a kind of dissociation with humanity. This lady told me that she felt a terrible yearning to be with her "old friends," whom she could not clearly define. Una mentioned that she had seen some evidence of them in dreams, but at this stage in my career I did not understand the full implications of that statement. At our first meeting, during intake, I felt that while there was evidence of sadness coupled with lack of energy and motivation, Una was not someone suffering from mental illness, nor was she on antidepressant medication. My assessment was that despite being chronically lonely, Una was not antisocial and even appeared to evidence peer engagement in her life. After I questioned Una further, I determined she was manifestly depressed over what she stated was "the absence of a meaningful connection with anyone who recognizes my real identity as a person." I saw that Una was grieving but quite functional. Yet there was an aspect to her discomfort that was clinically rather vague.

During the early stages of her session, I asked, "Are these missing friends people you knew at any time in your adult life?" Una answered no. We then began hypnosis, and in a shallow alpha state, I asked her, "Are you missing any childhood playmates who are no longer with you?" Again, her answer was no. As I took Una deeper into the middle and upper levels of the alpha state, we began to explore her most recent past life and even a couple of earlier past lives. Only a few friends dear to her began to crop up, although these souls were not visualized by Una as connected, because she was not yet mentally in the spirit world. However, she was visibly brightening as the session progressed. Una then told me that she wanted to see all her friends together, interacting with her, and this was why she felt so isolated and lonely in her current life. At the time, I thought this comment rather odd.

At this point in the session, due to my inexperience in spiritual matters, I was getting somewhat frustrated. More importantly, what I did not fully realize was the fact that this highly receptive woman was taking her trance phase into the deeper hypnotic theta state in order to help both of us. I did not know that Una was getting ahead of me and actually pushing herself from a subconscious mode into what we call today a superconscious mental state, which allows a subject in hypnosis to mentally reach the spirit world between lives.

Finally, in my bafflement, I asked Una, "Was there ever a time in your existence when you were *not* lonely because you were with a group of friends?" Suddenly, she cried out in excitement and said yes. I immediately commanded, "Go there!" What I did not realize at the time was the fact that I had inadvertently used a trigger word: group. To someone in deep hypnosis visualizing the afterlife, this means a spirit group of connected souls who are especially active together between lives and often incarnate together. Una was now crying with happiness, and with her eyes still closed, she was pointing to my office wall. "Oh, I see them now," she said. I asked where. She answered, "In my home." My confused response was, "You mean at home in one of your past lives?" "No, no," Una replied eagerly, "I'm in between—don't you see—in the spirit world. This is my real home, and my soul group is all HERE!" She then said, tearfully, "Oh, I miss them so much."

I was dumbfounded by what had happened to both of us and still did not fully comprehend what we had found together. With more questioning, I learned that no primary soul mate or supporting soul companions were in Una's current life, because she had been too dependent upon them during her past incarnations on Earth. This was a karmic learning lesson involving a prior spiritual contract for her current life. By not physically being with Una in her life today, members of her soul group gave her the space to grow stronger through the challenges of being alone. Once Una understood this situation in her life was by advance mutual agreement with her soul group and spiritual advisors, she began to relax, and her sense of loss diminished.

Over the next year, Una would contact me regularly with updates to say that life for her now had new meaning, and she was living it to the fullest because she finally comprehended her purpose, involving a need for courage and independence in decision making. She derived great comfort from knowing her immortal soul companions would be waiting for her on the other side. Una's new feelings of fulfillment, as an outgrowth of her first LBL session, caused her to realize that life was not governed by fate, or determinism, or some sort of divine punishment surrounding her loneliness, but rather by her own free will. This does not mean that I offer Una's LBL case as a panacea for depression; rather, it shows another avenue for the exploration of an unsettled mind.

I would like to quote Una's last letter to me, sent years after her session and just before her death:

> Michael, I am no longer a solitary being within myself. Rather
> than existing solely in my private world as before, I now find
> that I coexist easily with others because I am attuned to the fact
> we all live in a shared world where none of us need to be limited
> by boundaries. These days I find myself encouraging people in

distress to accept life and who they are and enjoy what is good and intended in our world. Thank you for this gift.

Una's session with me had sent cold chills down my spine with its profound, far-reaching implications. After she left, I spent considerable time reviewing her tape recording. Her case marked the beginning of my investigations into the afterlife, or innerlife, as some call this spiritual realm. I was now in uncharted territory. At the time, there were no books that I could find about spiritual regression methodology. The conventional wisdom among most past-life researchers during this period, and indeed for years afterward, was that memory recall of life between lives only involved a nonproductive grayish limbo of no consequence. Perhaps this attitude was influenced by the millions of adherents to an Eastern philosophical concept involving the absence of a permanent soul self in human beings who transmigrate from life to life without a spiritual essence of everlasting personal identity.

As for myself, I felt a compulsion to discover everything possible about our life after death through spiritual recall. This task would take years of quiet study as I worked with hypnosis subjects, designing a methodology that included an entry and exit strategy to the afterlife. While mapping the spirit world from a great many case histories, a magnificent truth became evident to me. I found that within the mind of every person lies the answer to the mystery of their life.

Finally, in 1994, my first work, *Journey of Souls*, was published by Llewellyn, followed by *Destiny of Souls* in 2000. These two books provide a foundation of understanding about life in the spirit world and reincarnation. In 2004, a third book, *Life Between Lives Hypnotherapy*, offered both the public and private hypnosis professional a functional step-by-step guide to spiritual regression methodology. Representing some thirty-five years of research, this text shows interested readers how information was obtained for *Memories of the Afterlife* by detailing the hypnosis process used with all the cases presented here.

I should like to offer a further word about these books in connection with endnotes. In this collection of cases, the authors may briefly allude to certain aspects of LBL methodology relating to their case that they are unable to describe completely without spoiling the pace of their short stories. In those cases where I felt more detailed information would provide the curious reader with greater understanding about a particular aspect of the afterlife, I offer endnotes with further commentary and references to my books, with page numbers on specific topics. *Journey of Souls* is abbreviated as JS, *Destiny of Souls* as DS, and *Life Between Lives Hypnotherapy* is listed as LBLH. As therapists, we honor the beliefs and perceptions of our clients during their LBL sessions. The endnoting in this book is not intended to detract from any inquiry by the facilitator or client statement, but rather to offer the interested reader additional detail on the same topic as described by many other hypnosis subjects reporting about their spiritual life. While there is some repetition with endnoting and page references between cases, I wanted each story to have the benefit of notes that applied directly to the subject under discussion and to stand on its own for ease of reader appraisal.

Although intensely powerful, life-between-lives hypnotherapy is still a relatively new field. The authors of this book will attest to the fact that when their hypnosis subjects find they have a definite purpose in life and do not lose their real personhood at physical death, this knowledge brings overwhelming joy. Each author has chosen a case from their files that best reflects a particular theme of special interest to them. In our editing, we have tried to select stories that offer a variety of personal situations for broad reader identification. It is our hope and expectation that these stories involving the conscious illumination of the soul will demonstrate a therapeutic form of healing that one day will be in general use everywhere among traditional therapists. I trust you will enjoy the cases that follow; may they bring you an awareness of what is possible in your own life.

Michael Newton
FOUNDER OF THE NEWTON INSTITUTE

LOVE
as a
CATALYST FOR CHANGE

Paul Aurand
(NEW YORK CITY)
PRESIDENT AND LEAD TRAINER FOR
THE MICHAEL NEWTON INSTITUTE,
INTERNATIONAL INSTRUCTOR, AUTHOR, AND
AWARD-WINNING MASTER HYPNOTHERAPIST.

Many seek life-between-lives hypnotherapy longing to know if they will ever meet their soul mates. This is a story of a young woman who has recently met her soul mate. But this time, rather than to be together, he has come into her life as a catalyst for change. As the session progresses, we find this is actually his second attempt to wake her up and help her learn the soul lessons she has been struggling with for lifetimes.

SASHA IS A thirty-two-year-old woman born in northern Europe. After a twelve-year relationship with Mark, the first and only man in her life, plans were made for their fairy-tale wedding. Two weeks before the wedding, Sasha's soul mate, Raul, showed up and rocked her world. Not knowing what to do, Sasha followed through with her wedding plans and married Mark. Despite keeping her commitment to Mark, she was torn and found herself pushing him away. She was never able to be really intimate with him, and a few months later, she moved away from Mark to live and work in Portugal.

They have been apart for almost six months. During their time apart, Sasha crossed paths with Raul again. They became lovers for a brief time, and then Raul moved on. Sasha was devastated.

She came in to our session feeling terribly guilty and confused. Sasha wonders if she is to be with her soul mate, Raul, or if she should stay married and go back to her husband, Mark. She is seeking advice from her guides and direction for her soul.

During an LBL session, we normally direct a client back to the most recent past life. On occasion, when there is an earlier lifetime of great significance, a client will go to that lifetime rather than the most recent one. That is what developed in this case.

The opening scene in Sasha's past life is of an Egyptian temple. She is a priestess named Sharoon engaged in spiritual studies. Our conversation about this life unfolds as follows:

SASHA: I am learning about spirituality, but I am also practicing manipulating people who don't work in the temple. I am able to influence them spiritually and energetically.

PAUL: Help me understand how you manipulate them.

S: I manipulate them to be obedient—to believe what I want them to believe. I do it through creating and sending images. I create a mental image of what I want them to do, and I send it. They can see it and feel it. It is very powerful! It is easy to influence them.

P: Move forward in that life of spiritual studies and manipulation. What happens?

S: I am killed. Yes, killed.

P: And how does that happen?

S: There are enemy invaders. They are entering the temple, and they are killing everybody. They kill me too.

P: What happens to you? Where are you in relation to your body now?

S: Outside, very quickly. I am just observing. I watch as more people enter the temple. But I don't feel sad; I feel peaceful. I am accepting.

P: Where do you go and what do you do?

S: Up and up, looking back on the scene. I see light, up and to the left. I am going toward it. I move toward it without any effort. It is very peaceful.

P: What happens as you reach this light?

S: (surprised) I am not very religious, but I see an image of a holy person with his arms wide open, welcoming me. I know this is a symbol of loving bliss. I can see now, it is my guide who is there. I feel safe. It is my guide Araton. He tells me everything is fine. I am doing very well. He accepts me, supports me, and loves me. He just melted into me; we are one. This is so incredible! It's a way of experiencing his vibrations. He is very wise and joyful, so bright and so pure.

P: Why does your guide merge with you in this way?

S: So that later on, I will know his vibrations, so that when I need his help and when I meditate, I will know he is with me. I will feel his peace and joy.

P: And where does he guide you next?

S: We are in a beautiful rose garden, sitting on a bench. There are pedestrian walkways. At the end of the path there is a building. It is white. As I look at it, I realize I can go there to ask questions, but I am afraid to do that.

P: And how does Araton respond to your being afraid to ask questions?

S: He says I don't have to ask questions if I am not comfortable now. He says I can do it later on.

 We are going to do some healing. I am to follow him. It is strange. I know he is radiating love, but I cannot feel it. He says we can fix it.

 Now I am in a healing chamber. From the top, it is like a machine producing different colored rays of light. (Sasha shakes in the chair.) I can feel that I am vibrating. I don't have to do anything. It is just happening. I am feeling very peaceful. There is a soft but penetrating pink light cleansing my body inside and out. (1)

P: What is it that is being cleansed from you?

S: There is still some kind of fear that I am holding in my (ethereal) abdomen that should be cleansed that is connected to love. It is why I had trouble feeling Araton's love.

P: Where does this fear associated with love originate?

S: From many lifetimes.

 This healing and vibrating goes on for some time, then Sasha reports it is complete.

P: With this healing complete, if we were to hold up a full-length mirror, how would you appear?

S: Clean. A blue color with some pinkish tints.

P: We know your guide's name is Araton, but what is your immortal spiritual name?

S: (long pause) I hear something like Kiya, but I am not sure.

P: Perhaps you can ask your guide?

S: He says this is a name from a past life. My immortal spiritual name sounds something like *Kashyapeya*.

P: And now that this healing is complete, where does your guide take you?

S: I am in front of a group of beings; there are five of them. We are in a round room. I feel so safe! Araton is with me. He is standing to my side and slightly behind me. At first, they all appear in the same brown color, but now the one in the middle is white, and one of the other ones is a reddish color.

P: What happens here?

S: I am just waiting. Now they are welcoming me. They want to help me live my life fully.

My client is now engaged with this group of beings, who are on her council, often called the elders, or wise ones. There is a long pause here while Sasha collects her thoughts and visualizes the council members preparing to work with her.

P: What are they communicating to you?

S: It is like a wall on the right-hand side of the room. It is sort of a screen. I see three scenes. In one, it looks like me giving birth, and there is someone next to me—a man I don't recognize. I don't want to see this.

P: What is your hesitation?

S: This man in the scene where I am giving birth is not my husband or Raul. I don't like that. I want it to be Raul.

They are showing me three scenes. There is one scene with the man I don't recognize. In this scene I am having a baby. There is one in the middle where I am with Raul, and this scene is very bright, although this is not the most probable or best one. Somehow I know this is true, but I don't understand why it is brighter than the other two choices. I am scared. (2) The scene to the far right is me with my husband, Mark.

Oh, I see. They are showing me I have a choice! I can choose to be with my husband or the other man. I can even choose to be with Raul. That is strange. I have three choices.

P: Do you want to ask them which choice would be of the highest good for your soul?

S: (long pause) I have asked, but they are not going to tell me. They say I must make my own decision, without their influence.

Here the council is having Kashyapeya, who in her past life as Sharoon influenced and manipulated many people, experience how important it is for one to be free to make choices in life. And as is often the case, they teach her this by talking to her about it but also by giving her the experience of choice free from even their influence.

P: (I pose one of the questions that Sasha has brought to me before our session began.) Perhaps you want to ask them why Raul came into your life as he did.

S: To show me how to relax and feel joy. He came to open me up—to help me open to other people. My closest friend has always been Mark. We were always together and had no outside friends. We were in a sort of shell or cocoon, closed and separate from others, in our own little world. Raul has come into my life to wake me up and break that shell open. He came as a catalyst for change! He came to help me learn how to love. That's why I now have many friends and am traveling the world for business. That is what has brought me here. (3)

P: (I ask another of Sasha's pre-session questions.) Do you want to tell them how guilty you feel about your relationship with Raul?

S: They say it is okay. It will be washed away. It already is. They say there is nothing to be guilty about. They say it was necessary to shake me that much so that I would make some decisions and make some changes in how I live.

P: (I pose another of Sasha's questions.) Do they advise you to go back to the marriage?

S: No. They don't advise me to go back. They say it is my choice. I have freedom of choice.

P: Perhaps you want to ask them what the best thing is now for your soul growth.

S: It is very strange. Now I feel sad and afraid. (After a pause, Sasha continues.) Acceptance and letting go of things—to let things happen. To accept life and let go. To let things happen and not to control them. To not manipulate things or people, just to observe, to see what happens. This relates to my lifetime as the priestess and manipulating.

This is scary. I don't know if I will be able to be with Raul. I know I want to be with him, but he has his free will too! I don't know if he wants to be together.

They show me on the screen how life with Raul could be. It would be nice. Spiritual and calm. I can see two children. I am not sure which country it is. It is a very peaceful and happy life, but he has to want it too.

P: You might ask them what the possibility of that is in this life.

S: It's only about a twenty or thirty percent possibility. Twenty percent.

I am scared it will not happen. The point is that I want it, and he does not. He has his free will too, and I am not supposed to manipulate it. He has to want it too. Oh, this is hard!

Soul lessons such as these are often a struggle to get, and Kashyapeya is really struggling here. She is so set on having her way that it is almost impossible for her to even look at the different possibilities for her life, let alone take in the deeper soul lesson her council is presenting her with. It can take lifetimes to resolve certain tendencies we carry in our souls, and this seems to be a pivotal lifetime for Kashyapeya.

S: They are talking to me about choices again. You have the freedom of choice. That involves others' choices too. I don't like it; I don't know why. I don't want this to happen. I am scared, really.

P: By showing you these choices, what is it they are trying to communicate to you?

Long pause, still struggling with what they are showing her.

S: All these lives (in current time simulation) meet at the same point in the end, but they are different (paths).

P: (I ask another of Sasha's pre-session questions.) Do you want to ask them if any of these three men they are showing you are soul mates?

S: (long pause) I don't know, I am so scared to see.

Kashyapeya is having so much difficulty accepting what her council is teaching her that her guide, Araton, steps in. He suggests we leave the council meeting for the time being while reassuring Kashyapeya that she will be able to return if she wishes. Araton takes her immediately to her soul group. (4)

S: We are already here! I can see my mom, Raul, and others. I see eight people standing in two groups, four on the left and four on the right. My mom is in the middle of the group on the left. And in the group on the right are Raul, Mark, and Andy (a new and close friend).

P: And who comes forward first?

S: My mom comes forward to greet me and then steps back. Then Raul comes forward. He is making jokes with me. He teases me. I don't know what he is talking about, but he is very funny and really joyful. He isn't that joyful in real life. He is often very distant and even cold, but here he is very warm and funny. (5) He says, "Take it easy. Don't push. Follow your heart. Allow yourself to follow the guidance." I am so scared. I am telling him I want to be with him. I feel the pain. "Maybe. Maybe, baby," he jokes. I am so angry.

P: Ask him why he came into your life now.

S: This was the last opportunity to change my life—to open me up and to show me there are many other possibilities. I was closed and shut down, and he has opened me up. He tried to do this for me before, in another life. I was quite reserved and couldn't open up to him. I didn't stay with him. That was very painful for him. This is one reason he is quite reluctant to be with me this time. He is afraid I will leave him, and he will be alone again. He says he couldn't bear that again.

P: What did you two agree to in advance of this current life?

S: Sometimes we are together, and sometimes we are not. In this lifetime, there are times we are together and times we are not. There will be a period without being together, and there may be another period after some time when we will be together, but he is checking other possibilities too. I must wait for him to decide. I cannot control it. He has to choose. I tell him that I love him. (cries, long pause) We embrace.

Now, Mark comes forward. Both Mark and Raul are in my soul group. He is happy that I am here, but he is sad that we have been apart. I too am sad about this. I tell him I am sorry if I have hurt him. I tell him I love him.

P: And what is the agreement that you and he have?

S: To be together. To love and support each other. To learn as much as we can from each other. To be friends. We are hugging.

I am confused. I am feeling this sadness and fear again. My mom and my friend Andy are there, just standing, looking at me. I feel their love and support. I want to move on, but there in the group on the right is that guy from one of the three possibilities shown to me by my council. But I don't want to talk to him. He is close to me, but it is hard for me to see him. I am so scared he is not right for me. My guide Araton is saying he can support me, and he is wondering if I want to talk. He says whoever I am with will be fine. My life will be fulfilled. This is difficult for me to hear, but Araton is telling me I need to work on acceptance. He is saying I have free will and there are different possibilities, but I am not sure which I should choose. I don't get this. He is telling me I need to go back to the council for this. (pause) We are now there. They are asking me what my question is.

After her initial meeting with her council and her soul group intervention, Kashyapeya is now far more ready to hear the deeper message that the council is communicating to her.

S: It is all about acceptance. All the best for me is happening. I still don't understand. Should I follow what is happening, or should I create my life? I don't understand. Should I make choices, or should I just allow choices to be made? Sometimes they can be made, and sometimes they have to be allowed to be made. In this particular situation, I can make the choice. I can leave Mark. I can choose to be with Raul, but I don't know how to do it if he doesn't want to. No matter what, I have to respect the choices of others and not manipulate them to get what I want.

P: (I ask another of Sasha's pre-session questions.) What do you need to do at this time in your life?

S: Meditate and calm myself down. Send love. Accept his (Raul's) free will.

I am asking the council if they can project some images about our future life together. See possibilities and open myself to the possibilities but be emotionally detached and not project them to others to influence things.

They are saying that I have a tendency toward stubbornness, and that I need to make the effort to move on and not stay stuck. I should move on with my life and follow my intuition. They say I already know what to do. No one is going to tell me what to do. I need to give free choice to others and not manipulate them. They say I can ask questions if I have any. I can have everything I want. I am very creative. I should respect the free will of others. There is a balance between creating and manipulating. I should create with love and acceptance. Soon I will have answers about where to live and what to do. They are showing me I can, if I wish, move from Portugal to another country—a colder place somewhere in Europe. I will be fine. I will have a good job, and I will have children.

Interestingly enough, six months after this session, while I was transcribing the recording for this chapter, Sasha contacted me and gave me a wonderful update on her situation. Sasha and her husband, Mark, have reunited. She is packing to move back to northern Europe.

Sasha told me:

> I set Raul free. I have accepted this lesson and have stopped trying to control things, and miraculous things are happening. I finally understand what they were telling me. I am learning to let go. Mark and I have reunited in more loving and supportive ways than ever before. I am moving back to northern Europe. I have successfully started my own business, and I feel stronger now. I always thought that I had no free will—that somebody would give me instructions for life or tell me what to do. But I have the power to choose, and I now give others the freedom to choose too. I have chosen to let go.

Clients seem to know the right time in their lives to schedule an LBL hypnosis session into the afterlife. Usually, a fork in the road of life precipitates this action. It is important to note that when we are working on these deeper soul lessons, once the session is over, it can take weeks, even months, to fully process and understand everything that comes to us in an LBL session. There is clearly a transition time between receiving the information, coming to an understanding of it, taking it into our soul, and integrating it into our life. Sasha's life is now moving in a positive direction, and she is focusing on her life purpose: to let go and enjoy life.

---

(1) Typically, orientation with our guides right after physical death includes visualizations of quiet, peaceful areas. This deprogramming is designed as a moderate measure in dealing with soul contamination rather than severe soul rejuvenation, which requires more drastic action. The spiritual garden-type scene as described in this case may also include what many call a cleansing shower of healing. The symbolism of flowing energy for purification is often evoked by the client reliving such scenes. See JS 54–55.

(2) There are a number of "I'm scared" expressions in this story by Sasha, the client, that demonstrate uncertainty with her spiritual visions. This sort of emotional fear does not actually come from Kashyapeya, her soul, even though Sasha is in a deep theta trance state. In a pure discarnate state, souls may be uneasy about a loved one still on Earth who is in trouble, or perhaps just before they appear before their council, but emotional fear from the central nervous system in a physical body does not exist for souls in the spirit world. For more information on soul emotion, see DS 43, 44, and 290.

What we have here with Sasha's visual reactions to her council presentation of three alternate current life scenes is an uncertain woman reacting to what she is seeing. She is engaged in a current life review within the now-time of the spirit world, where past, present, and future are all rolled into one timeline interview. This represents a "what if" exercise for the examination of possibilities and probabilities. With LBL therapy, the client may bring conscious mind transmissions into their unconscious, where the human ego becomes integrated into recollections of a soul ego. See LBL therapy, LBLH 190–194; life possibilities, DS 359–365 and LBLH 177; and council composition and therapy, DS 212–214, 256.

(3) The current life review Sasha is receiving from her council demonstrates the conflict we may feel by having more than one love partner in our life,

even though prearranged. Notice the dynamics between her two loves today. Sasha discovers it is Mark who is her primary soul mate over thousands of years of lives ("We were always together"). Raul has come into her current life, as he has from time to time in other lives, as a companion soul mate, also from the same soul group. He has come as a catalyst for change for Sasha because in this life and in her current body, she is a manipulator of love and must come to terms with what love is all about. See soul groups, JS 88–90, and soul mates, JS 250–251, DS 259–265.

(4) In LBL therapy, during periods of the session involving difficult scenes for the client, facilitators often call on the subject's personal spirit guide to assist. This is especially true with client blocks. In this case, the client was guided to mentally shift from a council scene to that of her soul group, and it was very therapeutic because she began to relax.

(5) A soul's immortal character may be in opposition with the brain and the emotional temperament of their human host. See duality of ego, LBLH 80–82, 183–187.

HEAD
to
HEART

JanelleMarie
(PLEASANT HILL, CALIFORNIA)
ALCHEMY INSTITUTE AND NEWTON INSTITUTE,
HEALING ARTS AND REGRESSION PRACTITIONER,
NDE SPIRITUAL CONSULTATIONS.

This is a story of an executive/music therapist's struggle with personal issues that have affected his family relationships and also appear in different forms in his business environment. His primary issues are deep-seated feelings of aggression and being too headstrong, along with an underlying lifetime pattern of feeling rejected and devalued.

As a result of his LBL experience, he has learned that leading from his spiritual heart center rather than from his analytical mind is a better way to live. He was able to release his strong, fixed mental pattern of what is right and what is wrong. He remembered the existence and the importance of the universal connection of all souls, which is musical in sound. And from his spirit guides, he received tools for working with his aggression and arrogance that, over time, helped to equalize his interactions with others.

MR. B, AN executive whom I have known for several years prior to his life-between-lives session, has struggled with personal issues that have affected his family relationships and that appear in different forms in his business environment. This highly respected executive, who is also an innovative music therapist specializing in autistic children, had deep-seated feelings of aggression that "make it difficult for my wife and children to approach me and feel safe." Their ongoing concern is when will he blow up.

In the initial discussion with Mr. B, I delve deeply to provide clarity for the questions that will be posed during the session. Along with this outward expression of aggression, he indicates, "I can't bear feeling insulted. Perfection must be maintained at all costs." He explains this by citing the following example: "When I arrive home from work and see the dishes in the sink, I feel insulted, as if my wife and oldest son treat me like the dishwasher. The dishes are not done; therefore, the house is not perfect." Mr. B sums it up when he tells me, "If the external does not fit or meet with my level of expectation of perfection, I take it personally and drop into my lifetime pattern of feeling rejection, and therefore, I feel devalued."

During his session, there were three stops where Mr. B was provided key tools to integrate into his daily lifestyle. These are relevant to his current questions for this session and his unresolved pattern of aggression. The first place of importance occurred in Mr. B's past life, where he finds himself standing outside in front of a cave entrance scolding, in a heartfelt manner, twenty or so people. The following excerpt is from this past-life segment:

JANELLEMARIE: What is your position in the village?

MR. B: I am a teacher/guru/hermit—the guy people go to when they seek advice or need teaching.

J: How are they receiving this information—this scolding to do better?

B: They are contrite and quiet. I am really very aware of my chest—sort of a spiritual heart I am carrying there. That is where I am coming from when I speak—the spiritual heart place—teaching from the heart.

J: Is there more to describe about this spiritual heart place?

B: I am powerful, but it is okay, because I have a balance between being powerful and not making anything out of it for myself. The spiritual heart is the place where the power and ego are balanced out.

Here Mr. B has connected with a forgotten part of himself. He is beginning to receive clarification and new awareness about teaching and leading from his spiritual heart, where he needs to begin to live within himself. Up to now, he was relating to others in an analytical manner, and he states, "I was relating from my head, and I had a very strong fixed pattern of what was right and what was wrong."

Further along in his session, Mr. B says, "I am in my bubble with my soul group." One of Mr. B's important questions for his soul group is related to sacred contracts and is revealed in this next segment of case dialog:

J: How are you feeling in this group?

B: I'm really glad to see them again. And I have a special connection to a soul named Ahrr, because I know him well in this life, and so I am a little bit astonished.

J: Can you tell me a little more about this?

B: Well, it's because Ahrr is a very dear friend who is very important to me in my life right now, and now I discover he is also a very important soul mate. As a soul, he is patient, consistent, steady, and very perceptive. (1)

J: One of your questions concerns sacred contracts—let's explore the purpose of your contract with Ahrr.

B: In my current life, his task is to set me back on track, because I am on the verge of going from the jokester to getting focused on my spirit. (2) With Ahrr, whether I see him in this life or in our soul group, whenever we talk, it is about his spirit or my spirit. There's nothing else we talk about. He's got this knack, both in the soul group and in this life now, where, whatever happens, even if it is a typo in an email, he makes it into a spiritual thing. And he's always dead-on; he's got this knack. And he is teaching me that talking about spirit doesn't have to be dry. It can be a lot of fun, and it can be funny too.

J: So his connection with you is tied to keeping you on track. Is this part of the sacred contract as we talked about—for your vocation and also for character building?

B: Yes, he's showing me that. I have known Ahrr since we were twenty and I was floundering. He is reminding me that, even at twenty, I really wanted to study the psyche, the connection between spirit and psyche, and everything to do with that. Ahrr is saying I have this special gift with sound frequency. I have a spiritual capacity to understand sound and the meaning of sound, and he's telling me to use that in conjunction with healing. (3) He is telling me I am on the right track with my assumptions of what are the right frequencies for healing, and I need to stop buying CDs, looking for the right frequency. He is telling me I need to produce the sound myself. Ahrr is pointing out the frequencies I have been researching—anything between first-particle frequencies down to cell frequencies down to the sounds of music— this track I have started establishing, I should continue developing and then publish. This publication has something to do with psychology. I'm not certain how right now, but I will be able to incorporate this study of sound frequencies into my field.

J: What is your feeling about what you have received?

B: Having Ahrr in a soul group is one thing, but knowing he is a close soul mate in my physical life is a big, big help and gives me support.

In the next segment of his soul group meeting, Mr. B describes another soul named Ghor: "He is sort of the leader of the group, and I admire him. He is the fighter for the group and for our spiritual advancement." The conversation with Ghor has an important focus and provides Mr. B with a key tool for becoming very present and shifting his aggression. The narrative picks up here:

B: Ghor is telling me when I have feelings of rejection and do not feel valued, it is as if I am looking into a mirror maze, like in a circus fun house. I don't know whether I am looking at myself or at the people who devalue me. It is a trap, and I am lost in there. I ask Ghor how do I get out? He says by focusing away from those who devalue you. Focus either on my spirit, spirit guide, or the realm of heaven. I'm too distracted by the physical. He is reminding me to look inside, because outside, for sure, you won't get your satisfaction. Once I connect inside, then I am in the present.

J: Does he offer you a tool for doing this?

B: First to touch my forehead to bring my attention there. Also, Ghor is encouraging me to pick up sword fighting again. I did that when I was young.

J: Does he mean literally or symbolically?

B: Both. Literally, sword fighting aligns the physical with the spiritual. Symbolically, using the spiritual sword will keep me focused on what is relevant and essential—to stay simple and not load myself up with all kinds of distractions. (4) And in particular, he is saying I need to drop appointments with all kinds of people who stir me up.

J: Is there more to describe here?

B: Yes. The fear of being rejected is actually a great, great tool. He is pointing out that when I am in the mirror maze, I am with the wrong people, and I am wasting my time. So this is actually a signal and a flag. It is a really cool spiritual tool, the fear of being rejected.

Another specific and very real-world tool was offered to Mr. B for keeping his aggression under control. During an important spirit-world stop, he met with his council. The following is the session dialog where the council interacts with Mr. B about his arrogance in his current life:

B: I'm being told I shouldn't be so arrogant. I don't quite understand.

J: Is there a tool for you about the arrogance, perhaps a specific place in your body or an attitude they can describe to you so that you have a greater understanding?

B: Ah, yeah. I know it all. I always pull my energy up into my head because I feel I have to know it all. I think I can control my environment this way, but, of course, that's not possible. They are telling me that's arrogant or that's the core definition of arrogance. Thinking this way keeps me in my head all of the time. I have to drop that.

J: Is there a way they can guide you into dropping or moving out of arrogance?

B: Yes. They have a very good way. They just suggested I clean the kitchen floor on my hands and knees. The energy will circulate through my body instead of getting stuck in my head. (laughs) All right—that brings the head down for sure!

J: Do they suggest how often?

B: Once a week, twice a week. (laughs) They nailed me. I thought I would get out of this one. They are really serious about this. I really have to do this.

J: Anything more?

B: This is so funny—really funny. I am being directed to do kitchen work. Most of the time I should be cleaning the kitchen. They are telling me to keep the kitchen spiffy clean. If it's spiffy clean, then I don't need to worry about my pretty little head. They don't think it was as funny as I tried to make it out to be. And I see my way of being funny about it was my way of trying to get out of it. But it's not possible. They are really serious about this one.

J: Is there more about this tool?

B: Yes. I need to teach my son to do the same thing—how to clean the kitchen and the bath.

Our session ended shortly after this dialog. Mr. B had a lot to process.

In the months that followed his LBL, Mr. B had the foresight to act on the tools offered in the soul group. Here he describes the enriching effect sword fighting had on his relationship with his son and how it assists him in shifting out of feelings of aggression and into being present:

> I engage in sword fighting with my ten-year-old son on our back
> porch. In using sword-fighting tools with my son, he has learned
> to express his aggression without fear of me. We both now allow

ourselves to express aggression in a relationship-building manner. Facing my aggression issue and integrating sword fighting in order to better deal with it has helped our relationship, which is very important and dear to me.

A second resultant effect is expressed in my work as an executive. In meetings, fellow executives express a rather high amount of aggression, of which I am often on the receiving end. In sword fighting, I learned to split the oncoming energy in half with the sword; the aggression coming at me is split in half and passes me by. Often in these meetings, I visualize a sword and am reminded of this concept. Since initiating this practice regularly, other executives have commented that I am so much calmer in meetings.

I also learned by touching my forehead, I can split my own aggression. This touching takes me inside, and it directs my energy to feel present.

As a result of following the council's serious advice, Mr. B tells me later:

I became aware I wanted some specialized therapeutic support for the aggression and feelings of rejection. Along with this, I followed the council's suggestion to scrub the kitchen floor every week and found I learned to be humble, a quality that cannot be taught, only acquired and maintained.

By doing this weekly, I realized I had been given a sacred tool for keeping my aggression in control. After one year of scrubbing the floor, Mrs. B said to me, "I'm impressed. You are keeping your anger in control."

One year later, Mr. B says there have been real-life benefits in maintaining monthly contact with Ahrr as a way of honoring this sacred contract he discovered in his soul group. He describes it in the following manner:

After several monthly conversations, I realized Ahrr had a contract with me in this life to make fun of me. By doing this, he shifts me out of my perfectionist attitude and my feelings of rejection and devaluation. I had the enlightening realization that he is the only one I would allow to make fun of my attitude, and this is an important aspect of our sacred contract.

Also, we both came to the awareness that all of us, as souls living on the physical plane now, are connected universally. There is a frequency to this connection, and it is musical in sound. Ahrr, in his typical form, challenged me to research this frequency, teach it, and publish it in Europe due to their long-standing acceptance of anthroposophy.

Mr. B now uses this frequency data with autistic children and their parents. He has found this sound frequency activates neuroprocessing language and enables some of the children to say basic sentences, when they were previously unable to do so. Also, he has taught adults about the use of these sounds for various physical illnesses such as multiple sclerosis, fibromyalgia, and sleep apnea. Mr. B says this special knowledge of harmonics helps to keep him humble. He now invokes existing harmonic patterns, and this allows him to truly teach and support his clients in their life goals. He no longer feels he has to pretend to be a powerful healer.

As an executive and department head, there were shifts in organizational dynamics realized by Mr. B. He has successfully integrated and utilized a roundtable format, presented in his soul group, as the model for his departmental organization chart and team meetings. The result of duplicating this conversation model caused equalization in his department position with that of his employees, thereby providing a safe environment for them to speak freely and to state opinions without fear of consequence. In staff meetings, he simply raises an issue and listens to staff input until a natural consensus emerges. By duplicating this productive and soothing dynamic, managers no longer see him as a threat and someone to obey. More projects are delivered on time and on budget, and there is a genuine upbeat feeling in his office environment.

We see in this discussion of Mr. B's session that the in-depth, basic, precious information he received, when taken to heart and acted upon, has an appreciable impact in his day-to-day lifestyle. The data also points toward a positive domino effect on the lives of those connected to him both personally and in business. Mr. B's final comment sums up the bottom-line effect of his soul journey:

Living from my heart versus my head has enriched my life. It has put me on a journey to equalize my interactions with people. I've stopped viewing myself as more important than others.

As a facilitator for life-between-lives spiritual regression, I never know where a particular client's soul journey will lead us, where the client will end up in life, or how the presenting issues and questions will be resolved. However, what is consistent are similar reports of unique and noteworthy scenarios reflecting the positive, insightful, empowering, and fascinating data received in their respective soul journeys. It appears there is an ability to use and integrate similar lifestyle tools easily and effectively as a result of a deepened connection to the client's personal soul life. I find the spiritual realm to be friendly, joyful, faithful, and beneficent toward those who are willing to embark on and embrace this deep, profound soul journey inward.

---

(1) I have found the public may have the misconception that all souls in a soul cluster group are primary soul mates. This is not true. Typically, we have just one member of a soul group who is an eternal, deeply bonded partner in our lives. However, they may not be with us in every life. The other members of the group are considered soul companions, and they often take supporting roles in our lives. If a soul from another group is working with us during a particular incarnation, they are called an affiliated soul. See DS 264–265 and LBLH 100, 120, 131–133.

(2) While I have mentioned different character types between souls in cluster groups before, this case gives us a different slant. Every soul group, especially in levels I and II, has a range of immortal character traits that complement each other. Mr. B, the client in this case, states that he is the jokester in the soul group. Ahrr has the reputation of being steady and perceptive, while Ghor is the courageous fighter. Presumably, others in the group are more quiet and thoughtful, or flamboyant risk takers. However, notice that Mr. B in his current life has an aggressive, obsessive human mind that is quite different from a laid-back jokester. Here is an excellent example of a brain that is not temperamentally in conjunction but rather in opposition to the character of the soul. See character types in soul groups, JS 142; body-soul partnerships, DS 384–394; and connections between body and soul, LBLH 181–184.

(3) Music is very relevant to this story, and music does play a significant part of what souls experience in the spirit world with vibrational, resonating

sounds that are manifestations of spiritual energy in terms of expression, communication, and healing. See JS 21–22, 43–44, 96 and DS 304–308.

(4) Having been a fencer, I can say that while Mr. B appears to be acting out aggressive behavior with swordplay in the later scene with his young son, there is more going on here. Fencing is a highly focused physical expression of the mind controlling rapid body movements, and it is a form of mental energy cleansing, as the story indicates. Historically, the sword has been called an instrument of spiritual self-purification. In Japan, for example, the blade is central to rituals of exorcism and thoughts of perfection.

3

When Children Teach
from the
Grave

Bryn Blankinship
(Wilmington, North Carolina)
Director of membership and lead trainer
for the Newton Institute, certified
hypnosis instructor specializing in
transpersonal hypnosis regression.

Candace came for an LBL session following the death of her two young grandchildren. She was seeking understanding and peace regarding the tragic event. She already knew that we are eternal beings, but by being able to connect in such a profound way with her grandchildren, she was able to feel the eternal nature of our relationships, which for her helped lessen the pain. Knowing that their connection to one another transcends time and space brings healing to her aching heart.

AS I GREETED Candace in the lobby of my office building, she smiled and shook my hand. I felt a sense of quiet strength and determination from her, which immediately caught my attention. Her beautiful hazel eyes looked at me through a veil of sadness that her smile could not completely hide.

As we made our way to my office, Candace didn't waste time with small talk. She had come today seeking understanding and comfort following the death of her two young grandchildren in a car crash four months prior. A third grandchild survived. Daniel was ten years old and Emma was just seven at the time of their passing. Candace was a devoted grandmother who found herself lost with them gone. She missed holding them, playing with them, and touching them.

Daniel had short blond hair, a warm smile, and friendly eyes. Like most boys his age, he was into sports, and his strong athletic build allowed him to excel at them. Candace and Daniel had been especially close. She described him as the kind of child who could sense that you were sad and find ways to make you smile. An incredibly loving and sensitive soul, Daniel was wise beyond his ten short years on this planet.

Emma was Daniel's opposite in many ways. With long black hair outlining the pale, petite features of her face, little Emma's body was slight and tiny compared to Daniel's. She had a mischievous twinkle in her eye and could at times be described as a naughty little pixie. When she would get caught purposely hitting her older brother, she'd just laugh, claiming it was an accident. She laughed a lot, but there was something inconsolably sad about her. It seemed to get worse as the time of their death drew nearer.

Candace's expression could not mask the pain she felt as she shared with me how they enjoyed spending time together biking, swimming, visiting the zoo, and watching movies. It really didn't matter what they did, as long as she and the children did it together.

As Candace spoke, her eyes drew me in. Her eyes are those of an old soul, possessing depth and wisdom. Dealing with her grief showed an obvious heaviness that was gracefully carried by her fighting spirit. She wanted to understand and learn from it—to not be consumed by the deep sadness that caused her to reach for a glass of wine more often than she would prefer. She knew this wasn't the answer. The nights were the hardest; they grew darker and the pain worsened.

We began the past-life regression in preparation for the LBL session that would take place in a few days. Candace easily regressed to a past life as a native hunter with beautiful black hair, wearing only leather skins and a strap with a holder for his arrows. In this lifetime, Candace was a male named Sequana, meaning blessed.

Sequana spent his days and nights in the forest in a time "before machines, boats, and the white people." He was gifted with the ability to get so close to the animals that they didn't even see him. He remarked, "I don't eat the animals but rather walk with them and get close to the doe to feel her beauty. Food is easy, it's just there—leaves, berries, water, fruits in trees, fish ... bears show us honey."

Preferring the seclusion of his cavelike place, his medicine was to live away from the tribe and among the animals in the forest. "My teachers are the spirits," he explained. "I walk. I feel the trees, plants—we talk. And the animals, we talk ... I shift my being to become them and learn their secrets, learn their medicine."

Quickly the journey carried us to a later time in Sequana's life. "I am old now, but not ancient ... my hair not so black, my body not so strong ... I have the magic and the medicine ... I love the heat from the fire and sit by it and smell the smoke. Women have come to me for my strength to give them children, but not to stay; my children are precious, desired, but I stay alone." Upon reflection, Sequana admitted that it was his mistake being alone because there was nowhere for his learning to go, no one to pass it on to. The women of the tribe would come to Sequana when they needed him to heal and for strength, but there was no other relationship between them.

Many individuals, whom Sequana recognizes, also play significant roles in Candace's current life. His father, Jenaqua, who has enormous energy, had been the tribal leader. Jenaqua taught Sequana and his twin brother how to work with the energy and to carry it for the tribe. He is now incarnated as Candace's father. His spirit now comes to her to hold her hand and offer comfort.

Sequana's twin brother, older by just a few minutes, serves as his link to the people and shares his same powers. As children, they played together with the nature spirits, the sun, the moon, and the clouds. He enjoys being around people, while Sequana prefers solitude. This twin brother is again a brother who is instrumental in Candace's life today, offering love, support, and strength. He helps her to hold the energy for the family during this difficult and tragic time. We discover "holding the energy" is a skill that Candace also possesses and is important to be drawn upon now.

As Sequana's life moves to an end, he is very old. "I need to rest; it's harder to breathe too. They have all gone. It's my time now." Sequana slips into death and finds his spirit standing outside of his body. "I just shake free from my body. I have my strength again. I know where I am going."

At the crossover into the spirit world, Sequana—as Candace in her most immediate past life—is greeted by loved ones (both human and animal). He is enveloped in a blue light "radiating from the heart of centered darkness ... this light is a deep, strong color like a gem that gets brighter and brighter; it moves and has sound, texture, and weight. It is like a solid light." It "washes off all of the sticky parts," rejuvenating his spirit body from the heaviness of his earthly body.

This native life gave Sequana the opportunity to refill the cup, so to speak, because it allowed for spiritual growth while having his basic survival needs met. It was about feeling the earth and knowing its souls, and to just feel the joy of the heat of the sun and the cool of the rain—balance. Learning to be of the earth gave him the knowledge of the plants and the medicines for later, when he would be a healer. "I have a list of things I need to be, so this was like class for the next lives. I made the choice to be alone this life but am learning that every choice is not the right choice. I will do it differently the next time."

Revisiting this life gave Candace access to this dormant reservoir of strength so necessary to carry her through this crucial time. Following the death of her grandchildren, it was essential to find the balance that she so desperately needed now. Clarity and unity of purpose would keep her energies from being scattered.

Before the session came to a close, Candace was advised by her guides that there was too much energy in her body, and it needed to be utilized in a better way. This was why she was having trouble sleeping. She was told to utilize the dreamtime and to eliminate the wine. Relying on wine took her further away from her purpose in experiencing these events. She was reminded of the importance of fully staying in the body, spirit, and energy of all that is life; she must come all the way into it and experience the whole of it.

Candace was given a lot to digest on this day. As she left my office, I noticed there was lightness to her presence. She seemed introspective yet relaxed after this intense session. I would see her again in a few days for the LBL.

When Candace arrived for her life-between-lives session, we wasted no time in getting started. She easily regressed to childhood and into the womb. In her soul state, Candace described the womb as "kind of like a waiting room; I'm feeling parts of me sliding into the edges, I'm upside down, can hear my mother's heartbeat that feels like a pulse and then ripples and flows ...

"I joined up with the fetus at seven months and am getting used to being in the body. I stay inside but I go out and look around sometimes. (1) My emotions control this brain. This body is female. I like incarnating as a male, but I need to try and be softer, yet strong. In my current life, I knew I was going to be a different kind of female. This one is full of challenge ... I need the emotions; challenges are obstacles that make it hard to stay on course ... nothing easy here."

Crossing into the spirit world after her past life, my client reports, "There are huge columns of light. One of the columns is me, but it seems to have no boundaries. I have a separate awareness but not a separate being now as I merge with this light and join to it. I am this light."

She is greeted by her spirit guides Gabrielle and Michael, who call her I-la. This is Candace's immortal soul name. Gabrielle is a pure gold color surrounded by rich purples, pulsating and flowing with pure love. Michael, her senior guide, has dark and glowing colors with the deepest of violets, displaying a contrast both of light and of solidity. I-la describes herself as having a bluish tone, not as deep as Michael's.

I-la moves to a huge temple with stone floors, then into a large library with many levels. She informs me that she needs to register that she's here before beginning the review of meaningful past-life experiences. As she stops to do this, she explains, "What we build on the earth is a pale imitation of what we remember from here ... I put all of the pieces in the big binder." (2)

The review begins. Her guides emphasize to her the value of spending time not only touching the earth but interacting with others. I-la, it seems, had experienced other past lives that also involved isolation and a tendency for her to seek solitude. I-la explains that "although I knew my plants, trees, animals, and birds from these lives, I needed to learn about individuals— their names—and to start having relationships with them."

It was noted that although I-la liked lives where she was devoted to the land, she did not slow down enough to take notice of people and details. The details are needed to connect with others to know them as individuals. They are the entrance to people. Each body has its story and its ego—"This I am still learning," I-la comments. I-la tends to be too much inside herself.

"I don't study here right now," I-la mentions, "I'm just depositing information that I learned (for a future time in the library). It's like charging myself by filling up on the details of my other lives. With some bodies it's more difficult to maintain soul identity, and there are other earthly lifetimes that are easier where I come to relax a bit." I-la explains that in recent lives, she has not brought a lot of energy into her bodies, but as Candace, she brought almost all of her energy, knowing what was potentially in store.

After finishing the review in this spiritual library, I-la moves through the courtyard to a large bouquet of energy where her soul group has gathered. She explains that "they are all gathered together. Since I am the elder in our soul family, when I come home we all spread out." Stepping into the energy, she recognizes various family members. "There are lines of connectivity with the soul group that wind from each one of us to each other ... sometimes the lines are lit and sometimes not." (3)

So I asked I-la to find the line that led to her grandchildren Daniel and Emma. She does, and they come forward; Emma first, followed by Daniel. Emma didn't have much to say. We are told Emma was not part of Candace's main soul group, therefore she is not a companion soul like Daniel but rather from an affiliated group. This was the reason the line to Emma was not as brightly lit as Daniel's. She loved Emma but the connection to Daniel was much stronger. Next Daniel appears. His energy is big and loving. He embraces I-la/Candace with his presence. Daniel informs Candace that he didn't mean to hurt her by leaving, and he likes knowing the importance he bears in her heart. She is comforted knowing he is happy now in his eternal home. He is learning too, and plans are being made for his next life. As souls, both Daniel and Emma volunteered in advance of this incarnation to teach the various family members through their leaving so early in life. Both souls apparently joined their human bodies knowing there was a high probability of violent deaths at a young age. Candace also joined with the same human family to experience the grief that followed. (4) For Candace, she is karmically overcoming her tendencies toward isolation and solitude in past lives (as had happened with Sequana, for whom it could be argued that he devalued family in favor of self-absorption). In this life, she must be strong and help her family pull together to work through the emotions of losing the children.

After a series of lifetimes of living in isolation (by choice or by circumstance), the departed children are teaching Candace to come out of her solitude and to bring forth skills she's developed from previous lives that will help her now to unify her family. Tragedy can unite or it can divide. She can use what she's learned to help the family heal. By remembering the children through stories and pictures, she can let them know it's okay to feel loss but also remind them that one day they will all be together again.

Children are the hope for our future. When a life is cut short, there is a strong impact on those who loved the child. Those left behind are given an opportunity for spiritual growth. Despite their tiny bodies, children are powerful healers. Although Daniel's earthly body was that of a child, his spiritual body is no longer restricted by the physical body. He is a very big and powerful soul. Candace believed that we are eternal, but losing her grandchildren had tested her beliefs. Experiencing Daniel's big energy now helps her to know that Daniel's (and Emma's) spirit goes on. Daniel is teaching Candace to keep her heart open. Life must go on, and she must be strong for her remaining grandchild, their surviving sister, who really needs her now. (5)

The effect of the tremendous exchange of healing energy between Candace and her loved ones was visible on her face. Palpable and transformative, it filled the room. Its healing properties restored her aching heart. Candace's face brightened as tears of joy streamed from her eyes. My eyes welled up too, touched by what I had witnessed. The power of spiritual regression in understanding karma in our lives is enormous.

Surprisingly, we didn't spend a great deal of time talking with the two grandchildren during the session. The powerful exchange went on for a while as its loving vibration lifted the heaviness from her being. This was more beneficial than any words could ever be. Her guides instructed her to take time at home to sit quietly to "follow the breathing into that quiet space ... visualize the lights coming, erasing the darkness and lifting the pain."

It was then time for I-la to go before her Council of Elders. These all-knowing beings are huge and luminescent. "These are the ones who send me to incarnate," she informed me. "They are the 'light carriers' and are here to bring enlightenment." There are seven of them.

Climbing up a mountain, she was led to a beautiful crystal building surrounded by a deep pool of emerald green water. I-la went inside the gates to where her council awaited her arrival. She stood before them as they complimented her on her progress through the hardships of her current life. They discussed how the lesson of sadness has held her back, telling her to go beyond the "sad" and to see the truth about babies passing. This would help her and her grieving family.

The elders reassure I-la that it is understandable to have despair sometimes, but she must move beyond it. Working through the energy and connecting with the light will lift her and those around her, making things different. They instruct her that meditation and being in dreamtime feeds the soul. Balance is needed between work and emotion. She must learn not to get lost in emotion or work in order to stay on track. This too is part of the lesson for Candace.

Alana, one member of the council who has been with I-la for many lifetimes, informs Candace that the purpose of Daniel and Emma leaving held different lessons for each family member. Candace's role is that of carrying the light and as comforter. The loss she has experienced will act to create more depth in relationships—a sort of crash course in learning about people and personalities. The qualities of gentleness and kindness that she's developed through lifetimes of living with the animals and in nature bear significance now.

She is to put out reminders of the children to the family to show them that although the children are not in a body, they are not really gone. Just as her father's spirit is able to come to her, they come too. Daniel's spirit often comes with reminders to help them grow from his passing.

As the LBL session concluded, a path was opened for Candace to return to the spirit world to visit the council whenever she needed. They instructed that she must remember to come, and that she can do this on her own now.

Our session ended there. When Candace arose from the timeless elasticity of the between-lives state, it was late in the afternoon. What had felt like a few minutes for her had actually been several hours, as we had started early that morning. I was honored to have been part of such an incredible experience. Something had shifted—for her and for me. What, only time would tell.

In the months since her LBL session, Candace has found relief from the tight grip of continuous pain that had held her. When I met with her to write this story, she looked good. She was smiling and happy, without the sadness in her eyes the first time we met. She shared, "After the children died, I found myself lost, without the ability to connect with my understanding of the universe, with my center, my soul, my heart. My time in LBL reestablished that connection. I found a sense of joy—momentary and

transient, but peace and joy again—after my session. It was not that I needed to be reminded of our eternal existence, but that I needed to feel and
experience it—to break through the veil of pain that hid my soul from me."

Candace has had contact with the spirits of her grandchildren since they
died, even before the LBL. She explained that the difference now is that "we
continue our relationship in a better way. My understanding of the eternal
nature of our relationships has lessened the pain of being without them."
She is able to heal *through* it rather than be restricted by it. And her meditations are deeper now; it is easier getting into them and staying there.

She also commented that pictures taken of Daniel and Emma during the
last few months of their lives showed "a distant look in their eyes. It's as if
they knew they would be saying goodbye soon."

Her heart is still mending, but Candace can now access that place in
her heart and soul where pain is understood and modified—where healing
begins. "I know we will dance together again," she says. "This helps make a
tragic situation more bearable."

---

(1) Souls are perfectly capable of leaving sleeping babies, adults, or patients in a
     coma for a while to roam around, perhaps visiting old haunts before return-
     ing. However, they always leave a portion of their energy behind for emer-
     gencies. See DS 79.

(2) Typically, souls find their permanent records of past-life accomplishments
     and shortcomings stored in places resembling earthly libraries. For more
     information and a diagram on the spiritual libraries containing life books,
     see DS 150–152.

(3) While we have magnetic gridlines on Earth, cluster groups of souls also have
     specific vibrational concentrations of energy rather like homing beacon
     locators; see DS 116. Transition to a soul group, JS 73–86. Lines of connec-
     tivity with individual soul group members, DS 276, figure 10. Also, compare
     with soul group placement, JS 176, figure 7.

(4) The possibilities and probabilities of events happening in our lives due to
     karmic influences may be difficult to unravel, because the laws of karma
     seem to favor elements of determinism in our existence on Earth to the
     detriment of free will. Yet this conclusion is not borne out by LBL research.
     While souls volunteer for karmic assignments in the life selection room
     before the next life, there is always room for free will choices and even a

change in direction with upcoming events in life. In this case, there was evidently a high potential of both children dying in a car crash at a given moment in time. However, there can be variables in this scenario. If the crash had not been quite so severe, one or both children might have survived. Perhaps their parents could have arrived at the street junction just before or just after the crash, or they might have decided at the last minute not to get into the car at all. See free will, JS case 26, 226–230 and DS 370–373.

As to reasons why a soul would choose a "filler life" of only a few years, this must be determined by an examination of karma here and the needs of the parents, especially the mother. Souls provide comfort and support during their time in the fetus and as young children who stand a high probability of dying young. We are told in this story that the children made Candace "blissful" with their presence, however brief. It would seem there are few major accidents in life, but these may contain a number of alternatives. For more on this subject, see DS 235, 359–363, 371–373, 383–384 and LBLH 177–178.

(5) The author of this story later advised me that Candace sat for a month with the surviving child as the little girl's condition went from critical to stable. When she was finally told that her brother and sister had been killed, she insisted, "No, they're standing right there," and pointed to the foot of her hospital bed. She was able to see and communicate with them long after the crash, as they provided comfort for her. It is believed that she continues to do so even now but just does not talk about it anymore to the adults in her life because it is too painful for them. The ability of children to see and talk to entities from the other side is quite remarkable.

4

COMPLETING
the
JIGSAW PUZZLE

Martin Richardson
(OXFORDSHIRE, ENGLAND)
SPECIALIST IN HYPNOTIC REGRESSION,
HYPNOTHERAPY RESEARCH, AND IN
HELPING CLIENTS CHANGE THEMSELVES.

When compiling a jigsaw puzzle, two elements are required: all the relevant pieces in combination with the ability to bring them together and complete the picture.

Dani came to experience LBL seeking a better understanding of herself and her place in the grand scheme of life. She wished to identify the major players in her soul group, the nature of the work they do together, and to recognize and get to know her spirit guide, the teacher of this soul group. Her thirst for understanding included the desire to check her progress on her soul path, to establish her direction, and to discover anything she should be doing to improve her learning.

The preparatory past-life-regression (PLR) sessions created, in Dani's own words, "the pieces of the jigsaw." Two ensuing life-between-lives (LBL) sessions allowed that jigsaw to be completed and answered many of Dani's questions.

THIS STORY IS all about Dani and her jigsaw-puzzle building. In the following account, the names in parentheses are those of the souls in Dani's current life. Dani's past-life experiences revealed that key souls are indeed interacting through different roles, and this key learning element forms a crucial part of her soul development.

First, Dani was regressed back to Wales in the late nineteenth century as Sarah. The souls of her father, husband, and children in this life were found to be members of Dani's soul cluster group, whose incarnated lives are intertwined with her own. For instance, Sarah's daughter Flora is her sister Lara today. While it was a hard life, Sarah had profound family relationships that resulted in Dani's first jigsaw piece—that of her discovery of the main lesson from that life: love and patience.

The next incarnation took place soon afterwards in England as a girl named Joy, and again we learned about the active role of Dani's soul group members. Her primary soul mate was her husband then as well as today (Kevin). Joy died rather young—at the age of fifty—of a heart attack, but from her family she learned trust and that happiness can be acquired from simplicity. This past-life lesson provided Dani with her next jigsaw piece.

Dani then regressed to the very first life she had experienced with the soul of Jeremiah, a family friend with whom she has a close affinity today. She returned to the time of the Roman Empire. In Rome, Dani was a man called Manas who made and sold clay pots for storage. At the age of twenty-five, Manas lived just outside the city with Leah, the love of his life (family friend Jeremiah today). As Manas moved forward to the next significant event in this lifetime, he found himself holding Leah, who was distraught at the loss of their child. Moving forward again, they now had two children, one of them Dani's current sister (Lara).

Forward again to the next memory: an encounter with a large crowd, shouting and jeering as slaves were given their freedom. Here, there was a healer called Samson (her aunt in this life) who used herbs to heal.

During the next significant memory, Manas experienced the time his soul left his body. He was aged fifty-nine, alone, thin, sad, and had just fallen in the street, with no one offering him any assistance. Manas had long since left Leah and the children in poverty, and he did not want to die without letting Leah know how sorry he was for her poor treatment.

Jigsaw piece number three: Dani discovered that as Manas, she was too selfish, didn't care about people, and lived purely for pleasure. The lesson was self-awareness, to show true feelings, and also the realization of the need to share oneself.

As her LBL facilitator, I felt it important that Dani experience the next life she had shared with this significant soul, known today as Jeremiah. She went back again to find herself as a female named Lita living in Greece. In this life, Jeremiah was her brother, Alta, and during the first memory, Lita was aged twenty-two, pregnant and hiding from soldiers. She was inundated with flashing metal (from the soldiers' breastplates), helmets with feather plumes, and lots of noise. She recalled being told to "wait here." The soldiers eventually departed, forcefully taking with them her husband and leaving Lita, Alta (current friend Jeremiah), and her mother (close friend Nikki today) to flee to the island of Rhodes. Moving forward in time, she recalled living in a simple home with a daughter of just two years of age (son George today). Alta was, in truth, her brother, but none of their community was aware of this; Alta and Leah were accepted as a couple and lived a happy life on their rural property. Moving forward in time again to Lita's late thirties, the next scene revealed another child, clearly part of the family but not her own. The child (her aunt in this life) had a burned, disfigured face and walked with a limp; her parents had died, and in Lita's memory, "no one but us would have her."

As we moved forward in time once more, Lita reported that Alta could not breathe and was feeling "a weight on his chest." Caring for him, Lita shed many tears as he slipped away from her and died. Lita's own life ended when she took a fall and found herself ready to die and to be with her beloved Alta (Jeremiah today) once more.

Another jigsaw piece: the lesson of love. Lita loved Alta, and she loved both her girls equally. She also learned compassion, for she was able to forgive the soldiers.

This series of past-life experiences illustrates that groups of souls incarnate together repeatedly, playing different roles in order to achieve important life objectives and to help each other. For example, Dani senses this
strongly in her close soul connection with Jeremiah, who today is a dear
friend she rarely sees but who has in past lives played very different roles as
her partner, brother, and lover. With this overview, Dani was able to make
comparisons with and understandings about her relationships in her current
life. But, she wondered, how do these souls relate to each other in the spirit
world between lives—and have the lessons learned from past lives been recognized and absorbed into her current life? Dani turned to LBL therapy to
seek the answers, and we began the first of two such sessions. (1)

The entry into hypnosis was slow, and Dani reached a deep level—we
had worked together many times before, and I already knew her to be an
excellent hypnosis subject. In the past life that preceded entry into the spirit
world, she was age nineteen, living near Canterbury, England, and about to
marry Terrance (husband Kevin today). Moving forward to the end of that
life, she was age fifty-four and alone, struggling for breath and dying just as
her husband found her. This was not a very hard life; however, its lessons
were significant, as we discover with Dani as she enters the between lives
state ...

She is met by her guide, Tian, who features both male and female sides,
stern and compassionate respectively. She has little choice; she has to visit
what she calls her "panel" first (also frequently called the Council of Elders).
On the way, Tian asks if she feels she has put enough effort into that life; she
remembers she had been expected to put more in, but she didn't—she just
"coasted."

In her visualizations, Dani is standing outside huge wooden doors and
finds these will not open until there is a sense that she has had enough time
to consider her actions in her last life in order to better understand it. When
she does enter, her panel appears to be strangely unfamiliar at first. Dani
would learn that we can be the co-creators of uncertainty with our first
visual spiritual images of new scenes. As Dani, she must learn to see beyond
what she initially fears. Artificial illusions—as masks—may be removed by

courage for greater clarity. She finds herself in front of the panel, but lower; looking up, she knows that the entities are not what they appear to be. Inquiring of her guide, she is told "you will see what you expect to see; if you expect to see something fearful, then you will." She is asked to be still and to trust; soon, the panel appears as it normally does, with seven members in total. (2)

During the telepathic communication with her panel, she reports, "I feel that I wasted time and was too quick to judge others; I didn't use the life in the way in which it could have been used—I didn't make it what it could have been." She continues, "I didn't really understand how I could make it different; I was lazy, I just took what came my way. I could have been a force for good in my community, but I didn't join in, I stood separate; the potential for healing within me didn't have a chance to show itself, even with my own children... I could have shared my inner knowledge with them."

She concludes, "I didn't use the life as I could have done; it could have been meaningful, and it doesn't matter how long life is... making meaningful connections with other people multiplies on itself."

Dani's jigsaw puzzle was now growing and was displayed to her with considerable relevance to her current life. The past lives she remembered had given her incredible resources, which she had not used or developed in her last life, but each one also bore significance in relation to her current life.

As this between-lives visit progressed, her panel symbolically showed her a flower—a beautiful rose opening up one petal at a time. Dani reported, "I'm opening up bit by bit—beginning to understand, beginning to show my beauty like a ripening flower. I am on that journey, beginning to understand and to glimpse what the flower could look like—what I could be. I am being given impressions of what I can truly be. If the flower receives the sun and water it needs, it will blossom accordingly—it has to be fed appropriately, too, just as I have to focus on what I need in order to achieve that understanding."

Dani then reported on the discussion and feedback relating to her current life. "I have to be more focused this time around; I am being told that just 'trying to be' is not good enough—I actually have to 'do' and not just 'try to do.' I am kinda sloppy in how I do things; I now know I have to give everything one hundred percent of myself and to do everything with intent. If I fix my intention, I have to follow it through—this relates to healing, mainly to healing. It is a gift I have—I have to build on that and not just fall back on it; the intuition is the first step, but the reason I have a brain is to take this further. It is not just about what I am being taught; it's about what I can apply myself using that teaching."

Having made this discovery, Dani ventured to her soul group and met the key players in her past and present lives; Jeremiah was the first to welcome her. She realized that her soul group's overall purpose is to "wake people up—we are making a difference to those around us," and this purpose is enhanced by the group's ability to see beyond what most people can see. One of her own soul activities is to increase her soul's healing energy. Dani described working with two members of her soul group—her current sister Lara and good friend Antoinette—working with "a ball of energy in my hands, but it doesn't touch my hands (it looks a little like a plasma ball). This healing energy is then thrown down like snowballs so that it can balance the negative energy created on Earth. This work is enjoyable, fun— dealing with all that powerful, positive energy is almost infectious and there is much laughter. It is a focusing of intention, a bit like doing Reiki—that's what Reiki is on Earth!"

After this first LBL, Dani reported that in a fully awake state, she received a huge download of information; it seemed as if she was being given all the resources necessary to catch up. Six months later, she came for her second LBL.

She regressed to a challenging life as Mary, whose brutal husband abused her. She was a simple woman with natural gifts of herbal healing; however, she found that she could not cope with all the abuse and gave up trying to live. This life was packed full of learning about how to be "on the receiving end," for in the life before this one, she remembered she had been a cruel male soldier.

Her second LBL proved to be a wonderful confirmation of the first. Dani viewed her Akashic Records in the library (3); the records initially appeared as a battered old book and then revealed multidimensional layers of meaning, through which she experienced a huge revelation: "I've come back to where I'm supposed to be via a different route—after a big deviation when I was seventeen..."

There were further discoveries in the place of life selection, in which she experienced confirmation that her current life as Dani has everything to do with healing: "I'm a bit behind where I need to be—I could have reached this point sooner, but I'm on the correct path. My enthusiasm is a gift, a tool to help people." At the end of her second LBL, a padlock was removed from the center of her heart, and she reported this as "a huge release."

Dani's jigsaw puzzle was finally coming together, creating a cohesive, focused picture. Our initial PLR work provided the impetus for Dani to develop herself further. Her first LBL provided her with confirmation, direction, and resources. The second LBL session highlighted to her that everything was now back on track in this life. In her own words, "I could sense that I had finally taken a leap off the edge of the precipice. I could fly or fall—but I didn't know where I was headed." As the sessions progressed, so did her understanding and resolve, and now the jigsaw puzzle is complete. Dani has undergone intensive training to become a qualified cognitive therapist and now has a full-time practice so that she can make her contribution in life.

---

(1) The dynamics of soul group interaction and the assumption of various supporting roles in the physical lives between group members is a vital part of spiritual regression therapy. For a client trying to understand the meaning of their current life and the lessons to be learned, it is very revealing to discover the souls of your friends and relatives in many bodies who have incarnated together with you for such long spans of time on Earth. See DS 128–129, 142–143 and LBLH 138–142.

(2) I suspect that Dani's initial visualization of her council members appearing as animals was by design. There is a symbolic overtone of negative transmigration here. Indeed, we are told that "if you expect to see something fearful, you will." There seems to be an expectation by Dani of some sort of punishment that feeds into Indian mythological dogma of reduction in rank to lower forms of life in future incarnations because she did not live up to her potential in the last life. However, readers should be aware that often

orientation by a personal spirit guide will initially address the soul's primary concerns of the life just lived after re-entry into the spirit world. See orientation, JS 69, and transmigration, DS 52, 203.

(3) Akashic in Sanskrit means "space," and Indian philosophy uses this term to describe a space representing a universal filing system that records every thought, word, and action in our lifetime. While people in trance may be influenced by a conscious memory of this well-known karmic term, more often than not in hypnosis, LBL subjects recalling spiritual libraries think of these records as their life books, diaries, or as representing a kind of celestial television set for their utilization. Visualizing the spiritual library is a profound experience in higher consciousness in an LBL session. See DS 150–152.

5

LIFE CHOICES
and
MOVING ON

Sophia Kramer
(NEW YORK CITY AND KIEL, GERMANY)
INTERNATIONAL INSTRUCTOR AND AUTHOR
SPECIALIZING IN HYPNOTHERAPY, REGRESSION,
FAMILY SYSTEMS, TRAUMA, AND RECONCILIATION.

In my LBL work, I often work with people who are griev-ing the passing of a loved one. They frequently wish to make contact with their deceased loved ones in spirit and seek answers on how they feel after their physical death. They will often feel an urge to have an exchange with them in order to be able to move on in their own lives. This can be a very healing experience that brings closure and acceptance, often paired with a blessing from the person in spirit for the one here on Earth, who still has to conquer the challenges of life. Then there are people who come for an LBL session because they wonder if they are on the right path and who want to know their life's purpose or gain insight into specific questions about their career, their family, or important life changes.

Here I will share with you my experience of an LBL session I conducted in South Africa that exemplifies the positive changes that happen when we follow our soul's purpose.

I AM ON my way to Johannesburg, where I have been invited to conduct LBL sessions. South Africa is a country of breathtaking beauty, full of rich culture, traditions, and originality. The country still struggles with its changes and adjustments after apartheid's injustice and imbalance. I feel that with my background in systemic therapy and regression work, especially the life-between-lives regression work and my passion for it, I can assist here and there with the healing of individuals and the core of this amazing country.

Andrew is a South African man in his mid-thirties. We had a phone consultation in which he stated that he'd had some experience with hypnosis, but this was many years ago. Meeting with him in my colleague's office, I see Andrew as a straightforward and extroverted man who describes himself as a "go-getter" and is successful in his work and focused on achievements and material comfort. He is married and has a small son. He doesn't observe any spiritual or religious practice and doesn't describe himself as particularly spiritual. But he is open minded and believes that our session will shed light on his questions.

Andrew and his wife are concerned about the future in South Africa, especially about the safety of their son and their second child, who is about to arrive. Even though they are financially settled and have a large extended family and many friends, they consider leaving the country. South Africa's future is the biggest concern for Andrew, aside from an inquiry about his life purpose and questions about some fears of failure and rejection.

Andrew responds very well to the induction and to the relaxation. His body reacts fine to images of safety and to affirmations of security. He gets so deep and relaxed that his voice is very soft, so that I have to be very mindful in understanding his responses. Regressed to childhood, experiencing a blissful moment as baby Andrew, he feels as if he is really there—he is the little baby, responding with a baby voice, bubbly laughter, and body movements that reflect this moment.

It is always an astounding feeling to witness the process of my clients—to sit with them in their experience and to tune in with the moment—on one hand, to sit in my place as a facilitator for their experience, and on the other to sit back to let them fully experience it from within. Baby Andrew is able to recall many details of his surroundings, which the adult Andrew would not have been able to recollect with his everyday, rational mind. This is especially nice for him, since he stated issues with his mom in our initial interview and here, as a baby, he is able to recall constructive recollections, which I anchor for him as a resource for the future.

In his mother's womb, Andrew is able to answer many questions regarding his body choice, his soul, and integration with the body. He realizes that his spiritual character is lighter, less serious, and more carefree. I ask him if he would like to pull in some of this carefree energy into his physical body, and he agrees. Then something astounding happens: Andrew starts to breathe heavily, pulling the energy down into his body, huffing and puffing, turning red and violet. I tell his body to accept it, to integrate it into each and every cell of his being. Then he relaxes with a glow on his face, feeling very happy.

After Andrew completes his "download" of carefree and joyful soul energy, the next step would have been to guide him to a past life, preferably his most recent past life. But Andrew's soul is eager to go right away into the spirit realm. He rises up, seeing some stretches of land below him, and experiences a strong pull from above. He perceives a tube of light, is pulled higher and higher, and trusts his divine help while leaving the heavy physical residue behind him. This light feels very comfortable as the space around him gets brighter and brighter. Following this pull into the bright light, his face becomes very happy, the sensation grows stronger and stronger, and then suddenly Andrew becomes very peaceful, very quiet, and tears start to run down his cheeks. (1)

Andrew states that he can see a light being who greets him with an embrace, enveloping him with loving energy. "He is here for me, he is like a big brother... he is my guide," Andrew exclaims. Andrew connects to Zecho, whose name he can recall and spell out for me. He is able to recognize his guide's energy, realizing that he had indeed felt it before. We then find out that Zecho calls Andrew by his immortal name of Estrell.

"Zecho is always with me," Andrew states with conviction. "We communicate with telepathic feelings." And then it happens again: Andrew/Estrell starts to download his guide's energy into his physical body, this one being even more dramatic than the first download. I witness him breathing heavily, pumping his body up with that loving, powerful force, his skin color turning red and violet again, and his body swelling up, tears running down his face, before becoming quiet and blissful once more.

Zecho communicates with Andrew/Estrell, telling him how pleased he is with his performance in this life and that his greatest achievement in this life is "being kind, honest, and simply being himself." Zecho states that he has been with Andrew/Estrell for a long time, throughout many difficult lives, and that he is proud of how well Andrew/Estrell is doing in comparison to other past lives.

Over and over in my work, I see that there is no judgment in the spirit world. We, in our human condition, critique ourselves and others, but our guides and council never judge us. Andrew is a man who is often hard on himself. He experienced a strict mother and often feels he doesn't accomplish enough. He struggles with self-esteem issues, and here in the spirit world, his guide assures him that it is enough to just be himself. He realizes that he is his hardest judge, and that we receive compassion and understanding in the spirit world.

Estrell moves even higher. "I am standing in a room, it is like a semicircle...lots of light...there are other beings, they are all dressed like Zecho, with brown robes...there is a lot of love...and humor." Estrell can count five council members, and Zecho is right there with him, standing in the background. (2) "Now they are all sitting down on the floor, and it is getting dark. I see a rounded roof...they ask me to sit with them...they are facing me...it is humbling for me to sit with them." I begin asking a few questions directed to his council members, but Estrell states, "They are hunched over, they are getting very serious...ohhh." Suddenly he starts crying heavily. "They show me Africa's stage today...they show me a picture of it...I feel the deep pain of it." I could see this was very agonizing for Andrew, and then he continued, "They tell me I can leave South Africa if I want...easy...it would be very easy." I ask Andrew if he would feel guilty if he decided to go away and leave others behind in South Africa, and he responds, "No! Not at all, they must do their destiny as much as I must do mine. I don't have fear. We all choose our own fate." He is still breathing heavily and is deeply moved by this. With his heart wide open, Andrew sends healing from this high source to South Africa. He embraces his own path and sends love and healing to all the human beings, animals, plants, and creatures in South Africa.

Zecho is also standing in the circle now, smiling at him. Andrew tells me, "He wanted to show me this lesson." Then one of the members in the middle of the circle communicates telepathically with Andrew/Estrell. "You can leave it behind comfortably. But go with gratitude; there is lots of good in South Africa. Be a messenger for the good of this country when you go out into the new world." Andrew/Estrell sees the planet Earth from above. I ask if he can tell where his new home will be. He responds, "All I can see is Australia." My client is zooming in, exploring more details about Australia, and his council continues to give him images and messages. Andrew/Estrell still needs to cry and grieve, but he starts to focus more on what he receives from his council. During this period, the impression of his council starts to shift. Andrew explains that "these are the same beings, also Zecho is here, but they are not wearing the dark robes anymore ... it is very bright ... they are wearing long, golden robes ... it is still a semicircle but bright and there is a podium ... on the left are the more important ones, the one in the middle is the most significant one ... even the podium is very radiant, it is out of glass, or rather out of crystal ... the ceiling is also out of crystal ... Zecho is with me, behind me ... it is like a university but a more formal setting, similar to a courtroom ... with light beings on the podium, they feel like wise judges to me." (3)

He feels in tune with the judges. "It is not bad at all, it's almost fun ... They are eager to share; they say: do not procrastinate, do it, go! The door of opportunity is open now! It will not always stay open." He looks at their faces; they smile warmly and again give him a picture of Australia. It looks bright and positive, then they give him a picture of South Africa. It looks like it is covered with a gray veil. At this point, I ask Andrew a few more questions regarding this life change, and he continues to receive messages in the form of visual pictures, kinesthetic sensations, and sentences. "People will come to help you and give you guidance. Just trust it. It will develop." (4)

Then Andrew/Estrell's council members give him a deep teaching. They confront him with his fear of rejection and failure. He suddenly feels himself transported back in the womb of his mother, while continuing to have the connection to above with his council. They show him that it was his choice to conquer this theme in this lifetime. He realizes that his mother also felt rejected by her mother, and that she was the perfect mom for giving him the chance to overcome his issues of failure and rejection. He is able to feel forgiveness and compassion for his mom. "She didn't know ... she made mistakes in life ... she and I had the same problem. Forgiveness ... that is the only way."

His council makes him feel and see the circumstances in his life. Andrew realizes that already as a fetus in the womb, it was apparent that this was one of his lessons his eternal soul wanted to accomplish. There is no such thing as rejection; Andrew says, "It is not about you ... don't take it personally. If the other people can't be in my space, it is about them, not about me. I am supposed to be more ME. And I have to lighten up, I am too serious. I need to be more of my true self. No one will reject my SELF! My self is connected to my eternal me ... This is really difficult to comprehend."

Considering that he has already pulled the energy of his teachings into his physical body twice, I ask him if he wants to do that again. And yes, before I even finished my question, one more time Andrew receives a download of his newly recouped information.

After this, it is evident that the session is coming to an end. In LBL work, it is really remarkable. You feel—you *know*—when it is done; the energy shifts, and the session comes to an end.

Andrew has one more glimpse of his council with Zecho present and feels a deep healing and rejuvenation in his body. He takes that in for a while, before I bring him back to the present moment.

This session shows several things beautifully. First, a person who is not an observer of a religious or spiritual practice, who doesn't meditate or do something similar, can go very deep and receive lots of information in visual, kinesthetic, and auditory ways.

Sometimes these messages are a lot to take in, and they come in downloads. Since the information is a lot to process for the mind and body, the download gives the human body and mind the information in the form of a time release. This can be easier for some to tolerate. It is also interesting how the council can assist us with major life choices and learning. Here we saw how the council, through graphic imaging, brought out the bigger message about the nation of South Africa.

Two months later, I heard from Andrew. He, his wife, and his son were in Brisbane, Australia. They took six weeks to travel extensively, to receive guidance and information.

He was excited to report that they'd already found the neighborhood they had decided to move to! About two weeks after that, we planned to meet for lunch in Sydney, since I was also there for work purposes. All of them were very happy about the experiences they'd had during their travels through Australia. Andrew shared that he felt such a shift since his LBL session that he is able to trust the messages he received and follows through with all the plans that were established with the help of his guide and council.

He said to me, "I am amazed at how easily everything falls into place. Since my LBL session, things seem to run perfectly, as if I am guided all the way. Many doors have opened! I've made new friends who are able to connect me with people who are competent to help me professionally. Through this, I already have several new opportunities and am looking at different options for my own business here in Australia! It is amazing to me how life changes when you follow your soul's purpose." Perhaps this is also due to Andrew's more positive attitude toward life.

His wife states how safe the environment is for their children and how many possibilities they will have with the educational system there. "It will be much better for our family life and for our children," she says. Even though they see so many possibilities in Australia, Andrew is committed to his task, which he received in his LBL. "I will tell the people about all the good and incredibly beautiful things South Africa has to offer. I will continue to be a messenger of our country and bring the best of South Africa to our new home. I made a commitment to Zecho that I would do this, and with fulfilling this promise, I follow my soul's purpose."

---

(1) The portal through which souls pass into the gateway of the spirit world is commonly called the tunnel effect. Bright lights are usually an accompanying manifestation. See JS 17–25 and DS 52.

(2) Placement at these meetings may give us an indication of a soul's developmental stage. For more details about the positions of souls, guides, and elders at council gatherings, see council settings, DS 204–207.

(3) Even under hypnosis, the human mind tries to make sense of what is being seen/remembered, using information already available through experience and prior knowledge. A subject may attach those references to the images they see at first before they allow the truer meaning to come into their mind.

   With the commencing of a council meeting, the formality of the setting can sometimes lead certain souls into misinterpreting what is in store for them. One would think the memories of previous council hearings (after other lives) would kick in immediately, but there are souls for whom this is not always true. Because of their conscious preconditioning on Earth, some LBL clients initially think they see a courtroom and judges waiting for them as they enter the chamber. For thousands of years, religious dogma and superstition around the world has predicted we are due for punishment and retribution for our sins at the time of death. This is all false. The spirit world is a space of love and forgiveness.

   The first thing souls see in the chamber are the elders waiting for them, usually sitting on a dais and perhaps in a semicircle. These positions can vary, but at first this scene can give one the sense of a courtroom with authority figures. In this case, Andrew recovers rather quickly and realizes the elders are not wearing dark robes. He also states they are smiling at him. In council meetings, the elders may be smiling or have a more serious look to the soul appearing in front of them, but it is not long before all souls know the meeting is designed to help them evaluate the past and plan for the future. For a more detailed analysis of this theme, see human fear of judgment and punishment, Council of Elders, DS 201–204.

(4) In this case, both sensory and visual images of South Africa and Australia were created by Andrew's council and "downloaded" into his mind. This was done during a deep LBL trance state to provide him with current informa-

tion and to assist Andrew with making choices in present, linear Earth time. By no means should the reader conclude that this sort of council coaching with current decision making will occur with everyone having an LBL session, but a variety of other clues are often available for our consideration. This case does, however, illustrate an important spiritual phenomenon in that we also have the capacity as souls in the afterlife to view past and even potential future events in terms of our participation. This review process is designed for growth.

It seems to me that the science of quantum mechanics is only now catching up with what our LBL hypnosis subjects have been reporting for years. Scientists are learning that subatomic particles, acting under the influence of vibrational energy waves, both record and store all images, animate and inanimate, on Earth. Events represent patterns of pure vibrational energy so that no human experience is ever lost that cannot be recovered for analysis in the timeless afterlife. Apparently, we leave fingerprint-like impressions of our own energy in all geographic locations where our presence has been permanently recorded. These energy waves also have the capacity to create a multitude of alternative patterns for possible future events in our lives. The council chose not to show Andrew what he might expect in the future for two reasons: the future is not set in stone, and also to even touch on what might happen in the future during Andrew's current life would preempt both free will and self-discovery. Even so, as we see with other cases in this book, past, present, and future exist in one continuum of now-time in the spirit world. See quantum application, JS 160, 195, 212, 221; past timelines, DS 168-169; future timelines and life selection, DS 360–365 and LBLH 175–178.

6

INSIGHT
into the
COUNCIL OF ELDERS

Deborah Bromley
(BEDFORD, ENGLAND)
EFT (EMOTIONAL FREEDOM TECHNIQUES)
PRACTITIONER AND TRAINER SPECIALIZING
IN WOMEN'S ISSUES, PAST LIVES, AND LIFE-
BETWEEN-LIVES HYPNOTHERAPY.

People who come for life-between-lives regression are usually very familiar with the books written by Dr. Michael Newton. It's not surprising that reading such inspiring stories about the afterlife awakens a deep desire to seek the experience for oneself. At the time of her LBL, Helen had no knowledge of Newton's books or ideas about the structure of the spirit world, so what makes this LBL fascinating for me is not only the freshness of Helen's spiritual journey but also the firsthand validation of the material in the books.

Sometimes the mind can construct doubts and expectations so that clients may come with a set of preconceived ideas about their life as a soul between incarnations. Fortunately, the guides have other ideas, and they gently direct the action and the energy to ensure the session is both revealing and fulfilling so the client receives the spiritual journey that meets their needs.

IT ISN'T POSSIBLE to describe the experience of LBL on the written page—it defies explanation. Your focus may be on your burning "this life" questions, but as soon as you are connected with the memory of your life as a soul, you are able to recall the limitless love that exists for you in this place—love that holds you and supports you through your incarnations, the love of your guide, the wisdom of your council, the deep connection with your soul friends—and it is overwhelming.

Once you have been immersed in this love, you cannot feel alone or in doubt. It is like having your connection to the spiritual Internet opened: by recalling your LBL, you can reexperience and reconnect with your soul intelligence. Then life's everyday struggles pale into insignificance, because you can put them into a proper perspective.

Meeting with the Council of Elders is one of the most important events for a soul to experience between lives. Thus, when clients in hypnosis recall appearing before these wise beings between lives, it is very meaningful to them. Usually, we are accompanied by our personal guides, who serve as our mentors, while the elders inquire about our progress and evaluate the results. For the still-incarnating soul, this forum appears to be as close to seeing divine beings as we get in the spirit world. What makes this case so unique in my experience is the fact that before her current life, Helen was actually invited by the elders to participate in the highest form of soul evaluation we know of in the spirit world.

Since these higher beings, whom we call the elders, have long ago finished their own incarnations, we cannot place them in hypnosis on Earth to learn their secrets. The compelling aspect of this highly unusual narrative is that Helen is probably being groomed to enter the spiritual vocation of a junior guide herself in the near future. It is possible that she was offered a brief indoctrination into the mysteries of a council meeting as a means of preparation. At the time this case fell into my lap, I was still in my first year of practicing LBL therapy. Today, I would have asked many more questions of Helen. However, even then, I realized that what Helen was describing to me was a great honor for her.

In the spirit world, an elder is above even a senior guide in development. This case illustrates what amounted to a training experience in advanced guidance counseling for a level IV or V soul who is ready to take on more management responsibilities, for lack of a better term. The essence of a soul's existence involves problem solving during their physical incarnations. Both guides and elders who serve as counselors for souls under their juris- diction are in the business of stimulating the gradual development of a soul's ability to improve on their decisions toward making better choices in each new life. This story reflects the impressions of someone who briefly went behind the scenes in a council chamber meeting to actually engage in the process of evaluating others at a level not normally experienced by a still- incarnating soul. The insight we gain about the elders from Helen's depic- tion of her minor role in soul assessment is illuminating, yet at the same time, she is apparently still too uninitiated as a council participant to know how indulgent the elders were in their treatment of her offerings.

Connecting with the spirit world while on Earth is called channeling by some; it's like tuning yourself in to the right radio station so you can listen to different music. Channeling is a skill that can be learned with dedication and practice, and it is through channeling classes that Helen came to experi- ence her life-between-lives regression, with the express purpose of making a strong connection to her own spirit guide to improve her channeling. But her session revealed far more about her own soul life than she could have anticipated.

The background to Helen's life is that she was born of mixed-race par- entage and adopted soon after birth by a Welsh family. She had a loving and secure upbringing but had always experienced problems with her weight. There followed clashes with her adopted mother and associated feelings that she was being judged for her appearance, although she knew deep down that this was not really important to her. She is a person who strongly believes it is your inner self-worth that makes you happy and fulfilled. She had been married but was now divorced, and she had one child, to whom she was devoted. However, relationships—her perceived lack of success with them and her subsequent failure to find someone to spend her life with—were a source of continuing disappointment. She had a background in personnel management and training but also had spent many years successfully working with disadvantaged children.

Helen relaxes easily into her LBL session and soon gets connected to her past-life memories, which will act as a springboard into the life-between-lives state. She finds herself in a field of tall grass in the sunshine. She is a young girl around twenty years of age named Shakira. She sees herself washing clothes in a stream with lots of other women; they are friends, they talk about their daily lives, and the atmosphere is happy, full of companionship and laughter. She lives upstairs in a small wooden hut on stilts and has a husband and a small son, Jacob.

Helen recalls:

> My husband is tall with shaggy hair, a beard, and his teeth are dirty. He is not a nice person. I don't know why I'm married to him. He shouts and drinks a lot. Jacob is frightened of him. I really want to get away from him.
>
> We are at a party, everyone is dancing. There is loud music but we are in a horrible smelly street, it's like a market square. My husband is off drinking somewhere, and Jacob is playing with his friends nearby. I'm carrying some fruit—pomegranates, I think—and talking to a friend, telling her I want to get away. My husband is really angry, though, because he suspects I want to leave him.
>
> I see him, he's coming for me, having a go at me, shouting and hurting me. He's yelling that I wasted money on the fruit. I'm running and crying, hiding in the corner of one of the buildings. Jacob and I are holding each other and crying—I have to tell him it will be all right. But it isn't—he has found us, and he's pulling me away to give me a beating—Jacob is watching him. He's hurting me really badly now, choking me. I tell Jacob to run.
>
> I'm finished now; I feel like I'm floating backwards, there are colors, floaty colors. It's such a relief.

DEBBIE: Any regrets as you think about your life and how it ended?

HELEN: I shouldn't have accepted what was going on, I should have moved away, followed my intuition, but I stayed. I cared, and I don't like to let people down. My husband hurt me, because he thought nobody loved him.

I'm in spirit form now and moving fast. Some people are coming to greet me—it's Melanie (daughter today), Sam and Ellie (close friends today). Oh! Mum's (mother today) coming too—she's puffing, running late as usual. That's just like her. They are clapping and laughing, they are all standing up—"You done well, girl."

I feel so happy and light—it's such a relief. Now I have to go to a place of restoration—that's what I call it. I go and relax in this other light. It's yellow/orange colored, and it just comes up and makes you glow, it fills you up. (1)

D: What is this for?

H: Well, it feels like putting your fingers in a socket. It's amazing. It recharges you after you have been away—I only need a little bit because I was young, but I didn't enjoy that last life, it was hard, so this energy is doing me good.

D: What happens to you after you have recharged your energy?

H: I'm going into this huge space, like a floating coliseum—there are loads of spirits here. It's like we are all waiting for something to start, for someone to come. It's like a seminar or conference. Understanding life purposes, that's what it's about. My group is over there to the side. I go and join them. (2)

Helen sees familiar souls whom she calls by the names they have in her life now—Melanie, her beloved daughter; her mum, and many friends. Gradually, she starts to describe them more in soul terms by their energy qualities. She knows their soul names too, and when I ask her, she says she is called Simene.

H: I can see Mum, Jason, and Melanie, these are the ones I work with the most. Mum—she has balance; Melanie has compassion; Jason—he has strength; me (Simene)—I understand unconditional love. (3)

We like to meet and talk in outdoor settings. I see us in a field. There is a feeling of freshness. We can be free here to laugh and say exactly what we feel. I can see that we are planning a strategy, putting a game plan in place. We have to do this together, because when we go off and have lives on Earth, we might be split up. So when we are together in the spirit world, we plan many lives ahead. That is how we accomplish our goals.

I can see us sitting around a square stone table, and in the center is a little bowl of golden nuggets—that's what we call them. Golden things like peanuts.

D: What are they for?

H: Well, we eat them but we don't, if you know what I mean. They're to help us when we are back on Earth—to give us recognition. We take in the little golden nuggets at key points in our plan; then when we are on Earth we get a feeling of recognition at that key point. It tells us we are on the right track or have met the right person. It makes sure we meet who we are meant to meet—to keep tabs on the plan. (4)

D: Like the feeling of déjà vu?

H: Yes, that's it. It makes you stop for a moment and realize something important is happening.

D: What happens next?

H: I'm in another nice field now. There are two of them—my guides, that is. Sirus—he is close to me, he is young and good looking, dark skinned. (laughs) I sense he is a more junior guide. He's got a lovely smile and deep blue twinkly eyes, he can be a bit naughty sometimes— we do laugh a lot.

In the distance, I see an older female in a floaty frock—she is senior—Opas is her name. She appears to me like an orange light over Sirus's shoulder.

I feel so at home, they know me so well. I need to feel the laughter but keep myself on track; that's what Opas is for. She knows all my weaknesses and reminds Sirus not to let me get too carried away. That's my trouble, I'm always looking for the love—the unconditional love, it's my main attribute—I don't see the bad stuff coming for me. Like my husband in that last life. It got me into trouble.

The feeling of being bound by their care and knowledge of me—it's amazing. So I get a little warning if I'm going too far, like an orange light in my mind reminding me that I should take care. Sirus has been told he must be stricter with me. He winks, though. He is showing me something important now—something that's going to happen to me.

D: In this life?

H: Yes, it's going to happen to Helen. He shows me where we are going to live, my business, my work and how it will continue—I am definitely on the right track.

A child will come and tell me I've made a difference to them. Because of that—I get recognition, something like an award—an OBE? (5) I get an apology and respect. It's a long time before it comes, but I'm doing all the right things now. The orange light in the back-ground shows me there is a new guide for me to work with, because I'm starting a faster pace in this life as Helen. (6)

D: Where do you go next?

H: I see myself in this light space. It's like marble but it's not, it's trans-parent. Ah! I see I am on a council, that's it—I am part of it, advising on the council for others. (7)

D: What does this involve?

H: It's like being on a board of directors. I'm just one of those people who are on it at the moment. I show unconditional love—that's part of my character. When we are discussing different persons (souls) that are saying this and saying that, putting across lots of different views on that person and what they need, how we can advise them without actually telling them what to do, I find myself saying, "Can they learn this lesson in a different way?"

You see, this council is a bit keen on tough lessons. If the souls have to go through probing questioning, I want them to have an alternative way to learn what they need to learn. I want them to have more love; that's how I see my role, if you like.

D: Tell me how it works.

H: Well, there are nine of us. I'm on the far right-hand side. I'm a bright golden-yellow color. (8) I can't really see over to the other side except when they are speaking, that's when the energy color or feeling of the speaker sort of lights up. I put in my view if things get a bit heated.

D: I can't imagine souls getting heated.

H: Perhaps heated is a bit simplistic. There tends to be a collective feeling of agreement about taking a firm stance with certain souls. I hear and feel the energy growing—that's when I have to chime in with my opposite view (to be fully engaged by recommending a softer stance and forgiveness). Then the energy sort of subsides and questions itself (a review and summation). I get commended for my view. I have to show alternative scenes (of a soul's life), like passing diagrams or drawings to the chairman—he is in the center. (9) I pass these tablets of stone with swirly golden writing on them, and everyone examines them as they are passed around. (10)

When we meet before a soul comes in, we always discuss everything that has happened in the soul's life in great detail. We review how our advice (before the last past life) has been heeded and note how each soul has reacted to our advice. Sometimes it is very hard when souls have severe troubles, which is evidence they have not remembered or heeded our words. At first, my impression is that the elders are always rather stern-looking with such souls who come before them. It is tempting to put my points to the council in favor of compassion and love, and even though I am right on the outside (of the forum), I have to make myself heard (telepathically). I am now being recognized more fully about the way I think is best. I feel I am providing balance and making a difference. It's all a question of getting the right balance for each individual case (between firmness and gentleness). That is why we spend so much time reviewing all the evidence (the council draws out about each soul). I have to speak up in favor of compassion and love, even though I am not placed close to the chairman. I think I am now being recognized more fully, and my view carries weight. The leader (chairman) is a very strong soul with an imposing energy. (11)

Helen then indicates she is moving away from this scene. She goes back to the field with her guides.

H: They are there together now, telling me what I need to concentrate on. They say, "You nearly got it; you've got more to learn, though."

As Helen has connected again with her guides, I ask them if they will answer the questions she has brought with her about her life now. Sometimes it's not in the soul's best interest to have easy answers, but in this case, they agree. Helen is able to see and hear what they say and report back to me. I ask her personal questions about her life, her work, her daughter, and relationships. She gives these answers:

H: I need to act more on my intuition. If something is wrong, I must accept it and act on it. I must have more faith in myself, in the things I can't see or touch. I must remember I'm not on my own, and they are there for me.

I thought I had to learn to trust people more (she has been very mistrusting of men in this life), but that is not so. I have to learn to have faith and not be mistrusting. Have faith and trust people until proven otherwise. I must not be suspicious. I can see now that I have gone too far the other way in this life, and it is stopping me from getting close to people. Not everyone is out to get me!

I should now connect more with them (my guides) in my everyday life. If I have a question, I can just put it out there and they will reply, so when I get a feeling or idea, I must go with it.

If I get a thought about what do, how to sort something out, I should go with it instead of analyzing things and pushing that original thought out of my head. That's because if I go wrong, he (Sirus) only has to come and get me anyway, usually by making something bigger or worse happen. If I listen with my heart, then everything will be okay.

Helen considers her temporary exposure to the Council of Elders and eventually says goodbye to her guides. There is a quiet time with them when she doesn't speak, and I know she is having a very deep and profound experience as they prepare to leave.

I remind her about keeping their images close in her mind and how they have advised her to connect with them. This was her goal for our regression—to know her guides, to be able to visualize them in her mind, to know how to call them and feel their energy. By having this experience, she will be able to lock the connection in her mind and recall it whenever she wants to have their support and reassurance. Her unique association with the elders has provided firsthand knowledge of spiritual counseling at the highest level.

She was very happy with her session and as a result is now able to fulfill her objective—to have a channel of communication, both for herself and to gain advice and wisdom for others, mainly friends and family. The knowledge of her guides, their unique personalities, the way they use their skills to help her and how this is perfectly matched with her own needs has allowed her to develop and grow toward a life that is more in line with her true purpose. I noticed she quickly made changes to parts of her life (career, business interests, and colleagues) without any regrets, and she made her daughter the focus of her energy. As that time is coming to an end and her daughter is going to university, now Helen is to realize a personal dream and relocate back to her native Wales. In doing so, she has listened to her heart and had the courage to follow the advice she hears without a backward glance.

---

(1) Healing energy for the returning soul—see JS 53–55. Also energy restoration for severely damaged souls, DS 93–109.

(2) Soul study groups—see DS 190–200. Assembly areas, DS 140–144. Guest speakers, DS 290, 373.

(3) Interaction within soul groups involves peer support between companion souls. There is a balance of each soul's strengths and weaknesses so when they are working together during incarnations, the entire group comple-

ments each other. See soul groups, formation, character traits and purpose in JS 87–90, 128–129, and 142.

(4) For more information concerning spiritual recognition classes prior to our next incarnation, see preparation for embarkation in JS 249–262 and DS 274.

(5) OBE: Order of the British Empire.

(6) Souls moving up to level III at the intermediate levels of advancement are usually assigned to a different specialized soul group and are assigned to a new teacher with particular skills in their area of study. However, we never lose our original personal senior guide who has been with us since creation. Movement to intermediate levels, DS 320–323.

(7) Placement in the council chamber—see DS 201–207.

(8) Brilliant, glittering gold energy colors as opposed to a flat or less vivid yellow—see LBLH 126.

(9) It is not unusual for clients to see their chairperson on the council as being larger and brighter than other council members. It has been suggested that this encourages the soul appearing before the panel to pay close attention to the chairman. Position and description of a council chairman—see DS 214 and LBLH 151. Taking clients before their council, LBLH 145–155.

(10) The client (Helen) was not asked what information she wanted to convey to the elders about the tablets she presented. One might assume they related to her own advice about love and compassion in some way. We do have information about signs and symbols that are used at council proceedings that represent an interpretation of ideas; see DS 224–242.

(11) While there is no question that the client in this unusual case has made some ambitious statements about the part she played with beings on a much higher spiritual level than herself, certain statements might well have been challenged by the facilitator, as the author suggests. This would include Helen/Simene lecturing the council about their lack of compassion and love toward a case before them. The fact Helen said that the elders were stern or severe in demeanor is subject to a wider interpretation in the context of this case as an indication of someone who has misjudged the normal practice of elder behavior. The author has shown us that the elder's indulgence of Helen/Simene is quite remarkable. It is clear we are receiving a narrow perspective by a temporary visitor who has not achieved guide status herself. Even so, in our work one must keep an open mind, because anything is possible in the afterlife.

7

LOTHAR
the
BARBARIAN

David M. Pierce
(PARADISE, CALIFORNIA)
RETIRED FIREFIGHTER AND PARAMEDIC
WHO PROVIDES PATIENT SUPPORT
AT A LOCAL CANCER CENTER.

When facing a difficult or painful situation, the degree of suffering one experiences may be significantly diminished when one finds meaning or purpose to the experience— even when the situation itself is not altered. What follows is the story of a man chronically plagued by a lack of energy. Unable to discover a medical cause for his condition, he began to explore the spiritual side of the question. A single life-between-lives session laid bare the root and reason for his state. Even though he still experiences low energy levels, with this knowledge he was freed of the suffering that used to accompany it, and he has even come to regard it as a palpable reminder of his growth as a soul.

PERHAPS WHAT STRIKES one upon meeting Mark for the first time is his apparent ordinariness—an average guy, slightly shorter than average, who works full-time at an average job. Like many people past middle age, Mark has a growing interest in things of a spiritual nature. For most of his life, however, Mark would tire easily, and he had to be very mindful about how he managed his energy.

Of this, Mark says, "I've always had a tendency to want to lie around more than most people. I'd feel like I had to manage my energy in a way that my friends didn't. It seems like the amount of energy I have is very limited, and I have to husband it very carefully. I'd been feeling kind of victimized by my own body—betrayed or something. I don't have chronic fatigue syndrome or anything like that. I'm able to hold down a full-time job and pretty much keep up with most people. So I don't have abnormally low energy, it just doesn't feel like what I ought to have."

After reading Dr. Michael Newton's work in *Journey of Souls*, Mark decided to find a practitioner of this type of hypnotherapy. "I had never done hypnotherapy before and thought this might be an opportunity to explore on a deeper level and gain more knowledge from a higher source."

Searching under the Newton Institute on the World Wide Web, he found several practitioners and selected the one he felt drawn to most strongly, even though it meant several hours of driving to get to my office. Since Mark had no experience with formal hypnotherapy, let alone a past-life regression, I was hesitant about undertaking an LBL session with him right away. After email and phone conversations, we agreed to see just how far we could get, and he was comfortable with the idea of returning for additional sessions if necessary.

On a sunny morning in early November, Mark arrived at my office in northern California clad in a T-shirt, faded jeans, and well-worn sneakers. While he sat on the small sofa next to my desk, I inquired about any new questions he may have and spent a little time recapping some of the questions and answers from his intake form and earlier conversations. Once I had finished outlining the potential course of today's session, Mark transferred himself from the sofa to a small leather recliner I've affectionately dubbed my "hypnochair."

Over the next thirty to forty-five minutes, I worked with Mark in the preliminary phase of our session. Gradually taking him deeper and deeper into trance, I provided him with opportunities to test and gauge his depth of trance and engaged in a series of hypnotic warm-up exercises aimed at vivifying his internal experience through various sensory modes—visual, auditory, kinesthetic, olfactory, and tactile. This initial phase of hypnotic work culminated with an age regression. Counting backwards from his present age, we moved further and deeper into Mark's past, superficially at first, and then pausing at ages twelve, seven, and three to examine mundane details more closely.

Mark seemed to be bringing up detailed childhood experiences as if he were experiencing them directly rather than simply recalling them. This was a very good sign indeed. I activated my sound-recording equipment and regressed Mark back to pre-birth, where he felt himself within his mother's womb. Almost immediately we hit pay dirt.

DAVID: Tell me what you're experiencing.

MARK: I just feel very floaty. I'm just me but a lot more primitive.

D: Feel your energy through this primitive me, this primitive self. Does this seem like a good fit for your energy?

M: It doesn't feel particularly good, no.

D: Tell me about that. What do you notice?

M: It's not what I'm used to.

D: Tell me what you're used to.

M: I'm used to being kind of a big, rambunctious guy with lots of physical energy and strength: a real strong kind of guy, kind of a warrior and womanizer. The body I have now is too weak, puny.

Mark later points to this revelation as "a life-changing moment for me. That was such a great question because I had never looked at it in that way before."

Curious to learn more about this rambunctious and energetic character, I guided Mark out of the womb and into a life prior to his current incarnation.

D: Notice that right over there, the passageway is opening up and the stream of time is still flowing back. In a moment, it's going to carry you through that opening, back into another life. Now, it may be one of those big, strong, tough guys, womanizing and really physical, or maybe a different life, I can't possibly know, but it's going to be very, very interesting. Are you ready?

M: Uh-huh.

D: Okay, let's go.

Mark's demeanor shifts, and his facial expressions change.

D: What are you experiencing now?

M: A Viking warrior.

D: Is it daytime or nighttime?

M: It's daytime.

D: What's going on?

M: A lot of looting and pillaging.

D: Some of your favorite things.

M: Yes. Oh, I'm having a great time. Steal some women, break things. Steal, take home the good stuff. Victory, always victory. We always win.

D: Why is that?

M: Because we're smarter, we're tougher, and we're more ruthless. No one can defeat us. Because we are the Vikings! And we are kings of our realm. And we don't put up with anything from anybody. We're the toughest and the baddest. We love to terrify people, and we do it on a regular basis.

D: What do you particularly enjoy about that?

M: It makes me feel very powerful. I love to feel powerful. It makes me feel really good. And I think I live for it, I just really want it more. Every time I kill somebody or rape a woman or steal some treasure, I feel just better and better. It's like a high.

D: How old are you?

M: About thirty.

D: So you've been doing this for a while.

M: I've been doing this for a while, yeah. It's a really fantastic lifestyle. There's no limits on me, I like that a lot. It's great.

While this information may have been interesting, entertaining even, it still did not shed much light on what had transpired that resulted in Mark's current experience of low energy. What had led to such a different choice of life experience presently? We needed the broader perspective available only in that space between lives. But to get there, we had to move to the end of this Viking leader's life. I instructed Mark to move forward in that life to the time when he died. He found himself in a cave about ten years later. Battle-scarred and no longer as robust, he was attacked by a faction of his own band that sought to wrest control from him.

Three men, armed with swords, close in. He is determined to go down like a Viking warrior and intends to kill them all, but he is too slow now. An opponent's sword catches him in the stomach, and in the next instant he feels a blade bite into his neck.

M: I feel extreme fear. A blade is slicing through. It's all happening in slow motion. I can't believe it. I'm shocked. After all the battles I've won, to lose one is just beyond my comprehension ... The shock I feel, and I thought it would be more glorious. It's not glorious.

D: What's happening now?

M: Well, it's like the blade is halfway through. Although it happens in an instant, it seems very slowed down.

D: Are you still in your body?

M: Yes. Okay, the head is separated from the body, and now I'm getting out of the body backwards. The body is no longer a complete unit, and therefore I cannot stay in it. I seem to be pulled out in a rather sharp fashion, pulled out through the back. I see my body leaving, going down, and I'm standing outside. I still love this body a lot. And I'm just watching it all. All the warriors are celebrating their victory of killing me. (1)

D: What's happening now?

M: I'm just there. I'm still there in some kind of a disembodied state. I feel very alone and very devastated, and I don't know what to do.

D: How long do you stay here before you move on?

M: It seems like a period of hours. I'm just there. I don't know what to do.

As the Viking starts to consider the life he was suddenly torn out of, he begins to see things differently from this startling new perspective.

M: Well, it seems that all the things I loved, my victories and my treasures, they mean nothing now.

D: What is important?

M: Well, I don't know.

Still confused and disoriented, Mark becomes aware of the presence of a pair of beings that have joined him. The beings appear to be almost entirely made of light, with the suggestion of a human form.

M: They are gently taking me backwards. I do not see where I'm going. They are a very comforting presence, but I'm somehow not interested in being comforted. I'm still very much feeling like the Viking warrior. I don't accept comfort. I am like a god to myself. But I'm going with them because there doesn't seem to be any place else to go. And they are taking me somewhere. And I'm trying not to be afraid, but I am afraid. I don't know where I'm going. Then it gets very dark for a time. It's almost like I pass out or lose consciousness. I'm going through some sort of transition. (2)

D: Okay. Pause and allow the transition—just let yourself gradually unfold into that transition in a very safe way. You've already experienced some really dramatic, startling things, so it probably won't surprise you that whatever this experience is, however different it may be, it is also unfolding. Now, allow things to proceed. What's going on now?

M: I seem to have lost my Viking body. I've become a ball of light.

D: How do you feel?

M: It's all a little strange. I'm not really grounded in this place yet. It feels very new to me and not at all familiar or comfortable.

D: Are the other two light beings still with you or nearby?

M: They are real close by. They are guiding me. Let's see, they are taking me to some kind of a classroom. And they are ... they are doing something to my energy. I am still very identified as a Viking. And I feel very much an aggressive energy. And I'm sort of angry. I don't like what's happening. I just want to fight with somebody. So they are taking me to what they call the adjustment room, where there are other people there that can deal with my aggressive energy. They are being very calming to me, but they are telling me that I am perfectly okay, even though the way I am feeling seems very out of place for where I am. But I'm so steeped in aggressive energy that I need some adjustment. I cannot be in regular society. (laughs) I've been taken almost to remedial education or something. (3)

D: A special place for people like you?

M: Exactly—to start over.

D: How are they adjusting the energy?

M: It's like they give me sort of plastic swords and say go to it, just start beating up things. It's like what you do with an angry child. They just give me lots of space and lots of time to just beat things, to beat and kill and be aggressive and just act out. But I'm feeling very weepy because I'm feeling all this love. (4)

   No matter how angry and threatening and aggressive I am, everybody loves me still. And it's okay. It's okay, I can't seem to ... I'm not really threatening to them. They don't react to me the same as people did in my old life. People would be afraid of me and go away. These people are not afraid, they just love me unconditionally. And gradually, gradually they open my heart. All the time, they just sit with me and let me throw my tantrums and whatever I do. (weeps) They are just there for me totally.

D: Are the same two lights that brought you to this place still with you?

M: They are still around, but they have turned me over to more specialized counselors who specialize in people like me. I'm just overwhelmed by the love!

D: It is overwhelming, isn't it?

M: Oh, so much! I'm so overwhelmed by the love! I gradually calm down, but it takes a long time. It takes me a long time to ... to pass through this energy, because there's a part of me that loves that aggressive energy.

D: Of course.

M: It just feels so free and so powerful. And I love it so much, I don't want to give it up. But I have to give it up, because otherwise I'll remain in isolation forever. They say that my love of violence is so intense that they almost had to retool me, or send me back to the source. But after much discussion, they decided to see it through. (weeps) Maybe I'm like one of the worst cases that have ever come back this way.

D: What made them decide to hang in there with you?

M: Well, I'm told that my love of violence has, in a way, created something good in me also. It's a unique experience that can be turned in a different direction. It gives me an extraordinary power and strength that could be used for good eventually. But it has to be honed and sent into a different direction. But they don't want to destroy it, they don't want to waste it. It's very, very valuable to the collective. And it is with great joy that I understand this—that there is nothing wrong with me, that I am just utterly unique. I have a need for intense experience. And that my ability to be violent can also be an intense experience to love. I can love intensely also. This is what my main lesson is. This is why they didn't want to reprogram me. Because I have something unique to offer. Because I went so deeply into violence that I actually turned that into love. I loved violence—I loved it so much that it became love. And so, it's like I'm kind of a unique subject because of my ability to turn violence into love. I have a unique understanding of violence for that reason, and that gives me something valuable to use later on.

Mark reports that his sense of time spent in this isolation felt like the passing of thirty years on Earth.

D: At any time during that thirty years did you encounter your primary guides? Did they ever check in on you?

M: That's a great question. No. When I say isolation, I'm talking *isolation!* Nobody comes around other than the specialized guides that are helping me through this, this transition. The ones I'm dealing with are very old souls, very experienced, and very powerful; they are able to control me with a glance, with a smile. They have incredible ability when they want to be commanding. Even I agree with them. They are sort of like the Hindu gods you see that look like devils or something. They can turn from beatific into horrific in an instant. It's even scary for me. (5)

D: It seems they can mirror what frightens you the most. Is it that they change themselves into your own fear?

M: Yes, they seem to have a unique ability to do that. I get the feeling they are pretty high-up beings. They are pretty evolved. (6)

Eventually, his period of isolation and adjustment completed, Mark meets with his primary guide.

D: Do you have more than one primary guide?

M: I seem to have one that I see right now, and there are others in the background. I'm seeing a man. He's like an old man with a white beard and very wise, kind of like a wizard. Very much like sort of a Gandalf type, although not exactly—no pointy hats or anything. He's like a wizard, an alchemist, a very wise man that's been through many, many profound experiences and lived many incredible lives.

D: In this realm, what does he call you?

M: Wow, that's a tough one. (pause) I'm getting Lothar.

D: And Lothar, what do you call this alchemist, wizard. What do you call your guide when you address him?

M: Kamon. Kaymoon ... yeah, that's right. Kaymoon, yes.

Mark went on to describe his education under the tutelage of Kaymoon. This included incarnations ("field trips," Mark called them) on other planets, many on Earth. Most of Mark's earthly lives were spent as one sort of warrior or another. Then it was time to examine Mark's present life.

D: What about your current body?

M: I'm running into a great deal of resistance with this question, but I want to discuss it.

D: Okay. In a moment, I'm going to count from three down to one, and touch you on this shoulder (touches Mark on right shoulder). The next time I touch you on this shoulder, just allow Kaymoon to speak through Mark's body so that I can hear him too. And if this is acceptable to both of you, just nod, and I'll know we're ready to continue. (After a pause, Mark nods.)

　　Kaymoon, the one that I know as Mark seems to have some resistance to the situation about his current body. Tell me about that.

M: (in a different voice, as Kaymoon) Well, he has great pride. He has a very prideful soul, and he has great resistance to going into this life.

D: Which life is this?

M (AS KAYMOON): This would be his present life (as Mark). He needs to go into a different kind of body now. And discover—(pause)

D: In what way? I mean he certainly seemed to kick ass in the last life.

K: Yes, but his ass-kicking days are over. What he needed to develop from the ass-kicking lives has been done. To do more would just be an indulgence. So he needs to go into a different kind of body now and discover what it is like to be a normal person, a real human being with feelings and a mind. But he doesn't really want to do that. He really much enjoys being the other.

D: So does that account for Mark's experience of this low energy? Is it just that he's been given a body that he's not going to be able to go berserk in?

K: Yes, exactly, his energy was cut down to the minimum. He was only given about 49 percent of what he could have had. And this was on purpose, to prevent any undue aggressive activity. He has been purposely weakened.

Notice that Kaymoon indicates that, in terms of energy, Mark brings to this life about half of what he could have had. This does not mean half of his total soul energy. As much (not most) of our energy remains in the spirit world during any given incarnation, 49 percent of what he could have had represents probably less than 25 percent of the totality of the soul energy that today expresses itself as Mark. (7)

K: He's having to learn a lesson here. So we're sending him in with less energy on purpose, so that he has to deal with the realities of having a body and cannot just run rampant as though he were a god incarnate. And it's been very successful.

D: So he seems to be learning well from these experiences.

K: Yes, but it's very difficult for him. It has caused him to do a great deal of soul searching, which is a good thing.

Although Mark still experiences a low level of energy, he is at peace with the experience, understanding it as part of the evolution of his soul. Says Mark, "It just explains so much about what I've been experiencing all my life in terms of my energy and the incredible disconnect between the energy I feel internally and the energy I have. It had always been something difficult for me to deal with. This (life-between-lives) experience has made it so much easier for me to accept my situation now and to deal with it. Now I can get past the frustration. Now I understand, and it has just made dealing with it a whole lot easier in terms of managing my energy. It (LBL hypnotherapy) was truly huge—really, really clarifying for me." (8)

---

(1) There are newly discarnated souls, usually at levels I and II, who are disturbed by a physical life just ended. They may wish to remain around the scene of their death a while because of unfinished business. Perhaps they were murdered, or a loved one left behind is in trouble, or they could feel nostalgia about the life they were not ready to leave, and so forth. For a number of reasons, they might not be ready to go into the light of the afterlife right away. See adjustment of souls right after death, DS 43–44, 56; discontented souls, JS 45; LBLH 69–70, and souls who have hurt others on Earth, JS, case 10, 50–51.

(2) It is not usual for nonincarnating restoration healers (the two lights) to arrive either at or near the death scene of a newly released soul. Despite the

severity of body damage and soul energy, souls are typically able to release from their dead physical bodies and make some progress themselves toward the gateway before being met by guides. Notice the skillful manner that the facilitator uses by guiding without appearing to lead his confused subject into the adjustment room with the help of the two lights.

(3) For more information on restoration areas as well as remodeling or reshaping soul energy depending upon the degree of soul damage, see spiritual energy restoration, DS 85–109, LBLH 107.

(4) This is a form of spiritual deprogramming.

(5) For solitude and isolation areas, see DS 3, 7, 67–69, 292; LBLH 105–106, 170.

(6) Souls returning to the spirit world after a destructive physical life can be shown the error of their ways through a variety of spiritual approaches: (a) They may be returned to a library setting for graphic self-analysis of their mistakes (see DS case 30, 164); (b) Often, our own soul cluster group takes a hand in reviewing what needs improvement from past-life shortcomings (see JS, case 21, 129); and (c) Our spirit guides may want to teach us a lesson about misbehavior in the life just lived by shocking the incoming soul. Notice in this case how Mark describes his brief confrontation with false demonic specters. For another example of this uncommon type of spiritual shock therapy involving a scene of demonic pretense, see DS case 18, 80.

It can be seen from Mark's case that not just our guides and council elders assist us with post-life rehabilitation. There are also spiritual specialists who rehabilitate souls by harmonizing damaged energy from souls contaminated by certain physical bodies; see restoration masters, DS 85–124.

(7) The author's note about delineation of soul energy is most relevant in the case of Mark. The average soul brings in about 50–70 percent of their total energy, as we have mentioned in other stories. But here, by saying half of what he could have brought, Mark's guide is indicating half of the usual 50 percent, or a very low 25 percent, as the author has explained. I should add that an advanced, highly developed soul might handle this low energy level well, but Mark is not in that category. Thus, we see that in Mark's life, his energy level is by design and not overconfidence on the part of his soul that can happen with some souls choosing a new body. See LBLH 101, 135–137.

(8) Some one thousand years ago, the Vikings had quite a time of abusing other cultures with their magnificent bodies and aggressive behavior. Even so, personal karma requires some radical adjustments in future body choices down the line to compensate for these combative lives, such as in Mark's case. The soul in one of my own Viking cases chose a life hundreds of years later as a woman without the use of her legs. See JS case 26, 224.

8

A
shattered
HEART

Trish Casimira
(GREENFIELD, MASSACHUSETTS)
EDITOR AND HYPNOTHERAPIST WHO
TRAINED WITH MICHAEL NEWTON AND
SPECIALIZES IN REGRESSION THERAPY.

People often seek past-life regression to understand the pattern of why their relationships go bad. Life-between-lives regression reveals that relationships with members in our soul group fulfill a contract that was agreed to prior to incarnation. At birth, we agree to forget that arrangement so that we can have the experience without any influence of memory. Even so, amnesic blocks can be removed through hypnotic regression.

Common questions are: What am I supposed to learn from all this? How can I identify the bigger picture? So often, the client's motivation to experience a LBL session is borne of the need to gain understanding and, perhaps, the alleviation of sometimes unbearable emotional pain. Oftentimes the resulting discoveries are unexpected, and relief is offered in a variety of ways that can be surprising. The following deeply moving account clearly demonstrates how such understanding, when combined with the power of forgiveness, can transform a life of suffering into one of serenity.

WHEN SAMANTHA WALKED into my office, her shoulders drooped and she feigned a polite smile. It was clear that her reasons for coming were affecting her deeply. As soon as she sank into the recliner, her eyes welled with tears. "You are my last hope," she whispered.

Clearly she was a very proud woman and seemed to feel her tears were a betrayal. She began her story with an apology:

> I am sorry to be so emotional, but my life is in ruins, and I have given up. Ordinarily I am very strong, but my life has been devastated, and I am here to find out what the hell happened.
>
> I was content three years ago, living alone in a lovely apartment. I had a thriving practice as an energy worker. My clients were faithful and sent people to me regularly. My relationship with Spirit was tight, devoted, and quite certainly the reason my healing work was so powerful. (1) After a long sabbatical, I decided to date again. A friend set me up with a man she thought might interest me. I met him in a local café. As I approached him, I heard one of my spirit guides say to me, "You are to be with this man." As he turned to greet me, I said to my guide, "You have to be kidding me! He doesn't even come close to my type; he's not tall, dark, and commanding, he is short, pale, and reserved."
>
> *Be with him* was the resounding message in my head.
>
> We had coffee and shared a piece of pie. He was very polite and witty but had no concept of the kind of spiritual path I walked. No way, I thought to myself, I cannot date someone who is a spiritual novice! So I listened to him chat, formulating my *No thanks, we don't have enough in common* ... speech in my head. He spoke some soulful wisdom that led me to think he was an older soul than he realized. I was curious but certainly could not see myself dating him. As I stood to leave, my no-thanks speech ready, Spirit said again, "You are to be with this man." I always trusted guidance that came through that strong, so I gave him my number and agreed to go to dinner.
>
> On the way home, I argued out loud with Spirit, yelling that this was not funny, not part of my plan, and why on earth should I be with a man who was my spiritual junior? There was no attraction, no spiritual meeting ground; how on earth was this supposed to work? But no matter how good a case I made, I was

quietly assured that I should be with him. So I gave up and dated him. Within a month, we were deeply in love, and in six months, we were discussing marriage. He was fascinated with my spiritual nature and absorbed my teachings like a sponge. He began to talk to crystals, although he'd laugh and shrug his shoulders in doubt. Nine months into the relationship, we were house hunting, making our plans for a future. And then one lovely Indian summer day, he announced he no longer loved me and would not see me anymore.

I was crushed with disbelief, and when I asked him why, he could not say specifically; he just knew he couldn't continue and did not want to lead me on.

Tears fell onto Samantha's silken blouse, but she refused my offer of a tissue. She had to keep pushing through, hoping to release this burden through her story.

I spent months in prayer, trying to understand. But there was no understanding to be had. My heart was shattered, my dreams destroyed, my whole world had crashed down around me, and my integrity was in deep peril. I was certain that Spirit wanted us together, so how could this happen? I'd listened when they told me to be with him. I'd helped him to develop a spiritual understanding; I'd even compromised my spiritual needs for the sake of the relationship. Yet he simply walked away.

I gradually sank into a severe depression. I lost clients and lost my ability to intuit their needs. If I'd been so wrong interpreting what I thought Spirit told me, how could I be trusted to see what my clients needed? My anger toward Spirit turned to apathy, and I gave up on even caring. I closed my practice, moved to a new city, and tried to start over. But honestly, it has been two years now, and I still cry every night. I have no joy, no interest in anything. I cannot pray. I feel completely betrayed by my guides. If my guides are all-knowing, how could they have set me up for this?

So I need to use this life-between-lives session to find out what happened. If he is my soul mate, as I thought my guides said, what went wrong? Mostly I need to know why my guides allowed this and what I was supposed to learn. From where I sit now, I have no faith; it did nothing but devastate every spiritual bone in my body.

Samantha went quickly into a deep trance and easily recalled her memories before birth. She gathered helpful information in the womb about her relationship with her mother. She continued the regression back to her most recent past life. She saw herself as an Indian scout who was ambushed by soldiers and remarked that it felt stunningly familiar. We moved to her death experience. She found that her spirit left the body moments before the death and so did not experience the pain of death. As she rose into the spirit world, she felt a moment of grace—a moment of freedom that was obvious as she relaxed deeper. She knew where she was going and had no need for a guide to escort her. She remembered her agenda and went straight to her soul group.

There were twelve souls in her group, and they all had blue auras. She was not surprised that they were an advanced group of souls. She first met with her ex-husband and wept as she recalled their agreements and why their relationship had to end. They had come together mainly to bring the children into the world; there was no agreement about love. She forgave him and herself for all the years of trying to make the marriage work. She exclaimed, "No wonder we had a love/hate relationship!" as she realized that he was the soldier who had killed her in the last life.

She met another former lover and understood their contract was to raise each other's consciousness. She met her dearest friend and several other people who had been instrumental in her life and recalled their agreements. She saw two people in her group without faces; her best friend laughed and said, "Oh, we haven't met them yet; it is a surprise yet to be!"

She looked around her group, but she could not find the man who had broken her heart. She looked at the groups next to hers, but he was not there either. (2) She decided to step outside her group and look around. Way off in the distance, she saw him—he was waving his arms above his head as if signalling for a rescue plane. She walked over, and they met in a cloudlike space with no definition.

"What happened?" she asked, with desperation in her voice.

He took her hand. "Don't you remember?" he said quite lovingly. "I am in a group of very young souls. No one in my group is ready to wake up. I was looking for someone to help me, because I thought I was ready to give consciousness a try. When I waved and called out, you heard me and stepped out of your group to meet with me."

"Oh, that's right; I remember now," she said.

He continued, "You said that you were going to be a light worker this time and that it would serve your purpose to assist me. I said I needed assistance, so it was a perfect match."

"But what happened?" she said. "I thought we were in love—I thought we would grow old together."

"Sweetie," he said as he squeezed her hand, "that was not part of our agreement. I said I was ready to try to wake up. I never agreed I would actually do it; I only agreed to try. You knew the possibility existed that I would not follow through. You said you were okay with that."

"Oh, my," she said in a soft voice, "I remember now. I agreed to help you. And this was your first attempt to wake up, so you needed someone to guide you. My purpose is to help people to understand their divine self, so helping you seemed like it was in line with my soul purpose—a perfect match, as you said."

Her brow wrinkled as she continued, "I have to tell you that my life is in chaos. I don't trust my guides or myself anymore. They told me to be with you, and I listened. I was so sure that we were supposed to be in a relationship that I let myself fall in love with you, thinking there was a greater plan that I just was not seeing. I was absolutely devastated when you left. I had changed my whole life to be with you. How could you just turn your emotions off like that? We were talking marriage, for god's sake; what happened?"

"Think back," he said. "What *exactly* did your guides tell you when you met me?"

"'Be with him,' they said; 'be with him.'" Her face softened as she worked to remember. "They did not say for how long. And now that I think of it, they did not even define what that meant. My heart was lonely when I met you, so I assumed it meant a love relationship. But we never agreed to fall in love. I see now that was my human self wanting love and security."

"Yes," he said. "I did love you, but it was in the moment—we were clear about that. Marriage was something we thought we were supposed to do with the feelings we were having. But that is not why we were together. You were showing me how to wake up, but I was not ready. And frankly, even if I had been successful in awakening, I think I would have moved on. You were my teacher, my helper, not my soul mate. Please know that I never meant to hurt you. I thought I was ready to wake up, but I got scared. Spiritual enlightenment would have required me to drastically change my whole life, and my soul is just not that evolved. I guess I will have to wait until the next life and try it again. Please forgive me for any pain my choice caused you."

They embraced as beings of light do, and in that embrace Samantha allowed her pain to dissolve and her hurt to be replaced by the understanding of their contract. Tears fell from her face as she said to him, "I forgive you, and I wish you happiness."

Samantha then visited her Council of Elders. She entered through a hall of light; the walls were transparent and extended up into forever; the floor was a path of light. Pillars marked the entrance to the inner chamber. (3)

Her guides wore robes of white, and white and blue color streamed up from inside the robes, illuminating their heads. (4) There were three elders, and she knew they all thought as one. The elder in the center began to speak to her telepathically. "You have done well to forgive. This is one of the keys in your soul evolution."

She felt as if her heart were more open than she'd ever experienced. The energy of forgiveness swirled through her mind, and she realized it was a major part of her life purpose. She recalled the times she had succeeded and failed at forgiveness. She saw that this latest experience was perhaps the hardest.

The elder spoke. "Your agreement states that you chose to be of service. Forgiveness is a requirement, and it is a necessary step in the evolution of your consciousness. You feel as if we led you down a path that hurt you, but do you see now that it was necessary to let you go there? You had choices to make as to how you would walk that path. You could have remained the teacher and simply served. Instead, you chose to listen to your heart, which was lonely. In your loneliness, you fabricated a future with that soul you were serving—a future that was not part of the agreement. We knew you might make this choice; we knew you might get angry with us. But we also knew that you had to be free to make this choice. We knew you would not rest until you understood the deeper meaning of this choice.

"You are quite determined. That is the nature of your soul, for as long as we have worked with you. You were allowed to walk down that path in order to test your own consciousness evolution. Do you think you failed? You did not. By allowing your heart to be broken, you learned more than you could have learned in any other way. And it served your purpose—to grow and to be of service. In this exchange, you were of service to yourself as well as to him. You learned much. We were willing to take the blame for a time, for even that was necessary for this growth. In order to forgive, you first must blame, accuse, or feel wronged. In this experience, you have manifested all of those. We gave you something to push against—to face the choice of judgment versus forgiveness.

"And so now you have yet another choice: to judge and hold on to the density of that lower vibration or to forgive him for jilting you, to forgive us for what you thought was misleading you, and to forgive yourself for not seeing the higher path from the very start.

"You have agreed that you are willing to feel whatever is necessary for your growth. We allow you to create that in very intense ways. Your heart seems to need a path of intense lessons, so we support you as you learn. There was no right or wrong choice. Each choice you have made has led you to the same critical crossroad: the opportunity to forgive. So tell us, how do you think you did with this choice? Are you in need of more understanding?"

Samantha smiled and told them she understood completely. They bowed to her and encouraged her to remember her strength. She thanked them for their grace, realizing that her soul work required her to use all the resources available. What better way to learn to forgive than to put your heart out there to be broken? When she looked at this lesson with the understanding of her immortal soul, she realized how brilliant the plan was, and even more pain melted from her. Her session was complete; she had received the answers she sought.

The forgiveness that took place during that session was remarkable. A year later, Samantha reports that her practice is thriving again, and her work is better than ever. Her sense of judgment and blame has been altered drastically. She no longer reacts to the emotions of the moment in the same way; she now looks for the gold that is not obvious. She is able to help others see that blame keeps them from seeing their lessons and that their hearts are trying to grow away from judgment.

By removing judgment from her mind, she is now able to clearly see that each person is following a divine plan, and she is now in service to help others be open to seeing that plan for themselves. Her heart remains open, and she now welcomes opportunities to understand that forgiveness is a loving teacher. She has begun dating again, no longer attached to the happily-ever-after fairy tale that always got in her way. Samantha now lives in the moment. Happiness is a choice, and forgiveness is her chariot.

---

(1) When Spirit is used in this way, it refers to the subject's personal spirit guide. Note that as this story progresses, the subject refers to "guides" in the plural. This denotes an inclusion of the elders of her council as well, because they were involved in her advance decision-making and current therapy.

(2) Community dynamics within and between soul groups is a significant aspect of the afterlife experience. In this case, Samantha has connected with a soul from another, much younger cluster group to work on a mutual contract for one life. See primary soul group placement, JS 87–106; secondary groups, DS 138–142; and interaction between soul groups, DS 287–290.

(3) Regarding council settings, readers may wonder why earthly structures such as libraries, classrooms, temples, etc., appear in spiritual visualizations of the afterlife. This is because souls from Earth associate the function of such ethereal spaces with earthly buildings that seem to them to have roughly the same purpose. The similarity between such client descriptions is uncanny. Thus, a council chamber is rather like a holy temple in the minds of many clients, with references to domed ceilings, marble floors, multicolored light illuminations, and so forth, that are associated with feelings of awe as the soul enters this space for their evaluations. See DS 204–207.

(4) Regarding colors of the elders, the robes of these wise beings can be of varied colors, depending on their high level of advancement and expertise in certain areas of soul development. Souls often see white, dark blue, and especially purple, the color of deep wisdom. See DS 218.

9

THE
white
GOOSE

Ursula Demarmels
(SALZBURG, AUSTRIA)
AUTHOR, WELL-KNOWN TV AUTHORITY ON
REGRESSION, AND UNIVERSITY LECTURER
WHO ENVISIONS A HARMONIOUS SOCIETY
RESPECTING ANIMALS AND NATURE.

This chapter describes very clearly the rapid, positive progress that can be triggered when a client is guided with sensitivity into the between-lives state. This case reminds us that we are all souls—immortal beings of light and love—and that through LBL therapy we can rediscover the soul state, in which our feelings and experiences are of a much higher quality than those retained within the human mind.

WHEN SANDRA, A pretty woman in her early thirties, first entered my Austrian practice, she appeared to be cheerful, confident, and slightly arrogant. I found this a little surprising, because when she originally wrote to me, she showed very little courage to face life and had already repeatedly thought of suicide. She suffered increasingly from sudden cardiac pain and feelings of anxiety, but no physical cause had been found. Even eighteen months of intensive psychotherapy did not help. She told me that she was never able to cry, even though everything appeared to her as extremely dreary and senseless.

As a university graduate with professional experience in various different areas, Sandra was very successful but joyless. She felt empty and had no friends. She had affairs with a frequently changing array of men, which left her feeling humiliated and used. She described her parents as "friendly and caring people" but now avoided any contact with them because she felt ashamed of their simple professions.

When guiding my clients into a past life, I usually go back with them to different stages within their current life and also into their mother's womb. But Sandra asked me to strictly avoid that. She wanted me to guide her directly into a past life. She said that she had always felt she was a very special person, one who wants to do something of great impact. However, she had no idea what this "something" could be. In her current life, Sandra never cared about spiritual matters. When she, by chance, read in a magazine about my book on the positive effects of spiritual past-life regression, she became curious, read the book, and was now here to experience spiritual regression herself.

It took a long time to guide Sandra into deep trance, as she suddenly became tense and afraid. I helped her by using an imaginative journey induction, visualizing a beautiful flower meadow. She then gradually relaxed. I asked her soul guide to choose a former life for this session that would best assist her, and then I regressed her into that past life.

My client experienced herself lying comfortably on her back for a long period of time, floating on a white cloud through a blue sky. During this, her trance depth gradually improved. Finally, I asked her to turn over and look down to Earth. Underneath her, she saw a soft green landscape with grass and trees. I explained to her that I would now count to three, and she would then have arrived at the situation in one of her former lives that would be most important for her current life.

URSULA: What do you see?

SANDRA: (suddenly trembling and intermittently gasping out through a barely opened mouth) It's a morass ... The horses can't move anymore ... firmly stuck ... dirt up to the knees ... I can't move anymore. (screaming) Everything is gray, only gray! This must be how hell appears! (whimpering) ... I must continue ... must continue!

U: Turn yourself. What is going on?

S: (heavily breathing) I have to throw away the backpack and the gun. No power anymore ... Oh god, they are shooting! They shoot! Those damned bastards! (whining) I can't anymore. But I need my gun ... They've hit a horse. (loudly) Ha, they didn't hit me, not yet! But why? This mess should end now!

Sandra had found herself in Russia during World War II, in the body of a desperate German soldier named Rainer. The situation was hopeless. The advancing cross-country vehicles were no longer able to drive through the intense rain. Instead, horse-drawn carriages were used, and even these were now stuck in the mud.

In the next scene, Sandra saw herself as a younger Rainer: a young man in uniform, just before the start of the war, together with his fiancée, Judith, in his parents' beautiful house. His parents were rich farmers.

U: How do you feel there?

S: Judith wants to separate from me.

U: Why?

S: Because I went to the military. (proudly) I will make a career! (laughs) Not just cows and pigs! ... She is Jewish. That does not fit with me, not with the German nation.

U: How do you feel about Judith?

S: She is very beautiful and elegant ... now she cries. I don't like that ... yes, we'd better separate.

Two years later, Rainer is in command of a group of soldiers controlling the Swiss-German border. They had caught a group of Jewish refugees; Judith was among them.

S: She appears scruffy, no longer pretty. Dirty. She stares at me strangely ... frightened ... now she looks away.

U: How is that for you?

S: Don't know. I move away a bit. Have to make a decision ... Jewish refugees have to be rigorously punished. (long pause)

U: Now! What's your decision?

S: (shouting) I'll have them all shot!

U: What do you feel?

S: (defiantly) It has to be! It is the law! I owe her nothing!

U: Are you present when she gets shot?

S: Yes. They all stand in one row with their backs to us, in front of a ditch, their hands behind their heads.

U: Did they line up that way by themselves? Look at this carefully!

S: No, my soldiers had to bully them. Some cry, beg for mercy ... one man breaks down, he whimpers. Women often are the stronger ones.

U: And what about Judith?

S: She does not cry. She holds a little child by the hand.

U: Is this her child?

S: I think it belongs to the man who just whimpered.

U: And how old is this child? Is it a boy or a girl?

S: A girl. Maybe four years old.

U: What do you feel?

S: Don't know ... what I always feel in such a situation ... a kind of emptiness.

U: Something else?

S: (slowly) Anger ... dreariness ... yes, and also agitation.

U: Feel these feelings carefully!

S: Yes, that power excites me.

U: What happens next?

S: My soldiers shoot ... they all fall into the ditch ... now it's over.

Soon after, Rainer starts increasingly to experience terrible pangs of remorse and night-mares. Sudden cardiac pain also appears. He volunteers to fight at the front. He hopes to die, but instead he was captured by the Russians.

S: I am in front of the barracks, meagre ... everything is gray and dirty ... there is hardly anything to eat, not even for the Russians. Have to rebuild houses. Useless ... they shoot again, those idiots!

U: Who?

S: Ours (the Germans). Everything is already smashed ... lots of German prisoners ...

An airplane dropped a bomb. Rainer was hit by the shock wave and catapulted away. He was injured on his left shoulder. As he bobbed up again, he saw a white goose sitting beside him, and its left wing was injured.

S: (astonished and full of awe) This white goose ... it is the purest and most beautiful thing I've seen for eons! (long pause)

U: What is going on inside you?

S: (slowly) That's how I once was, or could have been ... should ...

Russian soldiers came and caught the goose. One of them choked it. Rainer cried out and ran against them. A soldier beat the butt of his gun against Rainer's head. Rainer collapsed and immediately died. Something pulled his soul out from his body; then, for a long time, his soul was immersed in blackness. It felt lonely and lost. (1)

U: How do you appear now?

S: Like fog. No human shape.

Finally, it became a little brighter in the distance, and a white goose flew in.

S: (suddenly excited) This one is even more beautiful than the goose in Russia! It shines, and it is very big!

His soul was allowed to lie down on the back of the white goose, and then the goose flew them both away. Underneath, Rainer/Sandra saw a gray landscape showing the destruction of war. Sandra told me she felt very small, heavy, and tired. A deep sadness filled her, and suddenly tears ran down her face. As a soul, Sandra allowed herself to sink deeply into the white feathers, and she cried long and intensely.

S: (sobbing) I feel like dissolving into infinite tears, sprinkling the whole country.

U: (after the client calmed down a little) How do you feel now?

S: Lighter, and oh, the lands beneath me have become green! The horrible gray of death is gone! Everything is fertile again!

U: Where is the white goose?

S: Next to me. But now it is transforming into an elongated bluish light. (astonished) My soul guide! (2)

In retrospect, with the help of her soul guide, it became clear for the client what she had to learn from her former life that would help her as Sandra today.

S: I wanted to be someone special in my life today but I had forgotten the most important thing: my heart! To act from compassion.

U: How is compassion involved in your current life?

S: Today I am very different from what I initially wanted to be. I am treated rather badly, and I am alone!

U: What is your soul guide's opinion on that?

S: He shakes his head ... (surprised) He shows scenes of my current life to me. My parents ... I feel ashamed because I don't spend time with them. Now he shows me a woman. I know her from work. She's sappy ... (slowly) Hmm, I seem to have something to criticize in everyone and everything. I should let that go and instead be friendly, modest, and caring ... but I'm so tired!

The soul guide then brought the client's soul to a place of rest and cleansing in the spirit world. Underneath, she saw a small, light blue lake. She floated down and dipped into the water. It felt warm and soft and flooded through her.

S: I feel like I am getting more and more transparent, and lighter. I cannot say exactly where my body ends and where the water begins. (comfortably sighing) I'd like to stay here forever!

After a long time, the soul guide comes to fetch Sandra's soul.

S: He now wears a bluish, shiny, long dress. I cannot see the face, but... it's a she!

U: And how do you look now?

S: Like an elongated yellow fog. I have long honey-blond hair, and I am also female.

U: What's your name?

S: Tria.

U: Beautiful. And what's the name of your soul guide?

S: Tisana. She takes my hand, and we float up even higher... (happily surprised) Oh, there's my soul group! They say hello to me! (laughing) It's funny, each of them wants to be with me first. There are five souls. They look like glowing, yellow balls. All of them embrace me. (happy) Now I'm home!

U: Enjoy it! (pause) Do you know one or more of those souls in your current life as Sandra?

S: (sadly) No. I'm all alone on Earth.

U: Ask Tisana for the reason.

S: Another soul approaches. (horrified) Oh, no! It's Judith... she comes straight to me!

Sweat runs from my client's forehead, and she buckles on the couch. It takes me some time to calm her again.

S: (surprised) That can't be true. I don't deserve that. She smiles and takes my hand!... I hurt her so much, and she's not angry with me!

U: Has she forgiven you?

S: (very touched) Yes.

U: Feel that, and take it deep into yourself. Take a deep breath! Do you also forgive yourself?

S: (sighs deeply) I would like to. (long pause) Doesn't work ... it wouldn't be appropriate.

U: What is Tisana's opinion of that?

S: She looks very seriously and points to my soul group. They all appear so shiny!

U: Like you?

S: (sadly) No, I do not look that light. My yellow is somewhat dirty.

U: What does that mean?

S: (hesitantly) It is because I am not as fast in my progress as the others are ... it's an old problem.

U: Which problem?

S: (longer pause) On Earth, I forget ... about what has been so perfectly planned ... even my soul group helps me ... and then, as a human being ... I always want to accelerate, to be someone very special ... no respect ...

U: Like in your past life as Rainer. Look again at your Jewish girlfriend, Judith. Do you know this soul in your current life?

S: No! She surely does not want to be with me anymore! (suddenly sobbing) But yes, she is here again. She is my work colleague!

It turns out that this soul belongs to the client's primary soul group and has regularly incarnated with her, trying to assist her in her path of development. In her current life, she is Sandra's work colleague, who has repeatedly tried to initiate a friendship with her. She wants to carry out a humanitarian, highly promising project with Sandra.

U: What does your soul guide think of that project?

S: She shows me a scene from my childhood. I am a little girl, about six years old, visiting people who know my parents. They are reconstruct-

ing their house, and during that have completely forgotten about their
pet rabbits. Their cage is partly broken. It's full of dust and dirt—and
the rabbits have nothing to eat! I bring them water and grass from the
garden, although I make my short dress dirty while doing that. (pause)
I think I should do it—those humanitarian projects with my colleague.

U: How does that feel to you?

S: Somewhat strange. (long pause) But also delightful ... yes, that's it!

U: Is it okay for me to try to help you dissolve your heart pains and your
feelings of anxiety?

S: (longer pause) No, not yet ... I don't think so.

U: Go into communication with your soul guide. What does Tisana say?

S: She nods her head. She says that the heart pains are like a signpost to
remind me to listen to my heart ... to learn, to do good.

After Sandra returned from trance, she first appeared to be very relaxed
and more friendly. But initially, she had serious concerns that she would not
manage to bring the knowledge from the session into her daily life.

Six months later, she informed me that she and her colleague had,
together, actually undertaken the first steps to bring their idea of a working project into reality—helping people to help themselves. The idea was
to teach and support farmers how to change from mass animal farming to
breeding conditions with a focus on animal welfare, and to change from
mass plant production to organic agriculture. Their target was a win-win
situation for all beings involved.

However, Sandra's health problems had not really improved. I suggested
to her that she should consciously contact her soul guide every day for at
least fifteen minutes. It took another one and a half years until I heard from
her again. She now appeared to be very happy and enthusiastic. The project
had a surprisingly good start, and for the first time in her life, she was in a
loving relationship. She had also followed my suggestion to contact her soul
guide on a regular basis. Sometimes her soul guide, Tisana, comes to her
again as a white goose, allowing Sandra's soul to fly through the sky on its

back. When I asked Sandra about her feelings of anxiety and heart pains, Sandra thoughtfully said, "Wow, I had completely forgotten about them. They gradually disappeared!"

Spiritual regression into a former life, and most importantly into the life between our earthly lives, can be understood as spiritual therapy, integrating divine wisdom into our worldly experiences. Sandra's case is a good example as to how profoundly and thoroughly salutary the conscious connection with the spirit world can work. In my experience, therapy targeting spiritual growth and bodily and psychic healing is impossible without connecting to our divine soul. As a spiritual regression therapist, I know from countless sessions that a simple regression into a past life is not enough. It is of crucial importance to guide clients into their between-lives experience to obtain the information necessary for real progress. Professional experience is one important factor for successfully conducting spiritually oriented regressions. The other most important factor is the conscious contact of the therapist with higher beings in the spirit world before and during the session. During any regression, I keep on intensely communicating with the spirit world, and only by doing that is it possible for me to offer adequate assistance and support to my clients.

We are guests in this world, and we must remember that we are souls creating experiences in a human body and aiming to bring soul consciousness into a material form. As soon as we start, with trust, to commit to a higher divine guidance, we can obtain all the help that is necessary for spiritual growth.

In our minds, we know a lot. However, the quality of our existence is enhanced by connecting directly with our soul mind and learning that we are immortal beings of light and love. Experiencing the rapid, positive progress triggered by spiritual between-life regression, I always feel thankfulness and grace, and I am deeply touched. During each spiritual regression session, I accompany the client, and during that process, I also grow in awareness of our oneness. The deeper truth is that there is no separation. Everything—human beings, animals, nature, Earth, and the whole universe—all material and nonmaterial forms and the spirit world are part of "all that is": the eternal, divine source.

(1) Readers of past-life cases often comment about the disproportionate number of people in our time whose most immediate past-life incarnation was
in World War II. This is no accident. There are two primary reasons at
work here. The Second World War was the deadliest military conflict in
human history. Total premature deaths as a direct result of the war have
been estimated between 60 and 70 million souls, both military and civilian
casualties. Six million Jews died in the death camps. If a person's life is cut
short prematurely, their soul often returns to the next incarnation within a
short time period—say between five and ten years—to complete a normal
life span and attend to the things they didn't achieve earlier. Many souls
from WWII fall into this category. The second factor is the soul's need to
balance the karmic forces that lead to a violent, untimely death in the war,
such as in the case of Rainer/Sandra, particularly with Rainer's treatment
of Jewish refugees. As another example of karmic balancing from negative
WWII activities, see LBLH 61.

(2) Shapeshifting energy into different forms is a practice used by souls of all
advancement levels but particularly amongst personal spirit guides who
wish to achieve specific ends with their students. Usually, if this is going
to happen with a newly discarnate soul, it takes place soon after death, just
before, or just after passing through the spiritual gateway (DS case 4, 20).
To learn how souls practice this skill, see the space of transformation, DS
302.

In this case, the white goose is almost mythological in presentation
by a rescuing guide appearing in a traumatic death scene. Sandra's guide,
Tisana, was modeling as an animal victim and recipient of violence from
the sort of abhorrent behavior exhibited by Rainer's previous conduct as a
soldier against innocent Jewish refugees in World War II. The intention
here was to show Rainer the effects of cruelty inflicted on innocent living
creatures. The succession of increasing injuries inflicted on the bird in this
case mirrored what Rainer was going through himself in the last minutes
of his own death scene in the war. First, there was the physical damage to
the bird's wing and Rainer's arm and shoulder, and finally the fatal choking
of the white goose matched the blow to Rainer's head by the soldiers who
killed him. Through this symbolic vision, Rainer was made to see the consequences of his lack of compassion as a soldier himself. As he was leaving
Earth's astral plane, Rainer was carried away by a whole, uninjured bird that
was emblematic of liberation.

The white goose is also symbolic of purity, beauty, and peace, clearly representing Rainer/Sandra's soul alter-ego—that is, goodness and wanting to
do the right thing versus destructive behavior in the life just lived. Sandra
sees that in her own disturbed life today, she must act from gentle compassion, as the author of this story makes clear. When her guide, Tisana,

assumes the form of a white goose to fly Sandra into the sky, this visual lesson represents a melding of past and present timelines to represent bliss and the freedom to face life and to foster courage. It would appear that unlike Rainer near the end of his life (Sandra's past life), Sandra has found happiness through her acceptance of love by the spiritual forces watching over her.

10

THE
Wells Fargo
GUARD

Jimmy E. Quast
(EASTERN SHORE, MARYLAND)
HYPNOTHERAPIST SINCE 1993.
COORDINATOR FOR LBL CERTIFICATION AND
LEAD TRAINER FOR THE NEWTON INSTITUTE.

This is the story of a fairly advanced soul (1) who has already arrived at a level of competence in the spirit world that allows her to work with an amazing degree of independence as a teacher of very inexperienced and, in her own words, tender young souls. However, it is clearly not her nature to rest and be satisfied with past accomplishments. She is still striving to perfect within herself the lessons of sensitivity and compassion for others who may be vulnerable and in need of encouragement to find their own inner strengths. Therefore, she is working in specific ways to fine-tune her selflessness, patience, and humility, both in her spirit world endeavors and in her recent incarnations on Earth.

As you will see, this kind of soul work does not have to be boring. In fact, her most recent past incarnation could probably be used as the script for a rollicking good movie.

THE FOLLOWING LBL session was conducted a few years ago. The female client, Anna, was forty-four years old at the time. When we met, it was obvious that Anna was unhappy with her life, but the information on her intake form could not begin to convey the full extent of her misery. After about an hour of conversation with her, I was certainly more aware of the depth of her physical and emotional issues. However, neither of us would be able to appreciate the profound degree to which her life was about to change until the session was over. In fact, the positive changes would continue to accumulate for weeks and months afterward.

Anna's problems were not extremely unusual, but there were just so many of them. All of her life, she had felt that too many people were trying to take advantage of her. Referring to herself as everyone's doormat, she now seemed to be running out of energy, both physically and mentally. She feared and distrusted nearly everyone. She was losing weight and had dropped from 140 to 116 pounds within a single year, and found herself powerless to gain any of it back. She had been diagnosed with poor adrenal function, had developed an insatiable craving for sugary foods, and had become lactose intolerant. She told me she felt she had lost about 90 percent of her former personality and that, unless something changed soon, "I feel done with my life."

As if this wasn't enough, Anna was also having what she called "too many spiritual experiences"! She was having consistent dreams about a masculine figure trying to reach her, and she would wake up feeling a large presence in her house that seemed to be trying to get her attention. (2) These spiritual experiences did not frighten her so much as they caused her to wonder who this being was and what his purpose was. These mystical experiences eventually led Anna to look for answers in Dr. Michael Newton's books, which subsequently led her to me.

Before I do an LBL session with a new client, I usually prefer to have a session or two with them, working at a more basic therapeutic level. My process was somewhat foreshortened with Anna, in part because she was traveling a significant distance to see me and in part because my telephone conference with her gave me confidence that she already possessed a natural openness to transcendent spiritual experiences. I was also reassured by the information that her doctors had found her to be mentally stable, and she was not under the influence of any prescription medications of the type that can sometimes interfere with a person's ability to enter the hypnotic state.

Therefore, it was no surprise to me that Anna entered hypnosis very easily and very deeply by using one of her favorite places in nature as a comforting mental image. Once I was satisfied that she had reached a sufficient depth, I suggested she allow herself to be guided back to one of her more recent past lives. Anna began to tell me that her feet were hurting. Then, before I could figure out what that meant, she said, "I took these boots from a dead man, and they're too damned tight." Since Anna was not wearing boots, I realized she was vividly experiencing a different reality. So I began to ask questions.

JIMMY: (hiding my amusement) That's a shame about your boots. Can you tell me more about yourself? How are you dressed? What do you look like?

ANNA: Well, I'm wearing a puffy, white, long-sleeve shirt and leather pants that button up on the sides. I have a gray hat that's round on top with a narrow lip. I'm short, fat, and scruffy. Don't shave very often—maybe once every four months or so. And my hair is turning gray in places.

J: Okay, I'm starting to get the picture. Obviously you're a man. Tell me more.

A: That's right. And nobody messes with me. I don't cross anyone, but you better not cross me! I don't put up with nothin'.

J: I understand. So what do folks call you? What's your name?

A: My name is Wren. Some call me Wrenny. My partner's name is Max. He's new. Let me tell ya, I lost more partners because they just wouldn't listen to me. They hesitated, and hesitating will get you killed ... and that's what they did.

I soon learned that Wren was in his forties and worked for the Wells Fargo Company as a stagecoach guard in the southwestern United States during the Wild West era. His responsibilities included protecting the lives of the coach passengers and the contents of the strongbox that he and his driver, Max, transported through some very lawless regions between the six to eight towns they served. Wren wouldn't touch whiskey, even when he was off-duty, because he always wanted to stay alert. He rarely was able to relax. Even after delivering the heavy, iron-bound strongbox to its destination, usually a bank, he told me, "I don't feel safe. People are watching us, and they don't know there isn't something else valuable in the coach. We gotta get out of here." Wren and Max felt most vulnerable when they were leaving a town, so they tended to clear out suddenly, without notice, at high speed, and preferably with six fresh horses. Adding to their paranoia, there seems to have been a pox epidemic at that time, so if they didn't have passengers or valuables, they would always prefer to spend the night someplace off the trail, sleeping on the ground in a defensible location.

Wren always had a sawed-off double-barrel muzzle loader across his lap and four more loaded guns behind his legs under the seat of the coach. He repeatedly told me, "I'm small and I'm gettin' old, but I don't put up with nothin'." His guns were always well oiled, polished, and loaded.

Wren had a female horse named Buttercup. He said he always preferred a smaller horse, because he was so short himself and it was easier to climb up. He told me Buttercup was the love of his life. He never had to tie her up, because she always stayed close, even at night, and came whenever he called her. Wren said, "Buttercup is the only female who will come near me. I mean, just look at me. I'm ugly, uneducated, and I smell. I'm a mess, but not to Buttercup!" However, Wren did tell me how sometimes he might take a liking to an occasional female passenger on the stagecoach—even flirt with them a bit. He said, "I could only get away with that because their lives are in our hands." It never led to anything serious, and he didn't seem to want that anyway.

In spite of the constant challenges, or perhaps because of them, Wren loved his way of life. During his career, he had indeed shot and killed a few bad guys who had tried to ambush the stagecoach. "If I am challenged in a bad way, I kill on the spot—no hesitation. Our reputation is strong. The people in our towns respect us and pray for our safe return. They depend on us."

I asked Wren to move through time to the last day in his life. Within a few moments, he began to speak.

WREN: I'm in a bed. It's dark, but there's an oil lamp next to me with lace under it.

J: Are you sick or hurt or just worn out?

W: I got shot. They got me right here. (Anna pointed to her right side and said, "That explains why I feel pain here sometimes.")

J: Is someone taking care of you, or are you alone?

W: My sister, Clarisa, is with me. She's younger than me ... she's so good to me, but she doesn't like my way of life. Now I see she's rinsing out the bloody rags ... I'm bleeding pretty bad.

At this point, Anna briefly shifted her perspective back to the present to tell me that she recognized Clarisa as her sister Kimberly in her present life, and I could see that she was enjoying a sudden, deep feeling of renewed closeness and love for her sister.

As wonderful as that revelation was for her, within a few moments, Anna just wanted to get back to Wren's predicament. In a matter of seconds, I was probing Wren with questions about how he had gotten shot. Was he on the coach when it happened? Did he know who shot him? His responses were all very vague. It seemed to me that he just didn't want to talk about these matters. He also didn't want to give up on living. He remained true to his tough, invincible nature right down to his last few breaths. At the end, he was not in pain but simply could not breathe. Finally, in his words, "There was nothin' I could do but LET GO."

I asked Wren to explain what, if anything, he was experiencing after letting go of his physical body, and he told me, "I'm not there anymore ... I'm surrounded by clouds now." He couldn't see into the distance because of the clouds, but he knew he was away from Earth. "There's nothing here but peace, just peace. The misery is gone. I'm safe now. You don't have to do anything here." After a minute or two, the clouds had gone, and he could see something far away that was shaped "like a shoehorn with a light in it. But it's not a shoehorn, and I'm moving toward it." As he drew closer, he said, "This is a place—a nice place—and it feels like Earth, but it's not Earth. It has trees and flowers and grass like Earth, but the colors are brighter. I've been here before. This place is just for me ... I don't have to worry about anything here. I can rest here ... this is MY place, where I rejuvenate. I can feel it happening… I am being filled. Everything in me is being healed. I don't need anything else."

Wren became silent, so I asked whether or not he could tell me, in terms of Earth time, how long he usually remains in this place of solitude and rejuvenation. His answer was "somewhere between about 100 and 200 years." After many LBL sessions, I have come to understand that the client, at this point, is operating in nonlinear time. Therefore, one cannot directly compare linear Earth time to what they are experiencing. This allowed me to use a very interesting and handy technique. I simply told Wren, "Let's honor this 100 to 200 years by remaining in silence for two full minutes of Earth time, during which you can experience the passage of as much time as you need in this place of solitude in order to fully rejuvenate your energy." (3) After two minutes of silence, I softly asked Wren if he felt he was finished and ready to move on from this place. He told me he was done, that he could feel a difference: it was a feeling of wholeness. I could tell that Wren was now quite changed. Based upon my past experiences with LBL regressions, I understood that Wren was now becoming better oriented to this larger reality, regaining his awareness of himself as an immortal soul.

I learned that this soul's immortal name is Karaa (pronounced *care-AHH*—emphasis on the last syllable). Karaa describes herself as feminine, very tall, slender, and graceful. (4) This is about as different from Wren as anyone could imagine. She currently has retained 85 percent of her energy, meaning that Anna only took 15 percent when she incarnated. The combined data from thousands of LBL sessions conducted by Dr. Newton and others have indicated that the average quantity of energy brought by souls into their physical incarnations typically is between 40 and 60 percent. By giving Anna a relatively small amount of energy, Karaa has accomplished two important things. First, Karaa has retained enough energy to continue doing some special work in the spirit world that she is very passionate about. Second, as Karaa points out, Anna's relatively lower amount of energy causes her to have a feeling of longing for the other side, her true home in the spirit world. This makes it possible for Anna to be more open to receiving assistance from home, even though it can also cause her, as a human being, to feel weak and intimidated on some occasions.

Karaa does have a guide named Sariel (pronounced *sah-ree-EL*, emphasis on the last syllable). He has a more masculine energy but does not come around as often as he once did. He is always available to Karaa when needed, but she says she rarely needs to call on him.

The color of a soul's energy is always of great interest because it reveals so much about a soul's level of achievement. To me, Karaa's energy is extremely interesting and rather unusual in its color arrangement. She has a great deal of blue energy, which indicates she has a very high level of experience, but she usually prefers to hide her admirable accomplishments by covering herself with the dull grayish white coloring of a much younger and inexperienced soul. I couldn't understand this until she took me to the place where she does her work. It was a crystalline building perched on a crystalline pedestal, where one must carefully adjust oneself before entering.

KARAA: This place is very old. But it's not just a place—it's alive!

J: Do you mean it's alive the same way you are alive?

K: (emphatically) Better than me! You must have respect for this—tremendous respect—before you can enter. You always stay humble ... mustn't show pride ... that's not good for *them* if I show pride. I teach them how to be more than they are, but I have to be very gentle with them.

J: So you are a teacher?

K: Yes, that's right. But I have to be very careful with them. I cannot show off (this is a reference to her blue energy color), because they look up to me. They are so young—faint white lights. They want to learn, but they're very timid. You've got to be careful, because they have total trust.

J: Does this mean that you tone down your own energy when you are here? How do you appear to them?

K: That's right. I'm a soothing grayish white color. My gown has creases, or folds, and I only allow my light blue color to show as streaks in the shadows of those folds.

J: That actually sounds rather elegant to me.

K: (with a secretive but emphatic tone) It is!

J: So how are you different when you're away from this place?

K: I'm brighter, and I let more of my blue energy show sometimes,
but that could be intimidating to the little ones. I'm really not that
advanced (souls at this level of advancement tend to be incredibly self-
less, so this statement actually helps to confirm her achievements), I
just know how to do this job—preparing new souls to move on to the
next level. I do it really well, and I love doing it.

Further questions reveal that Karaa works quite autonomously with six
to eight students at a time, with a fairly constant turnover. She occasionally
takes some time for socializing with other souls at her own level, but actually does very little of that. As our session went on, this relatively advanced
soul did not take me to any of the other common sites that we frequently
encounter in the spirit world during LBL sessions. Even though I probed
and questioned, there was not much else she would reveal.

Karaa did point out that the goal of her incarnation as Anna is primarily
twofold. She must stand up once again for herself and others the way Wren
had done, but this time in a small female body, without the help of "an arsenal
of sawed-off shotguns." Also, she has to take on the role of nurturer. Initially,
Wren does not appear to have many redeeming qualities, but further exploration revealed that Wren's attitude toward the life was not as cold, uncaring,
and murderous as his words suggest. According to Anna, he was admired in
many western towns as a courageous protector of people's lives and property.
The message for Anna is that while Wren was physically vulnerable in the
badlands with his job, this did not deter nor diminish his capacity to act when
necessary. The strong, masculine figure in Anna's dreams that led her to me
was apparently intended to show an embodiment of her real self in Wren.
Recalling the life of Wren in session demonstrated her true capacity as a soul
to overcome adversity with strength and independence.

I was expecting the session to continue a bit longer when Karaa suddenly announced that it was time to wrap up this visit. That was a surprise,
because very few LBL sessions are ended with such a dismissal. So we followed her suggestion and ended the visit.

When I brought Anna out of her trance, I felt I had not obtained as much
spirit-world information for her as I would have liked. But I got over that

quickly when she opened her eyes and shouted, "Oh my god, that woman is so strong. She's amazing! It felt so good to be her again! It's so important what she's doing to encourage the little ones! And that Wren... amazing! He showed me what it's like to be a man. I understand now why men act the way they do... Wow! Was all of that stuff real?"

Following this session, Anna's life began to improve rapidly. Her energy returned immediately. She began to have an unexplainable craving for healthy food—and gained ten pounds within six weeks! She was both pleased and puzzled to find she had lost all desire for sugary foods. And can you imagine Anna's surprise when she discovered she was no longer lactose intolerant? Apparently, Anna's digestive system was the most vulnerable part of her physiology in regard to her long-term self-esteem issues. What we feel emotionally and our state of health are not separate. By recovering her memory of who she is as an immortal soul, Anna has been empowered to believe in herself and pursue her dreams.

At the time of this writing, it has been eight months since Anna came for her LBL session, and she tells me that she now feels a sense of determination and purpose in her life. People no longer frighten her. She says, "I'm comfortable now with some people who used to make me uncomfortable. Equally important, I have become uncomfortable with a few people that I have really been needing to get away from, but I couldn't face it before. I'm not a doormat anymore—I don't have to put up with that anymore." (Sounds like something Wren would say!) Other remarkable changes: Anna no longer fears death and has acquired the ability of perceiving ethereal things that are not available to the usual five senses.

Anna recently told me that a few months after our session, she was visiting a flea market where there were a number of antique guns for sale. She has no real interest in guns, but she was attracted to one gun because it looked just like the one Wren always carried on his lap. While she was looking at it, a man approached and asked if she had an interest in old guns. She said she was only intrigued with this particular one, and before she could figure out how to explain herself, he said, "That type of gun was used by the old Wells Fargo stagecoach guards." She told me that the price was a little too high for her budget but that she now regrets her decision not to purchase it.

Anna's work continues in her present incarnation, and judging by the very positive mental, emotional, and physical changes that have occurred in her life following this LBL session, she is making gratifying headway toward realizing her soul's goals. Furthermore, now she knows it.

Anna's case is an example of a relatively advanced soul who is attempting to perfect selflessness and sensitivity toward others. Karaa's approach to her work as a teacher demonstrates how very focused she is on mastering this kind of compassion. Therefore, in her most recent incarnations, by experiencing the fine points of feeling vulnerable herself, she is steadily refining her compassion for others who feel vulnerable. As Anna, she is truly fine-tuning this experience by facing it without most of the protections that were available to Wren. The most immediate result is that Anna has now been energized by this new perspective and has undergone more healing and relief than she ever expected was possible. (5)

---

(1) For case comparisons between beginner, intermediate, and advanced souls, see JS 123–200.

(2) Archetypical images in dreams and dream recognition: DS 24, 28.

(3) We see many case examples in this book of time not being linear or absolute in the spirit world. In this case illustration, 100 years on Earth may seem as though only 100 minutes have passed for a soul in the afterlife. Deliberate time distortions by experienced LBL facilitators, as in this case, can be an effective therapeutic tool in many spiritual settings for slowing down, freezing, or speeding up timeline action during an LBL session; see LBLH 161.

(4) While souls are pure forms of light energy, they can assume any shape that pleases them in the afterlife.

(5) When examining the stages of development for any soul, progress may go forward or backward during many incarnations, depending on the karmic challenges. Each body occupied by the same soul in different lifetimes has its own brain, central nervous system, emotional temperament, and so forth. Aside from gender differences here, while Anna and Wren may appear to be complete opposites, nonetheless they do have the same soul. The immortal soul character of Karaa is simply coping with a new set of circumstances in different environments. The soul's task is to overcome such obstacles in each life by seeking the best solutions in order to achieve productive lives. The soul grows progressively stronger by this process; this is the secret of incarnation.

LIFE
on the
WING

Rifa Hodgson
(VANCOUVER, CANADA)
BORN IN MOSCOW, SHE COMBINES DEEP INNER
SPIRITUAL WORK WITH A SENSE OF ADVENTURE.

Among the many fascinating discoveries revealed during years of life-between-lives hypnosis regression is the existence of hybrid souls. (1) In Destiny of Souls, Dr. Michael Newton describes hybrid souls as those of "mixed incarnation origins" who "have memories of actually incarnating on alien worlds before they came to Earth." Often gentle, sensitive, and older souls, hybrids can have difficulties adapting to this planet and may have chosen to incarnate on Earth in order to experience a difficult challenge; they can feel isolated, different, and experience problems in creating relationships.

The following account is about such a soul. Lindsay had experienced severe health problems during her current life, together with a sometimes-painful sensitivity to her environment and the people around her. Through LBL therapy, she gained clarity and understanding. Since her session, she has been able to continue her life with renewed purpose and in considerably increased comfort.

WHEN LINDSAY, AGE fifty-one, contacted me about past-life and LBL sessions, she was concerned whether her current extreme fatigue would allow
her to participate fully. I discovered that she had experienced severe birth
trauma and had been battling with ill health all her life. She'd had aches in
the area of her spleen for as long as she could remember, and she constantly
avoided crowds and noisy places because they made her feel overwhelmed
and physically sick. Lindsay had never been able to create a deep connection
with anyone because she felt different and somewhat isolated. I also found
out that eight years before, while working in Africa on an international
development project, she'd been bitten by an insect carrying five viruses.
Eventually the viruses cleared up, but she was left with an exceptionally bad
post-viral condition: chronic fatigue syndrome.

Eight years later, with the use of conventional and holistic therapies,
Lindsay's health had improved considerably. She had also begun to work on
herself and others with healing energy, but she was still experiencing stubborn and debilitating insomnia, which proved resistant to both conventional
and alternative remedies.

During Lindsay's first past-life regression session, we explored several
lives. None of these was directly related to insomnia, but as she received the
lessons of those lives during the hypnotic state, Lindsay found parallels with
her current life. She observed:

> I hadn't completed things in those lives to my satisfaction... In
> this current life, there is so much work I have to do, yet I can't
> do it. I cannot be sick and do the work; my body just can't handle
> it... transferring all that energy. I am very aware of time... the fact
> that time is going by. It's been hard to relax and allow the healing
> process to be completed. It makes me feel sad, somewhat aimless,
> helpless, and disconnected.

I asked Lindsay to go directly to the origins of feeling sad, aimless, help-
less, and unable to do the work. She became very emotional and tearful as,
haltingly, she recounted:

I have wings ... I am a sort of a yellow/golden color with wings, gliding, not flapping, gliding ... and a tail ... kind of like an insect, very large ... it's shaped like a wasp or lizard, but my head is very strange. I came to this planet to do some energy work, and I can't! It's difficult ... it's beyond my abilities at this point ... it's too hard a task ... I try to manipulate the energy, but I can't, I don't have the skills. I am reaching beyond my skills level ... I want to do too much, too soon. We are all very eager to transform the planet ... we orbit around and work, then we rest. We don't need much sleep here.

I asked, "If you take a rest right now, what happens?" After a long pause, she replied, "It's funny ... I just drift, allowing the planet to evolve on its own, and it comes along just fine ... I don't need to push so hard."

As this memory filled her, Lindsay realized that there was no need to push so hard in her current life. She must focus on her work as a healer and first heal herself.

Immediately after the session, Lindsay drew a picture of herself as this flying being, and a couple of days later, she wrote me a letter describing the flying body she had experienced in her PLR session.

I remember being of a soft yellow/golden color, with two wings, a head, and sort of a tail. My head had bumpy features where the face would be, but there were no eyes, ears, or mouth. Instead, there were four antennae—roughly the length of my head and neck combined—extending out the top of my head. The antennae moved independently of each other and were flattened into a sort of oval shape, rather than being round (like the difference between linguini and spaghetti). My skin (there were no feathers) had a sort of smooth, rubbery, gel-like texture. The wings, on the leading edge, were roughly similar to a gull wing, angled back at the half-way point; the back edge of the wing wasn't smooth, but rather had something like uneven blobs extending a bit from the body of the wing. My body shape was loosely similar to that of a cuttlefish, except there was no long fin around the perimeter; instead, there were more of the uneven blobs similar to the back edges of the wings (although these were fewer than on the wings).

Along with a number of others like me, I was orbiting around a very small planet in its early stage of formation. It consisted of an orange and red swirling mass of a heavy gas, which moved like liquid. We were working to evolve this planet quickly. My antennae were used to pick up the results of the changes we were attempting to effect, and with that information, we continually modified the energy we were sending to the planet. I remember having difficulty with this work; I was focusing too hard, and I was getting in my own way a bit. By relaxing and coasting in orbit for a while, I found that the various elements of the planet began to slow down and coalesce into more evolved states, with primitive land masses beginning to form. This concept of relaxed intention is something I'm continually working on in this lifetime, as well. (2)

I've never seen anyone so eager and determined to start a life-between-lives session! A tall, quietly striking woman, Lindsay arrived at my office half an hour earlier than our agreed time, beaming with anticipation. She brought with her a sense of urgency; there was no more time to waste.

During LBL, Lindsay received the answers to all her burning questions and discovered much, much more. She found out that she is a mature hybrid soul incarnating to the planet Earth with the specific mission to carry out planetary work. This became quite obvious right in the womb, for in order to prepare the groundwork for this important job, her soul joined the fetus at a very early stage. With growing understanding, she gave me the reasons for this:

LINDSAY: Hard work, no vacation time ... there is a lot to do in this life. We have to make lots of connections ... with the mind. The relationship has to be very finely tuned ... with all the work we have to do. Want to reach the patterns earlier ... I ... we ... do a lot of unusual work with this mind.

RIFA: Like what? You said "unusual."

L: Oh, it's like when, instead of driving an old station wagon, you drive a high-performance sports car; the wiring will be lots trickier and harder to maintain, but I will be able to do much more. I have to do a lot of energy work for this planet. I need to be able to be more creative... my body has to be receptive to... almost "playing" with the energy... be willing to experiment on ways of working with energy... She (Lindsay) is working with energy she has never before encountered. Before, there was no one there to teach (this is Lindsay's soul talking). The realizations came with increasing confidence. She has to be able to listen to me to be able to do this. It's tricky work, because we are working with a high voltage and... we can harm the body, and there are no teachers... It could be risky, so we have to be well attuned and listen closely to each other to do the work... it's a team effort, so I have to first heal the body and release all the baggage from other lifetimes... then do it in time... so that I can do the "planet work"... so I have to accomplish one before doing the other... so it's going be tight. I have waited a long time for this.

R: How did your birth trauma contribute to the lesson you need to learn during this life? Why was this birth trauma needed?

L: So it (the body) was compelled to work with energy, because it was the only thing that would help heal it, and that will raise the interest level enough... to keep working and working with it... and so that I could get to do the planet work.

R: Do you have any experience of working with planets? This isn't your first incarnation of doing this?

L: No, I love this, I love working with the planets, we work on the planets' elements... it's like... like a poetry... it's like a dance... it's so beautiful, combining all the energy with the elements. It's like creating a cosmic... like a soup; and making a planet that people can actually live on. It's so beautiful, and even if... they... won't... it's such a lovely place in the sky. (3)

R: You've done this before, numerous times, haven't you?

L: Yeah, this is what I do.

R: Where do you do your planetary work?

L: This isn't the first time with planet Earth. I missed it ... I missed doing it so much. And here you get to do this ... you go to my planet, you are doing it from a distance, you are ... not touching, but here you get to touch everything and ...

R: "Here" means on Earth?

L: Yeah, you have to be in it ... it's like ... it's like making a soup and eating it too ... you have to experience it at the same time; it's wonderfully fulfilling this way.

After these insights and during a visit to her council, to whom she referred more as colleagues, Lindsay received an explanation about her insomnia.

R: During the life as Lindsay, what does insomnia teach you—what does it remind you of?

L: (immediately) Ah ... ! (an "a-ha" moment; she smiles)

R: You've got it!

L: This is so good ... (laughing) Ah ... oh ... it's multiple things—one is that it's teaching me that things are getting to be a little critical here now ... I do need to relax more about it and do as much as I can, because, ah ... a planet is meant to evolve, all I can do ... is the best I can ... with the time I have ... and that relaxing will allow me to follow it to deep sleep ... also, in the other incarnation ... in my home dimension, you don't sleep so ... it's a bit of trick, it's allowing me to ... now think ... that I am wasting my time sleeping here.

R: So, on a subconscious level, you get very upset that you are wasting your time during your sleep?

L: Yeah ... because I don't have any sleep, I use the time on something else. I need to remember this ... that sleep is part of being a human. It is a very productive part, allowing the soul to rest when the body is sleeping and the body ... to heal also; there's something else ... it will come, they say—you are on the right track ... with the things I am doing and with the sleep issue resolved.

R: What was the significance of being bitten by the insect in Africa?

L: Being bitten? Oh, that was really helpful ... I was bitten by that bug about ... eight years ago. Twelve years ago, I'd started doing ... receiving energy work and learning how to do it both on myself and others.

  I made a lot of progress, healing myself with the energy work for the first four years, then I sort of leveled off; I wasn't able to dig down deeper. Had I needed this body just for getting from point A to point B, it would have been fine, but I needed it to be able to do the planet work, otherwise the energies would change, so ... I needed to completely disassemble everything, repair and ... put it back together again. The only way to do that was to get very, very ill ... and that's where the bug came from.

During the extended healing session that followed, Lindsay found out the origin of her chronic spleen issue.

L: Yeah, It's always been an area of sadness ... I think it's ... I wanted to come to this dimension to learn about Earth, and it has been rewarding; the people have been so helpful ... I did miss my own group ... I did, it has been a homesickness ... the spleen area is where I carry the sadness of being away from home.

We created a direct connection between Lindsay's spleen and her original dimension so that simply by breathing into the spleen, she would be able to connect to her home.

  As the session progressed, I asked Lindsay why she was drawn to experience LBL at this time.

L: She (Lindsay) was stuck on some level, and with the sleep thing, was backed up against a wall; she was so sleep deprived, she couldn't function and progress, and this proved to be a hurdle. She had to get over it in order to achieve anything, because nothing else was working anymore, absolutely nothing; ah, and so many other decisions hinging on ... to be able to sleep and to be lucid enough to act on them ... and she just needed a reminder ... it has been difficult for her to acknowledge ... the kind of work she does and the direction she is going with it ...

Then, as understanding deepened:

It sounds so strange, and she really knows very few people who have a clue what she is ... hardly anyone ... she's much ... less able to discuss it with anyone ... so creating this sense of understanding within her-self ... at this point ... is important ... in order for her to move on with this work, because it's time to move forward much more quickly, so many other things ... puzzles were in place, and she needed this help to get through the "stuck" part.

At the end of the session, Lindsay was totally exhausted but very pleased. LBL had given her an understanding of who she is. It clarified her purpose and gave her the encouragement that she is, indeed, on the right path.

The LBL session gave her an explanation of the flying dreams she could remember ever since her childhood. It seemed that Lindsay wasn't surprised at all; in fact, she identified with the incarnation in her flying body much more than her incarnation in human form. (4)

It explained so many other things too: why she had always felt extremely uncomfortable and overwhelmed when in a crowd, hearing the voices of people around her like a constant, intrusive noise and feeling almost as though she had been sucking in all the pain and despair around her. She could also now understand why she had never been able to connect with anyone on a deeper level.

Perhaps the strongest impact of her LBL was that Lindsay was now able to connect with her history. She discovered her own origins, the origins of her unique abilities, and also that there were others with similar abilities making similar, mutual efforts.

Lindsay observed, "Knowing that I belong 'somewhere' makes me feel that I belong more 'here.' When I own who I am, it's projected forward, and people relate to me differently than ever before."

Now, a year later, her spleen area is feeling great, and her sleep pattern is gradually improving. Lindsay is now carrying out intensive energy work, releasing her own baggage and healing herself as well as others. She learned and is putting into effect this important lesson: she must first heal herself before she can finally do the work she came to do here on Earth. This, in her own words, she describes as "the planet work."

At the end of the LBL session, Lindsay was totally exhausted but very pleased. She had discovered an explanation of her flying dreams that she had remembered since she was a child. Actually, she felt more related to the incarnation in her "flying body" than her incarnation in human form. Her experience in deep hypnosis gave her explanations of many other things, such as feeling extremely uncomfortable and overwhelmed in a crowd, where she sucks in all the negative energy of pain and despair around her, and why she has never been able to connect with anyone on a deeper level. Lindsay told me in session that her council said there may be some upcoming change in her personal life—a special man from her home dimension may join her within a year or two. "How would I know that this is 'the one'?" she asked of her council. "Oh, it's easy," they said, encouraging her. "He will have the kindest eyes and most beautiful smile, as well as goofy, silly shoes; you will know."

While I was writing her story, Lindsay called me to report that a special man had indeed come into her life, just as the council had predicted. (5)

---

(1) Hybrid souls are rather rare in human society, and typically an LBL facilitator might have less than 5 percent of their yearly caseload who are hybrids, originally from alien worlds. During their first incarnations on Earth after experiencing life on another planet, hybrid souls often have difficulties, but if they can survive these early lives, great contributions to our society may follow. See DS 100, 154 and LBLH 165–166.

(2) Hybrid souls now on Earth as former alien creatures. See JS 192–193.

(3) Planetary healers involve two major spirit world professions of advanced souls: (a) healers of the environment, or ecological energy specialists (DS 113–115), and (b) harmonizer souls who balance the energy of planetary events and human relationships (DS 330–331). It would appear Lindsay is in training for the second class of specialists. Highly advanced souls not in training for specializations do not seem to incarnate.

(4) Human dreams about flying with alien planetary origins—DS 348.

(5) In the spirit world, before we enter our new physical bodies for the next incarnation, certain triggers of recognition may be provided to help us

connect with significant people who will impact our next life in some way. The fact that Lindsay was advised about a man she would meet by the council is not typical. Normally, this information comes to the soul in a recognition class, or preparation class, just before embarkation into a new incarnation. Our personal spirit guide is involved, but often this work is handled by guides/prompters to reinforce what we might have been told earlier between lives. See JS 249–262.

12

Small
is
Beautiful

Angela Noon
(East Grinstead, England)
LBL training assistant and editor
for the Newton Institute and
registered hypnotherapist.

In utero regression, the process of taking clients back to just before the time of their birth in the current life, is one of the many fascinating stages of the LBL process. Here, clients can become reacquainted with their soul consciousness, sometimes for the first time since birth, and remember how they were able to think as immortal souls while they made the necessary adaptations in preparation for human existence. Experienced souls often gain profound insights that are then expanded on during the visit to the interlife. The following story describes the LBL experience of such a soul.

JESSICA WAS A joy to meet and to work with. It was clear that she simply wanted to discover as much as possible through her LBL session. Before she came to experience LBL, she had already made a number of far-reaching life changes, including a courageous career move that took her away from a demanding corporate environment and into the development of her own business as a life coach. Here was an inquisitive, intelligent, fun-loving woman with refreshing energy and a seemingly insatiable thirst for knowledge. At just five feet in height, Jessica's physical appearance is ultra feminine and petite, but her personal presence in the room feels huge. Married to Sam and the mother and stepmother of five children, she and her husband share a deep love of the natural world, and Jessica loves animals, particularly dogs and horses. She and Sam have a strong sense that they are soul mates. Jessica and each member of her birth family (parents, a brother, and three sisters) have demonstrated strong personalities, but Jessica's keen interest in all things spiritual is quite unique within this family group.

Achieving a deep level of trance quite quickly, Jessica easily accessed some early, happy childhood memories. Although her childhood had its issues, years of subsequent personal development had ensured her view of the difficulties was now clear and uncomplicated. Then she regressed to the time in her mother's womb, not long before her birth. Her first reaction was surprise that she could hear her mother's heartbeat and that it sounded "strange." Soon, the strength of the emotions she was feeling from her mother became overwhelming, and we had our first inkling of this compassionate soul's desire to help and heal others. Through tears, she told me that her mother needed an enormous amount of love and support, and she provided this by sending her mother healing in the form of golden light, explaining, "I just think it and she finds comfort." At this stage of her LBL session, she also discovered that her journey to spiritual enlightenment would not be taken alongside any of her siblings. And then she observed:

> My body is going to be small in this life. In other lives, I have
> been taller, more predominant, usually a leader. It's going to be
> interesting working in this body because I know so much. My
> small body means I will have to pace myself and lead from a

different perspective. I will have to show people what I know, so they will listen to the content and not just be predominantly aware of my physical presence. When you are small, you have to make your presence felt in a different way. This body is exactly what I need now: bubbly, soulful, and full of fun. (1) It will take me quite a while to understand my role this time, and I chose this life challenge because I thought it would be fun.

This is borne out in my knowledge of Jessica's life experience; for example, she created her huge career change during her early forties. Then came further important revelations. Not only were the entry into this body and integration with the brain and its circuitry "simple and exciting," but she "could also see the great potential of this particular combination." When I questioned her about the nature of such potential, she replied instantly, "I am a teacher, and this will present me with entirely new facets on how to teach."

I will spend very little time on Jessica's subsequent past-life regression other than to describe that, ultimately, it was a reassuring experience. Her most recent past life proved to be one of rest and ease. She knew that many previous lives had been difficult and challenging—in large, dominating bodies and involving challenges both physical and mental—but this particular life provided her with a vitally important insight: that "life does not have to be a struggle." Her soul left her body with no effort and with no regrets, and her overriding feeling was "coming home ... I'm here again." Jessica meets her guide, who she says has appeared in many dreams in repeated incarnations as Old Father Time. She reports that they have no need to name her soul or his—they just know each other—but for the purpose of this LBL experience, she calls him Time.

In her current life as an inquisitive, learning soul, Jessica is a keen reader—it is no exaggeration to write that she devours the written word. Therefore, I was not at all surprised when Time first took her to the library, in which she could review this and other lives. (2) Standing behind her and to her left, he gently told her to "relax and enjoy; there is no hurry." She takes her time and discovers much. "From the book, I somehow get images and senses, not pictures. The life I have just come from indicates to me that I should not push against life, because I have already learned so much. I don't have to struggle to teach others—just carry on doing what I am doing now and allow others to make their own decisions." Gently, Time reminds her that she is not responsible for their decisions, telling her "these will come in their time, not your time."

Jessica discovers a blank page in her book. "This is to remind me. I have been incarnating for such a long time, it's to remind me that I have a choice. If I want to go back after this physical life, I have a choice—I can move on to the next stage if I choose. This is somehow linked with the reminder that there is no need to struggle. I am part of the change—the incredible change throughout the world. It's important that what I am doing is not for me but for the world. Rewards for humanity will be huge because of all we are doing."

Prior to this session, Jessica had not read any of the LBL books by Dr. Michael Newton, preferring to wait until afterward to compare her own experience with that of others. Her guide leads her onward, and she describes a vaulted corridor leading to an enormous special room. She recognizes where she is going: "Ah, yes, this is the council."

Jessica then commences an enlightening visit to her Council of Elders. One of the members is a female dressed in green. With delighted recognition, Jessica realizes that this being helps and guides her when she is with the clients she coaches and strengthens her "knowing" as she carries out her work. Another member, who also radiates feminine energy, is dressed in a natural linen robe and answers Jessica's enquiry as to why she feels so strongly about feminine wisdom as opposed to male-dominated religious dogma. Jessica learns that the world is changing, and the feminine age is returning; the world has been so immersed in strong male energy that it has forgotten its balance. "She is here to represent all we are about—Earth—there will be a significant change, that's why I feel so strongly, it will be in my lifetime. Her linen robe is to remind me to protect myself using natural things—no artifice, just natural processes. Her message is to remind me that I know the beginning. I recognize balance."

After this information-filled visit to her Council of Elders, Jessica asks to visit her soul group. Here she discovers Sam, her husband in her current life. "He is hugging me—it's a relief and it feels wonderful. We have so much learning together. We are choosing the lives we want—there is no doubt that we'll keep finding each other (in this life, Sam is Jessica's second husband). He's telling me that he knows what he needs to learn and he's learning it. He's even put on muddy boots to show me that he is down to earth and fully grounded!" (This is a particular acknowledgement of Jessica and Sam's love of the natural world and of growing natural produce.) In their current incarnation together, Sam is helping Jessica to remember she needs to be in the natural world and to be grounded, perhaps to balance her inclination to spend more time in the spiritual plane. Music is a strong, shared focus of attention for them both, and at this point, Sam transmits to her a particular song that reminds her of their shared goal; the choice of music is private, so I do not press for its identification.

Meanwhile, Jessica has moved on. She discovers that she and Sam are part of a very small group of souls. She tells me "they are quiet, I do not recognize any of them from my current life, but I know them. We are developing as a group. I get the sense that Sam and I are exclusive, and these souls have recently joined us. They are translucent in color; Sam is yellow with muddy boots, and I am olive green with a tinge of yellow." According to Michael Newton's research, a clear yellow color indicates courage and perseverance, and the appearance of green in Jessica's core color indicates her healing abilities. (3) Enjoying a sudden clarification, Jessica realizes that she and Sam are this group's teachers, and their translucence may be an indicator that these are young souls. She and Sam are in a new role, and the group is new, so this is a group of learning. As yet, she is unaware of the full scope of their duties; she simply knows it is all about energy. Then, thanks to her own guide, Time, she remembers she is learning to be a junior guide.

Time gives Jessica a signpost with which she can recognize his presence in her life. In this current incarnation, she never wears a wristwatch. He will show her a vision of a watch on a chain, and if she sees this when she is

experiencing doubt about whether or not to act, she will know he is prompting her to take action.

I expected that Jessica might wish to visit the place of life selection
in order to discover more about her diminutive size in this life, but she
declined. "This is now complete. I can come back to find out more, and I
will be learning from my dreams."

Jessica and I have remained in close contact during the two years since
her LBL experience. We share many interests, and I have witnessed firsthand her healing and teaching abilities. Immediately after the session,
she told me that her first, overriding impression was of the complete and
unconditional love that exists in her Soul Home. She was delighted with the
understandings she gained about her siblings, and particularly her relationship with her husband and soul mate, Sam. She gained insights into how she
can help Sam in this life, and she confirmed her deep inner sense that she
will never need to doubt him.

During her return to full awareness in the reintegration process, she was
reluctant to come back from her expanded consciousness and resume her
current body's limitations, and it was especially hard for her to move away
from an environment in which communication is purely telepathic. (4)
This is clearly her preferred choice as an experienced soul. But she felt that
her LBL had taught her not to worry so much about physical things. And,
indeed, in her current incarnation she has embraced a great deal of what she
learned in our session. At the time of writing, it is two years and four months
since her LBL. During that time, she has sought attunement to the different
levels of Reiki healing and is now a Reiki Master, thus combining the healing and teaching of her soul's path. Her intuitive abilities, assisted by her
"green guide" who walks with her when she exercises her much-loved dog
each day, have expanded greatly. She was delighted to discover that her Reiki
healing abilities extended to animal healing, and she has set up a canine and
equine healing service unique in her area. Jessica's life-coaching practice has
developed into an intuitive healing and guidance practice; for a long time,
she has been intuitively interested in crystal healing and has now formalized
this by studying to gain an internationally accepted qualification as a crystal

healer. Jessica has founded two self-development groups in which her developing teaching abilities are much appreciated. She is in no way hindered by her small physical size and is learning that her students will listen to and appreciate the content of her teaching; she doesn't need to "push."

It was indeed a great privilege to work with this enlightened soul and, most importantly, to witness and share her subsequent development. Jessica's LBL experience provided her with many valuable insights, tools, and signposts; most important, perhaps, is that she continues to apply these to her daily life.

---

(1) Life and body selections are an important aspect of LBL hypnotherapy, because these visualizations provide therapeutic answers to so many client questions about why they are who they are in this life. See DS 355–381 and LBLH 175–180. Also see souls joining a fetus, DS 384–394 and LBLH 49–51.

(2) Spiritual libraries not only contain all our life-book records but are also spaces designed to review how the soul has progressed or regressed. The reliving of past events through live action is also provided to the soul; see DS 150–164 and LBLH 163–168.

(3) Where green does exist, a total green core color often begins the level IV stage of soul development; see LBLH 126. Because Jessica has not yet reached the deep blue stage of development, she may not realize that it is a bit early to think about ending her incarnations. She may also be slightly ahead of Sam in development, but the two of them could have been assigned—or are about to be assigned—to their own specialized training group of like-minded advanced souls. As the case indicates, being assigned to train younger souls is the first step toward junior guide status. See soul movement into specialized cluster groups, DS 320–323.

(4) Communication by telepathy is the spirit world norm and is so comprehensive, as far as total perception is concerned, that clients often want to stay in trance with their spiritual existence rather than return to a full consciousness state, where verbal communication often leads to misunderstandings in human form.

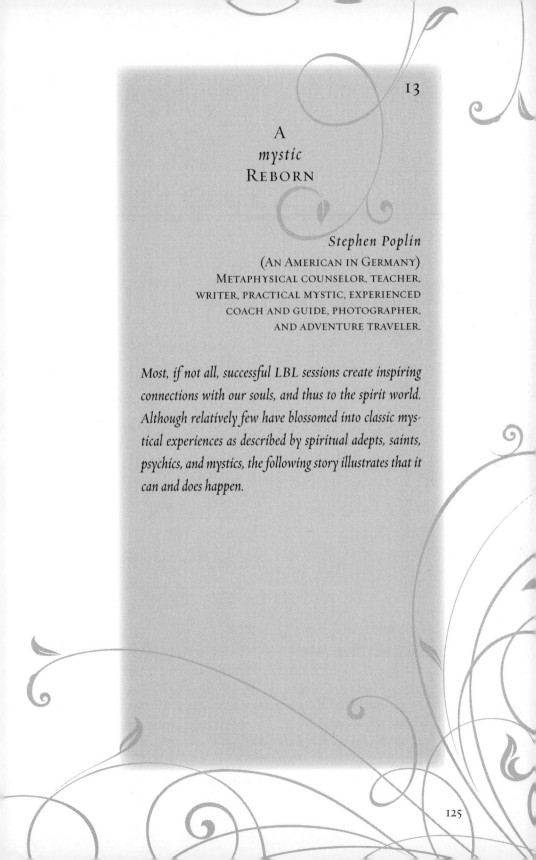

13

A
mystic
REBORN

Stephen Poplin

(An American in Germany)
Metaphysical counselor, teacher,
writer, practical mystic, experienced
coach and guide, photographer,
and adventure traveler.

Most, if not all, successful LBL sessions create inspiring connections with our souls, and thus to the spirit world. Although relatively few have blossomed into classic mystical experiences as described by spiritual adepts, saints, psychics, and mystics, the following story illustrates that it can and does happen.

As an artist, Anne probably had many inspired moments while drawing and painting, but she had left the financial insecurity of the artist's world for a lucrative but demanding job with a large corporation. Her present existence was one of team projects, long hours, and deadlines—not the classic arena for poets and muses.

Anne was a pleasure to work with, partly because she was personally motivated and proactive. She was interested in astrology and felt attracted to what she called "a celestial art of the heavens" that influences our planet. We began our initial spiritual regression session some four years ago, and throughout our association, an ongoing interest for Anne has been how to better understand and fulfill her life's purpose. She wanted to know more about herself and how to express herself in the various roles we all play— co-worker, partner, friend, investor, and homeowner. She was especially concerned about how she could build a bridge back to her work as a visual artist.

Anne wrote up her own perceptions and memories of our hypnosis sessions together, and I present them here with little editing. Note the details that a visual artist would appreciate:

> The session occurred in my home, with me lying on the couch with a blanket and Stephen sitting in an adjacent chair. He took me through the initial steps of relaxation, breathing, and counting backwards. As he suggested, I felt myself, Anne (or more precisely, the conscious analytical mind), shift off to the side, where she could observe without interfering.
>
> Stephen offered questions and comments throughout to guide the session. I won't mention all of these. Rather, I'll focus on the events of the journey that occurred.
>
> The first thing I see is a giant eye. I know that it's a god. (1)
>
> Then, as if I had stepped back to view the whole being, I see it is a Michaelangeloesque god, the father being, with long, white flowing hair, beard, and a white robe. It's as if we're in the clouds looking over a landscape of mountains. He is pointing, and I understand I'm being directed where to go.
>
> I look down, and I see that I'm wearing exquisitely luxurious shoes made of soft, silky material embroidered with flowers and

inset with jewels. I'm wearing a Renaissance-style gown, and
I'm sitting in the private interior courtyard and garden of an
aristocratic home. At first, I feel like the beloved daughter of this
home, a young woman, but then my perception shifts, and my
child, a little girl, is there with me. I understand the place to be the
home of my marriage. There is much happiness and beauty here.
I love my little girl; she is adorable, mischievous, about five years
old and running around the garden, playing. She has a remarkable
head of black curly hair, which is why I call her "my little storm."

In her present life, Anne is childless, but this causes her no regrets. I have
noticed that many advanced souls who have had children in past lives are
either neutral about the wish in this life or open to Fate bringing a child.
They are often very good uncles, aunts, and godparents. (Of course, many
advanced souls may choose to have children, which is a spiritual contract
and an honor.)

As Anne continues her narrative, notice her surprising realization of who
or what she really is in this vignette!

The scene shifts, and I seem to be at the top of a castle lookout,
like the balcony of a turret. I'm looking down, and below I see a
dark-haired young woman riding her horse off into the distance. I
am very sad to see her leaving. I realize later I am the same woman
as before but I'm now dead, and my spirit is looking down at the
young woman, who is my little curly haired girl now grown up. I
was killed during some form of warfare or invasion. She has vowed
to avenge my death, and she is riding away to join a battle.

Anne was pleasantly surprised to learn that this dark-haired daughter
is presently a colleague and friend at work named Sarah. They have joked
that they were probably together in some past life … and indeed they were!
Although the presence of others in our lives often provides a rich and meaningful focus in these sessions, here I wish to present Anne's clear and colorful
past-life and between-lives memories and how she integrated these experiences to perceive her present life in an expanded and profound manner.

As Anne continues her soul journey, the age-old idea that we will get our rewards in heaven actually becomes clear ... but not in the traditional sense. We now accompany this soul upwards, at home in spirit:

> From there, the vortex, I arrive at a place I know at once is home. When Stephen asks, I tell him it is the pearl place, the place I go to when I make art, and again I weep, telling Stephen that I'm very homesick to go back.
>
> It is not me, Anne, experiencing and telling this; it is another being now, one who knows the pearl place intimately. It is very beautiful here—everything seems to be made of crystal and light and pearly radiant hues yet at the same time is kind of formless. There is a group of people sitting nearby, a little below where I am. They are all shining and made of light, and I know that they are all artists of one form or another ... writers, poets, painters, dancers, actors, and so on. Further in the distance, I can see more shimmering shapes of people coming and going, as if they, like me, are leaving and returning here. Some of them look like kings and queens, but I know they are actors in Shakespearean plays, wearing their costumes. When I look back at the other group of people who were sitting closer, I am surprised to see my friend Sarah looking up at me. (2) What I see is not quite the human Sarah I know, though; it is the highest, purest aspect of her being, and I'm very moved to see how beautiful she is.
>
> Stephen asks about the pearl place and its people, and I tell him we are a spherical way of being. When I say this, I see the pearl place as if from a distance; it is a sphere made up of all our spirits joined together. In the pearl place, even though we have our individual spirits, we are equally joined and part of the shining sphere. (3) I tell Stephen this in a very matter-of-fact way, as a being who simply knows this.
>
> Then I see the god from the beginning of the journey looking down on us. I tell Stephen he is not from the pearl place, not like us. We are like the grasshoppers from the fable about the ants and grasshoppers—we love to play and laugh and make beautiful things, and here, unlike the fable, there is no punishment. I tell Stephen the god made us because we make him happy. He has many responsibilities, and he comes here for relief. Then I see

my channel opening in the crystal, and I start walking through it. Stephen asks what this means, and I tell him we each have a place, like this, where we go alone. The channel opens into a kind of arena or valley surrounded by crystal rock cliffs on either side. Sometimes they appear like crystal (4), and sometimes they are like rocks. I am in the center, and I'm holding a rock or a crystal in my hand. I tell Stephen this is where we come to learn things and then, when we're ready, we move into the belly of a woman. I can see, or I know, that from above, the channel and the arena look like a womb and a vaginal passage.

One can tell from Anne's description how moved she was. There were tears in her eyes and a beatific smile on her lips. She was in ecstasy. In this in-between place between the Earth and the cosmic pearl sphere, she imagined that I touched her hand, but my sense is that this was an association—and a touch—from a life long ago.

I'm spellbound by the place and kind of drift peacefully there. Because he thinks I might fall asleep, Stephen lifts my arm. The instant he does so, I become Father William walking, hand on staff, up a rocky mountain path within a landscape that opens up toward the back area of the pearl place. I'm in a monk's garb, and I feel the sandals on his feet, all covered with dust from walking many miles on his travels. I must be in a deep trance at this point, because Father William is more vividly present in my body than anything that happened before; my voice changes, and his voice speaks through me, conversing with Stephen. He lives near Siena, in Italy, living like a hermit monk in a little hut in the woods. The local people bring him food. He has many manuscripts in the hut, some of which he reads and some in which he writes. He is an old man now and very weary. He tells Stephen how he gave up all the pleasures of love, family, and friends to serve God; how he learned many languages, studied many teachings, and how he traveled to spread God's teachings to the people. Stephen asks about Father William's teachings, wondering if his god is the Catholic god. Father William laughs and says God's love is for the people, and he is merely an instrument through which that love can flow. I feel that Father William is a very wise, compassionate soul, pure in heart and motive. Stephen asks if Father William regrets leaving family, friends, and the possibility of marriage behind. He gives a soft smile and points upward, saying, "What greater love is there than this?" (meaning God's love) Then he says, "Besides, I have the bird to keep me company."

Now I can see a tree branch outside the window of the hut, and perched on it is a rainbow-colored bird who sings beautiful songs for Father William. The bird transforms into an image of Christ wearing blue and white robes and pointing to the flaming sacred heart. Father William has accepted much hardship gladly to follow the path of serving his god. Still, I can feel within him a great weariness.

Stephen asks how this life ends, and I see Father William setting out on his travels through the woods. For the very first time, instead of forging onward, he stops to rest by a stream, to enjoy the peace and beauty there. And he dies peacefully while sitting there by the stream, slumping over onto the grass.

Stephen asks me what significance Father William's life has for me, and I begin to weep again, saying, "It can't be like that, it was too hard, too hard." And then I see the god, back in the pearl place, who takes me into his arms, saying, "It's all right, you're not meant to be the father this time, you're meant to be the child...the bird who sings the songs of the sacred heart."

This was such a beautiful and poignant experience, and I felt a deep gratitude to witness this journey. In my Earth-time, many hours had passed. I knew, however, that to Anne, in this state of bliss, this was not long at all. She was outside time, in a lovely place of serenity. Surely an advantage of doing a house call (something I rarely do) is to allow the reclined sojourner to float in the ecstasy and to savor the many memories and feelings for as long as possible. Anne was full of heart and spirit, and I saw that these grand feelings could continue. It was time for me to go but not time for the curtain to fall and the play to end. I reset the stage, suggesting that she remain lying down while I quietly left.

Then Stephen readies me to end the session. We talk a little, then he leaves. But after these remarkable experiences, I remain in a heightened state of awareness for several days. During the evening of the session, I once more experience, amongst other things, the god comforting me and taking me on an elevator, descending down to a floor, where I get out. I ask him, "What am I supposed to do now?" He gives me two suitcases; I take one in each hand, and he says, "You have everything you need in your two hands."

Little did Anne know that the suitcases were more than symbolic. In the next few months, she heard an inner calling to move further south, to a warmer place that Father William would have enjoyed.

Anne floated on air for days! The soul had awakened—or perhaps, more precisely, the soul had a clearer access to the everyday conscious mind. The corporate world was now not so interesting.

Notice how Anne proactively engaged with the memories and revelations as she concludes her narrative:

Other remarkable things occurred. Although I knew I could return to "normal" reality, I continued to allow the experiences to wash over me. It was as though a curtain had opened and revealed another reality, literally the tangible experience of a spiritual reality, and I wanted to stay in its flow. A couple of days later, I visited Stephen's office for another session, in part to help me process the remarkable things that happened. I took the subway and walked several blocks. All the while, it was as if I was floating in another mystical reality. I was able to cross busy streets without looking at the cars or traffic lights—something I'm normally very cautious about. Many people turned their heads as I passed and smiled, as if sensing the presence in which I was immersed. After talking with Stephen, we did another regression session. This time, I was a white bird flying south to an island in the middle of the ocean. I find a mountain on the island, and the god from the previous session is at the top, waiting for me. I sit within his arms like a child with its father, feeling the beauty of divine love. Then, as the white bird, I fly back north. Below me I see the USA, specifically Florida, and I see the bird land there. Although in the past I had thought about moving to Florida, I now fully understand it's a place I'm meant to be.

I would have to write much more to fully describe the significance of these sessions and follow-up events for me, but it was akin to the Caravaggio painting "The Conversion of St. Paul," in which, having had an experience of God, St. Paul literally falls off his horse. Since then my life has been an attempt to come to terms with the experience. Subsequent readings have affirmed to me that what happened was akin to the first stage of awakening— or a call to the mystic path.

Anne moved from the colder climate and bought an apartment near the ocean in Florida. She found many ways to relax and to enjoy life, including getting a puppy to accompany her on beach walks. Since the session, she has taken a very profound turn in her relationship with her body and her health. I learned about the positive changes through later correspondence:

I'm conscious of wanting my body to be stronger for, and more inviting to, spiritual experiences like this. Prayer, meditations, and self-hypnosis helped me to finally quit smoking and, more importantly, completely surrender the desire to smoke. I'm also more conscious that my food is comprised of life forms, and that I wish to eat, for sure with pleasure but also with thankfulness and in moderation. In similar ways I seek to be aware of my own negative energies and habits, and in a gentle, self-forgiving way, transform them into more positive practices.

I was especially impressed with Anne's profound professional changes. She is planning on going part-time with her corporate job and has already downsized her possessions and pressures. Her new attitude at work is nothing less than amazing. Simplicity and serenity are her companions now.

I knew that our spiritual sessions, especially the life-between-lives integration sessions, were of profound value to Anne, but when I asked her to share more of her journey for this book, I was very moved and humbled to learn the extent to which she was positively affected. My sense is that she had always been ready and willing; now the time was right, and I had the tools to offer her at the appointed time. The rest was magic and divine grace.

Anne is looking into ways to aid others in and out of the workplace and to artistically express herself again, be that through painting or singing the song of the sacred bird. The attunement is reached, and the mystic is reborn. The artist is again connected to the muse—consciously.

Three and a half years after our first hypnotic session, Anne shared the following with me:

> My daily life has changed dramatically. Although I had gradually returned to a less heightened state, I nonetheless still felt the call of the divine, and I saw and continue to see the indescribable love I had felt in every living being. I strive in all my actions to be attuned to this spiritual realm, to be as close as I can come to the perfect love and union that was revealed to me. In the classic terminology used by mystics, I am now on a path to seek the unitive state, a oneness with God. I now see my desire to eventually return to art-making as something I would do to serve this greater realm of spirit.
>
> Before, I walked in one world on the Earth plane. Now, I am consciously learning how to live and walk between two worlds: the Earth plane and the different aspects of the spiritual plane. I am interested in all spiritual traditions and practices, and study subjects I had no particular interest in before: shamanism, Buddhism, Taoism, Christian mysticism, psychic development, tarot, transpersonal hypnosis…
>
> In everything I do, I seek as best I can to be a channel for the divine love from the spirit plane.
>
> As I reflect upon all these changes, I would have to say the opening to the divine through this session was probably the single most important event of my life.

---

(1) The subject in this case uses a number of religious symbols to describe her feelings about the divine experience she is having in her LBL session. Some involve archetypes such as a robed holy figure with long white hair or metaphoric visualizations with an all-seeing eye or more traditional Christian declarations. For an overview of deified entities reported by large numbers of hypnosis subjects, see references to the Presence in DS 243–251 and God in JS 122.

(2) First encounters of friendly spirits: JS 27.

(3) Spherical visions during the soul's transition phase home: JS 73.

(4) Visualizing crystal enclosures, stones, etc. are common with LBL clients. They appear to represent the balancing of vibrational energy that enhances thought and fosters rejuvenation of the returning soul. See meaning of spiritual settings involving crystal, DS 91, 134 and LBLH 106.

14

The
weather
Whisperer

Susan Wisehart
(Chicago, Illinois)
HOLISTIC PSYCHOTHERAPIST, LICENSED
MARRIAGE AND FAMILY THERAPIST, AND
AUTHOR OF *Soul Visioning*.

Elaine's story illustrates the effectiveness of LBL hypnotherapy in helping a client to gain clarity and direction concerning relationships, issues needing resolution, and the purpose she came to fulfill in her current lifetime. A mother of two and former professional in the corporate world, Elaine had been in couples counseling prior to coming to me for an LBL regression. Her marriage was very troubled, and she felt disempowered. "I was giving my power away to the point where I was no longer taking care of myself or enjoying my life," she explained.

After Elaine's session, I followed up with interviews after one year and again after two years to determine the long-term benefits that LBL brought to her life. The following is an edited summary of those interviews. Elaine's path has already begun to take an intriguing direction toward a most unusual mode of service to humanity and our environment.

IN MY ROLE as a holistic psychotherapist and a marriage and family therapist, I often work with people who want insight concerning their purpose
as a soul, their purpose within their primary soul group, and the lessons that
they incarnated to learn through their relationships. I look at all relationships from the perspective of the soul. What soul contracts were made prior
to this lifetime? What does each relationship and life situation have to teach
us? What patterns persist from previous incarnations that are still affecting
our relationships?

I have found that life-between-lives regression facilitates a deeper understanding of how we can clear the unconscious barriers that interfere with
our ability to create a joyful, soul-inspired life. When we become aware of
our soul contracts with people in our present lifetime, with those we have
known in other lives, and with those in our primary soul group, we may step
out of the victim role and appreciate that we have chosen our experiences
as our classroom.

During Elaine's LBL session, she easily regressed back to some of her
happy childhood memories, then into the comfort of her mother's womb,
eagerly anticipating her birth into this lifetime. When I transitioned her
from the womb into her immediate past life, Elaine remembered a significant lifetime as an African-American mother working in a tanning factory:

> I was surprised to find myself as a woman who had been raised
> in a low-income environment in New York City. I was very poor
> and had beautiful children. I was beaten in that life because I was
> black. The beatings were on the left side of my body. Interestingly,
> all of the medical ailments that have plagued me in my current life
> have been on my left side—a broken leg and arm, stitches on my
> left side from birthing my children, an epidural that worked on my
> right side but not the left, and injuries to my left side from a dog
> attack. When I run, I drag my left leg. I am working to balance
> that out, allowing that left half of my body to be just as celebrated
> as my right side.

It is revealing to note that the left side of the body is considered the feminine side, and many of Elaine's past lives were experienced as a woman in a

subservient role. For example, in another past-life regression, Elaine discovered that as a small child in China, she was immobilized in a box to prevent her from struggling as her feet were bound, and she lost her sense of freedom. To this day, Elaine has claustrophobic feelings in any close quarters. During her LBL she recognized that her ex-husband, whom she describes as having power over her in this and other lifetimes, was the village foot-binder in that Chinese incarnation. Her present-day soul mate was a friend in that Chinese life who used to unbind her feet and take her for rides on his back.

> In my current life, I have been athletic with a predominantly masculine side. In the corporate world, I was viewed as a very strong-minded person. That strength was never accepted readily from a woman. So I am balancing those issues through my mothering role. I teach my children that women can be strong, not only emotionally but also physically.
>
> My death in the African-American lifetime came when my lungs failed; I had worked for a glove manufacturer, breathing in the tanning chemicals they were using. I remember having a lot of difficulty breathing at my death.

I transitioned Elaine through the death scene into the spirit realm, where she was warmly received by her guides:

> The between state was this amazing place of love, energy, and acceptance. My spirit guides were not in human form. They were more like light beings, so when I needed to recognize them, they showed me various parts of a human form or symbols for me to identify them by. I was standing in the center, and everyone was moving around me. They were so happy to have me there. I realized that I am never alone, and the love that these spirits shared for me was unconditional. I felt tears of joy rolling down my face the entire time.

Elaine was welcomed with great celebration by her primary soul group of people important in her life. Her soul mate in her current lifetime greeted her and took her to the library, where she was shown important information about her life purpose.

ELAINE: One individual in my primary group, whom I later recognized as my soul mate, walked me over to this book (part of a vast library). Although I didn't feel intimidated, I didn't know what he wanted from me. I was told that I needed to keep learning. The four words in the book—awareness, discipline, education, and fortitude—have become very important reminders since then, guiding me about what I need to develop in my life. More was revealed to me at my meeting with the Council of Elders about what these words meant.

SUSAN: Who else did you recognize in your soul group?

E: My deceased grandfather was there. I began seeing auras as a child, and he not only helped me feel understood but accepted me for the scattered, wild child that I was. I recognized my father (who is alive today), one of my sisters, a high-school teacher of mine who had committed suicide, and a woman who calls herself Malena. Malena is not incarnated now but has always been an all-knowing, maternal figure in my life. I have known her in my heart and sensed her around me since I was a little girl.

It was wonderful to recognize the one soul who most understood me, who was the most nurturing. He is my current partner in this life. I realized that my relationship with him needs to be nurtured in this lifetime, and that it is my destiny to be with him.

S: How did that destiny unfold for you?

E: I finally had the courage to do what my soul knew was right for me. I understood my marriage was over but didn't leave my husband right away because I felt it was my duty to let him know about my growing awareness of the spirit world. We had conversations about that, but I realized that he was just going through the motions of listening, and that deep down, he did not respect my spiritual path. It was difficult for me to say, "I need to leave now." He was angry at first, but eventually I was able to move on. He has also moved on and remarried. We share the parenting of our daughters.

Elaine's relationship with her husband was materially based. Once again, she realized, she had stepped into a subservient role and had lost herself. She did not feel supported or understood for her spiritual growth and passion for life. Elaine eventually confronted her fears of leaving. She knew that in this lifetime, she needed to leave behind the role of emotionally abused victim. (1)

S: What else did you learn in that relationship?

E: To stay true to myself, I had to learn courage and fortitude. I have to remain balanced and focused in my relationship with my ex-husband and not give my power away. I also learned in the LBL that I must embrace the human experience as being imperfect. That's a big one for me. I'm not a perfectionist, but I am hard on myself. I always had to be number one in the race, I always had to be the best, but I have learned from the LBL that imperfection is perfection.

As her LBL continued, Elaine experienced a meeting with her Council of Elders, where she was further instructed about her life purpose.

S: What was your meeting with the council like?

E: It was lighthearted. I was standing in a room with white marble floors and a semicircular table, and there were three light beings of indigo and gold colors. Their message to me was to lighten up: "You have a lot of work to do, but you can enjoy doing it." They repeated the importance of developing awareness, discipline, education, and fortitude, because these were the qualities I needed to develop in my current lifetime to fulfill my purpose.

Part of that purpose is to remember my wholeness as a spiritual being and to express that knowing in my life's work. There is something significant that I need to do to help Earth's health and awareness, some purpose related to weather and geologic changes. When I am in a meditative state, I become more attuned to weather patterns and seismic activity. I can tell what the weather is going to be like before it happens. I sensed an earthquake that happened in Japan a couple of weeks ago.

Elaine's weather-related purpose became much clearer to her many months after the session, as she explains below.

E: The LBL taught me that I need to become more conscious (aware) of my inner guidance, through which I can receive the instruction (education) for developing my talents. Also, I realized that I need to develop the strength (fortitude) and discipline to stay focused on my spiritual path.

My meeting with the Council of Elders and the entire positive LBL experience gave me the confidence to move forward and make major life changes. After I left an emotionally abusive marriage, in which my spiritual interests were ridiculed, I met my soul mate, and he supports all levels of my being. I am the happiest I have ever been, and I am developing my talents to be of service to this planet. (2)

About a year after her LBL session, I spoke with Elaine to find out how her life had changed. She had already benefited greatly from the experience. It gave her the insight and courage to be true to herself. Guided by the recollection of her soul's purpose, she was able to leave a relationship that was not working for her and to be with her soul mate. This was an important step, to be able to be herself in a loving relationship that fosters her growth. She broke a multi-incarnational pattern of subservience and valued herself enough to follow her soul's guidance and purpose for her life.

Elaine and her new partner were clearly happy and well suited to one another, and shared a common purpose to be of service to others. The children were benefiting by seeing a loving, respectful, balanced relationship between these two people. They were negotiating the challenges of a blended family with love and maturity. Elaine had gained self-confidence and was more in touch with her intuitive capacities. She continued to apply awareness, discipline, education, and fortitude to every area of her life.

Two years after her LBL session, I again contacted Elaine to discover what further developments had occurred in her life. She is now happily married to her soul mate. Their blended family is working out the adjustments that come with the transitions of a new family constellation. Her current husband has done his own past-life and LBL work, discovering the patterns and lessons that he carried into this lifetime.

Elaine continues to grow in her spiritual pursuits and studies. She shared an incredible story about how her life purpose is unfolding, which is to help facilitate this planet's healing and to find a balance between humanity's needs and Earth's environment.

My new husband and I felt drawn to travel to Peru, strongly sensing that we would meet the people that we needed to meet. Because one of our flights was cancelled, we had to take a 6½-hour taxi ride through the Andean mountains to our destination near Lake Titicaca. At I AM, we randomly picked a hostel to stay in. To our surprise, it was one block from the home of the author of a book that we had recently read. He also runs a tour business there. When we visited, his nephew offered to conduct a tailor-made tour of the sacred islands on Lake Titicaca. After we told him our story and interests, he offered to take us to little-known places and perform some of the spiritual rituals that aren't normally shared with tourists.

One of the islands he took us to has two temples—one for Mother Earth and another for Father Earth. He arranged for us to stay with an indigenous family on this island. Our hostess told us a bit about their life and how difficult it had been. We were there in November, and it hadn't rained since June. They were very worried, as almost everything that they eat comes from their back yard.

We did a ritual to ask permission to go to the 13,000-foot summit of the island. At the top of this sacred place is a circle temple made of rocks. Our guide shared a beautiful ceremony in his native language and then said, "We have about fifteen minutes to do whatever you feel you need to be doing, because it is starting to get dark." Intuitively knowing exactly where to go, I walked to a cliff that overlooked the lake, and I meditated with the intent of bringing rain to this parched soil. With my eyes open, I saw before me a grid. I was physically shaking, feeling intense heat and energy. I started to doubt myself: Who am I to think that I can bring rain to this place that hasn't had rain in five months? But then I felt I wasn't alone. There were other energies facilitating this, and I needed to stand fast. Right behind me, I sensed an amazingly strong source of love and acceptance. I stayed for another five minutes, then I felt my work was complete.

As we took our first step down toward the trail, the first raindrop fell. It poured all day and all night long. The woman with whom we were staying was elated and grateful, exclaiming, "Now you have to stay!"

Elaine's apparent ability to manipulate weather patterns is consistent with many Native American and shamanistic traditions that acknowledge people who are known as rainmakers. Although it may only have been a coincidence that rain occurred just after her experience, and there might be other explanations, to Elaine it was a powerful validation that she is on the right path. Her confidence in her abilities has grown tremendously after this amazing demonstration. Elaine is committed to her life purpose of helping the planet with weather-related issues.

Elaine's story demonstrates what can happen when a person is ready to change their life and reclaim their true self. Her LBL session helped Elaine to know that she is never really alone. The last time I saw Elaine and her husband, they were radiant and happy in fulfilling their mutual purpose of service. I look forward to following Elaine's continuing progress and achievements.

---

(1) We often see a repetition of the same karmic lesson over a number of lives. The immortal character of the soul, which changes slowly over time, does play a role here when you consider that the individual human temperament and emotional chemistry of each body is different. The notion that we routinely clean up all our past karmic lessons at the end of each life is not really accurate in most cases. Our work on various issues often takes longer. Also, for more analysis about the assumption of being partnered with the "wrong" person in life, see LBLH 131–132.

(2) I should stress the fact that rather than appearing before a panel of judges in front of our council, clients quickly realize they are facing a group of wise

guidance counselors who are typically gentle in their questions. In most meetings with the soul, regardless of our past mistakes, the elders do not tell us what we should do in our future but rather allow us to find ourselves through an indulgent Socratic approach. See DS 210–212.

15

Two
Suicides

Joelle McGonagle
(Portland, Oregon)
NGH-certified hypnotherapist and
registered counselor specializing in
mind/body/spirit regression therapy.

This story illustrates how life events are part of a greater plan and how contracts with our soul mates are carefully arranged to be a part of that plan. Grief is a hard lesson, but in this case, we see how Rosanne is able to understand why the experiences of her tormented life are meant to help her grow.

ROSANNE CAME TO me because she was suffering greatly from the lingering grief and inner pain resulting from the loss of two of her closest and most cherished family members. They had both committed suicide.

Over the years, she had tried many things to heal—conventional therapy, traveling, staying home, and burying herself in her work, as well as spending significant time off of work. Since she loves art, she also tried art therapy, as well as expressing herself in several art mediums to try to release her deep, lingering grief.

Nothing seemed to help. Of this period in her life, she told me, "My life had been shattered. There was a huge black hole inside. I just couldn't recover." She also complained of experiencing recurring nightmares, of having suicidal fantasies herself, and of crippling low self-esteem.

Rosanne grew up in a dysfunctional and emotionally cold home. Estranged from her verbally abusive mother since early childhood, her older brother, Ben, had been her only ally and the only one in her family she felt she could trust. He was her surrogate mother, her protector, and her best friend. Her father was seldom at home and was emotionally distant when he was there. She and her brother were extremely close all through her childhood. She felt he was the only one who really loved her, and her only positive childhood memories were of the two of them playing happily together.

When he was just seventeen years old, Ben committed suicide. Although her family tried to convince Rosanne it was an accidental death, she knew the truth. He had overdosed on their mother's large selection of prescription drugs.

Rosanne was devastated and would remain so for many years to come while she struggled with her guilt and self-blame, shame, anger, abandonment, loneliness, and self-esteem issues. Even today, she felt there must have been something she should have or could have done to change things—that if she had somehow been different, Ben would still be here with her today. For years, her mind replayed the days before his death, over and over again.

It is a testament of her inner strength, as well as of the dysfunction of her family, that she was the one who ended up making all of the arrangements for her brother's funeral, casket, and burial. She was only fifteen years old.

She grew up to be a struggling, middle-aged single mother of two adolescent sons. Her youngest son, Andrew, was diagnosed as bipolar. During his adolescence, she watched helplessly as he began to develop the symptoms of schizophrenia. After several rocky and agonizing teenage years of roller-coasting emotionally and physically, he too committed suicide. He was also only seventeen years old.

Rosanne was now completely and utterly devastated. Convinced that if she had just been there for him more—been more loving, more understanding, more *something*—this never would have happened. She now believed that she must have been a very bad parent as well, and her self-esteem was at rock bottom:

> When my son first died, I went to a therapist. We did a lot of
> work together, and I finally was able to go back to work, but my
> soul was gone. I was just too broken to pull it together anymore.
> I was on medication for depression, but the inner pain was so bad.
> I thought I deserved my pain.

Perhaps the most damaging belief she was carrying was that she no longer deserved any happiness or good things to come into her life. She believed that since these terrible events had happened to her, the inability to prevent the two suicides proved that she was not worthy of any additional love, joy, success, or happiness in her future. She began to have more graphic suicidal fantasies, envisioning herself jumping off a cliff in a beautiful white dress, at last no longer feeling her emotional pain.

This is the road my client had been down when she came to see me over two years ago. I felt we needed to do some preliminary hypnosis therapy sessions to prepare her for the intense and in-depth experience of spiritual regression.

We began by doing some conventional hypnosis sessions: using suggestions and imagery to help her feel more relaxed and at peace. We then did some childhood and past-life regression sessions as well. These initial sessions helped her to release some of the grief and emotional pain that she was carrying, and begin to identify and untangle some of the distorted beliefs that she had acquired in other lives and accepted as true in her current life.

We explored a few related past lives in which she struggled to survive, often hungry, scrambling to get enough food day after day. One of her beliefs that we uncovered in these sessions was that life has to be hard. Some of the other beliefs and themes we found in these lives were that no one really cares; there's not a lot of joy in life, only moments of not being afraid; and children die often. These lives all contributed to her current belief that life has to be arduous.

There were many past lives where she experienced demanding work. In these lives, she experienced a variety of limitations and restrictions. She said, "I don't have a choice. I don't have enough of anything, not food or clothes. I'm cold and hungry most of the time. There were lives of unfairness and inequity as well; as a serf, a slave, and a poor farmer. My head was chopped off in one of these lives." At this point, I decided it would be best to postpone Rosanne's immediate past-life review until we were ready to enter the spirit world. (1)

As we moved deeper into the relationship between these former life issues and her challenging life today, she had the momentous realization that all of these difficult lives had helped her to understand and explore the many faces of powerlessness.

To balance this exploration, we also reviewed a few of her happy, loving, and peaceful lives as a way to strengthen Rosanne's present human ego by integrating her soul's past experience of being safe and loved.

Our childhood regression sessions focused on helping her to resolve the still-troubled relationship with her current mother. Still self-centered, unhappy, and unable to get outside of her own needs, her mother was unaware of the pain she had caused her daughter. And remembering all this in our childhood regression sessions, Rosanne still felt like her victim: "I feel so cheated. So much would have been different if I had been nurtured," she told me sadly.

After these initial sessions, my client began to feel more at peace and centered in her life. She was less depressed as well. It was now time to do the life-between-lives session.

The results were spectacular! Rosanne was able to connect deeply in her session with the souls of both her brother and her son, seeing and knowing them to be glowingly happy and at peace. She remembered and at last understood clearly that the three of them had lovingly planned this life together to challenge Rosanne's courage.

During the beginning of her life-between-lives session, as we move into her prenatal experience in the womb of her mother, Rosanne realizes that her mother's coolness began here. "She doesn't want to be pregnant with another child. It's like I'm not human. She doesn't want me." Rosanne feels herself armoring herself against the rejection she knows will come.

As we continue with our session, I regress my client into her most recent past life. She finds herself as a frail young woman of eighteen, living with her family in a small village. She remembers her cozy home, her busy, happy family, and the younger brother she loves deeply and often cares for.

Caught in the crossfire of a battle in World War II, she dies alone in the mud near her family's small thatched-roof home. "We can't outrun the tanks. The ground is vibrating. I'm disoriented: on my hands and knees, I can't get up. I can't stay with my family. I'm terrified. I don't understand what's happening. It looks and smells like hell. I never get off that hill." And finally, "I'm high up now, looking down."

She realizes that even in her immediate past life, she was aware of feeling that if she had just been stronger and faster, she might have been able to save her brother and herself. This theme was to be continued even more strongly in her present life.

As she floats away, it's very bright all around her. "I think this (the brightness) is just to make me feel good. I love the way it feels."

Eight purple lights then surround her. Her first thought is that they are spiritual guards of some sort. "They want to talk to me, to make sure there's nothing left over from Earth. They know if you're carrying something traumatic back." They fade away, and she realizes they were loving, rejuvenating soul beings who were there to help her come home. (2)

She then says, "I'm not alone anymore. A friend is helping me now. It's the light that was surrounding me, letting me know he's here. I think it's my spirit guide, Jason. He's a clear, bright light. I'm a simple shape now—a yellow-orange light.

"Now I'm rolling on a grassy hill. It's pure joy, so healing, it's like being a kid again. It's healing me from that life. My little brother (from the life just left behind) is there too. We're like two little puppy dogs, rolling down the hill. There's no judgment here. I could be any age. The grass is so green and soft. The hill is just perfect. All the colors are so bright."

Then she is aware of a white marble bench where she and Jason go to talk about her recently completed life. (3) But Rosanne wants to meet right away with the "old wise souls," as she calls them, and doesn't want to stay on the bench or join her soul group.

As we arrive at the space of the Council of Elders, she finds herself in a Greek setting where there are white marble pillars. She is joined there by six "wise white- haired beings in white robes" around a table that she experiences as being a little above her. (4) She comments that they seem larger to her than she is. They wait quietly until she is ready to begin. The two beings in the center begin their meeting.

They communicate lovingly to her, helping her to remember that the key focus of her current life has been courage. Her main goal in this life has been to be stronger and more courageous by demonstrating to herself how strong she can be in the face of intense pain and adversity.

She remembers clearly now that her immortal soul self has orchestrated in great detail the adversity of her difficult, lonely childhood and the challenges of her life as a single mother. Even the two awful suicides that affected her life so deeply were carefully planned in order to challenge and bolster her courage and inner strength. She understands that this life is only one in a whole series of lives planned to help her gain the strength and courage that her soul is seeking. The difficult past lives we had explored were some examples of this lesson.

The elders want her to know that her son, Andrew, is an old soul who had done just what he had agreed to do to help her to grow, and that she had helped him down his path as well.

A difficult and headstrong child, she had been able to give him the freedom to be himself, keeping him safe without judging him. Because of her support and love, he had a full life during those seventeen years in spite of his mental illness. Letting go of him after his death was part of her challenge in this life as well, she realizes. And she knew that she had fulfilled her part of the bargain.

In addition to shedding light on a variety of other questions that Rosanne had about important events in her life today, the wise ones also remind her of her need to differentiate between her strength and her stubbornness. She realizes that while stubbornness is sometimes considered an offshoot of strength, courage and stubbornness are very different qualities.

The elders also communicate to her that they want her to rejuvenate herself more often. They tell her she needs to protect herself more from her own guilt and self-blame—that she has been too hard on herself. "I need more self-love. It's all OK." She realizes with certainty that it has never been her fault or lack of tenacity that has created these challenges in her life but rather the careful planning and agreement of several souls to help Rosanne's soul become even stronger.

At the end of her time with the elders, they remind her to take responsibility for her psychic gifts, something she'd had a hard time acknowledging until then.

Rosanne sees her son Andrew outside of the council chamber, and she goes to meet him. He appears to her now as she was never able to see him in this life: mature, wise, bright, and strong, an older man. "He thanks me for the strength and courage I had demonstrated when he was growing up. He's asking me to keep being strong for his still-living brother. He's sorry he had to put me through so much pain."

Her dear brother Ben is there too. "He's being a goofball. He wants me to be happy, to laugh, to find joy. He loves me." She asks him why he left her. "He's showing me now that his path was closed off early in this life, and that his death was also a part of the bigger plan. We both needed to experience his death for our growth. I needed to find the strength and courage to move beyond it."

As our session continues, the powerful events of her life are now shown in their true light. Rosanne now fully understands that rather than being a testimony to what she does not deserve, her life has been a carefully planned way for her to exercise and fortify her soul's inner strength, wisdom, and courage. "I'm being given the chance to redo some things. I see that now."

She also realizes that her various physical ailments are caused by being so hard on herself. "I need to lighten up. No matter how you prepare, things happen." She is also told that she can get rid of her constant physical pain by not being so stubborn. "I need to learn the difference between stubbornness and inner strength, and learn to let some things go, because I can't control everything." She is grateful as the session ends.

Today, two years later, with these powerful and life-changing insights, Rosanne has been able to go from being a victim to consciously connecting with the inner empowerment she has so long been seeking. As the pieces of her life fall into place for her, Rosanne continues to leave her identity as a victim behind.

She understands now that "Mother set me up for not having courage— by giving me no foundation and no grounding. She made me believe I was weak if I asked for help. That made me seek out many ways to take care of myself, which ultimately helped to create the inner strength I was seeking. All this was by design."

As she continues to shift her perspective from victim to empowered, Rosanne has been able to identify many instances of her own courage and strength. This has greatly helped her to find peace in her life today. She sees the courage it took to go on after her beloved brother died. She understands that she made a conscious choice to be brave after her son died so that his teenage friends would be better able to go on with their lives too. And she continues to have insights daily.

The understanding and knowledge she gained in her LBL session has been absolutely life-changing for her. She has been able to move forward in her life at last, leaving behind her sense of horror and never-healing wounds that the suicides had created. And knowing that these two close family members are doing just fine and are exactly where they are meant to be has given her the peace of mind that she was searching so desperately for in life.

She knows clearly now that she is to go on with her life with joy and happiness. "I'm learning to relax and enjoy life. Things aren't black or white anymore. Love is everywhere. They want me to see the rainbows."

---

(1) Death scenes in the client's most immediate past life are usually the most effective way to bring the LBL client through the gateway into the spirit world. This is because that life represents the most recent entry into the afterlife, so their memories are more vivid. See LBLH 65–73.

(2) Apparently, this client's soul entry did not require immediate restoration of energy at the gateway. See DS 90–92.

(3) One often finds these idyllic scenes as a prelude to orientation. See JS 53–70, DS 90–92, and LBLH 109.

(4) Because of human stereotypes, the elders are often portrayed in the minds of hypnosis subjects as old, white-haired beings—mostly men. This sort of visualization denotes beings of wisdom in the human mind, so the characterization is applied to spiritual council settings. The more advanced souls usually report the elders as being genderless. Also, we often hear about a raised dais, or table, for the elders above the soul before them. This visualization too denotes authority in the human mind. See DS 212 and LBLH 148–150.

16

Spreading Universal Energy
through
Music

Peter Smith

(Melbourne, Australia)
Director of Operations and instructor
for the Newton Institute; practices
and teaches hypnotherapy.

This is a story about energy. At the core of our soul being lies an amazing energy that we can integrate into our lives in so many ways to feel better about ourselves. This is Jeremy's case, and it gives insight into how the energy fields of individuals can interact for a collective purpose. Once these aspects of energy are brought to conscious awareness, our thoughts change, our outlook transforms, and, most importantly, we can share this wisdom with others.

JEREMY BEGAN MUSIC at the age of seven and was playing professionally while still in school. Today he performs all over the world.

As Jeremy matured, he was drawn more to exploring within, and life-between-lives hypnotherapy became the next step after the book *Journey of Souls* was given to him by a friend. In 2005, he was one of the first in Australia to undertake this amazing journey.

As he went deeper and deeper into the relaxed state, Jeremy traveled back in time to the life of Flight Lieutenant Frank Norbert. Frank was born in the Cotswolds, central England, in 1906. Before World War II, he had been a civilian pilot, and in 1943, at thirty-seven years of age, he found himself in a Lancaster bomber over Hamburg, flying bombing raids for the Royal Air Force.

> PETER: Where are you now? Describe to me what is happening around you.

> JEREMY: I'm sitting in our plane. We call her Sassy Sally. I've handed her over to the bombardier, and we've just dropped our load. She goes better without the load, the wheel feels good. There is a bit of twine wound around the wheel, we are a little superstitious, better to leave it. Twenty-seven missions, and we are still here.

> P: Move forward in time, Frank, to the next event of significance. What is happening now?

> J: We are back over Belgium ... being attacked ... only time I've ever wanted to fly a fighter. I love Sally, but we are sitting ducks ... can hear the shells hitting the plane ... LOUD ... I never thought you'd be able to hear them ... chaos on the intercom ... should have thought about getting out ...

> *Frank's plane plummets to the earth. His soul left his body on the way down and followed the plane to the ground. (1) All the crew was able to bail out except Frank and one other. As Frank floated in a soul state, surveying the wreckage of the plane, he noticed a presence nearby.*

> P: Who is there with you?

J: It's my guide, Phineus—he is laughing at my stubbornness. He is wearing a coat and a hood, and now he has chosen a gnome form. (2) I still feel I should have been able to fly the plane. Phineus is saying you can't fly a plane with one wing. I keep thinking I can do something no one else can do.

P: By what name does he call you?

J: Ismuth.

P: What does your guide have to say about the life of Frank?

J: I learned courage ... to be brave for the others—one of them was only eighteen. I made them brave. Now he's laughing at me, as I always want to be perfect. I've done this a lot. It is possible to fly a plane with one wing; you can even fly a plane with no wings if you know how.

Phineus takes Ismuth to a quiet place so they can debrief the life of Frank and distill the lessons learned.

J: He's telling me I was a bit abrupt with people and is giving me examples. I didn't mean to be unkind ... although I was good at pushing people away to get the job done. Now I understand from my guide how I could have done more in the lifetime as Frank to help people feel better about themselves. To use my energy in a better way ...

P: Do you know a lot about energy, Ismuth?

J: Yes.

P: Why do you know so much about energy?

J: It's what I do ... I use it ... I can put some here, put some there, leave some with somebody or put it all together and really make something happen.

P: You mean leave your energy, rather like an imprint of the rapport and warmth you want to convey to people? Leave them a residual echo—a brief sense of your presence?

J: Yes.

P: Did you do this as Frank, the bomber pilot?

J: No.

P: Are you an energy specialist, Ismuth?

J: Everybody uses energy, though some find it hard to hold it. They can't hold it and use it well.

P: What do you do that others can't?

J: Keep people warm (comforted).

The definition of warming people reflects Jeremy's ability to use energy to help people feel better about themselves, which is certainly what he is doing today as a musician. Sometimes, in certain bodies, souls get so caught up in the mindset of that body and the tensions of its environment that their natural talents are inhibited and they don't do the good work they are capable of in a particular life. As our session continued, Jeremy, as the soul Ismuth, spoke of Ganymede, the third of the larger moons of Jupiter, where he learns and practices the art of light and energy. (3) He can also work in different dimensions from our physical existence. He left a portion of his energy there to continue his studies while he came back to the life of Jeremy to bring new skills to Earth.

An amusing reflection came from Ismuth. Jeremy buys many batteries and takes them with him when he travels—far more, in fact, than he will ever use. This is how the concept of "taking energy with him" plays out in the physical realm.

Ismuth gave another example of how Jeremy uses energy in day-to-day life. He spoke of a time when a door was locked and others tried to open it without success. Jeremy then walks past the others and puts his energy into the lock. For him it opens, much to everyone's bewilderment.

Ismuth goes on to explain more about energy:

ISMUTH: The energy is not one thing, there are many tiny bits. The trick is to be gentle and get them all working together. You direct your energy and then work with others to direct it as a larger group.

P: Ismuth, what should Jeremy do next with this energy?

I: He should combine his energy with others who also do this type of work. That's why he has to get ready, so everyone can use their energy at once, so everyone can feel the warmth (benefits). I can see how the energy looks if we get it right.

Ismuth described how everyone has the ability to use vibrational energy and how it is far more powerful when we all use it together. In the life of Jeremy, Ismuth has chosen music as the way to send energy. Ismuth described how the physical existence sometimes gets in the way of the energy. Music offers a way to bypass this and bring harmony to the world (4):

When I play, it's me. Music is the window to see into the calm ... when I play, it is for everybody. It's like the tide runs the other way. I get past the body and send energy straight to the soul.

This is an important lifetime for Ismuth, for a pattern is being broken. Over many lifetimes, Ismuth has been attempting not to get caught up in the physical aspects of human form.

A review over lifetimes showed Ismuth as a Viking named Kantor, who in his early years was very physical. However, toward the end of his life, he felt differently; he found his sword brought him no pleasure, and he craved peace.

A second life was also viewed—this one as Captain Morgan, a British Navy captain who was delivered into the hands of the Spanish in the 1800s. He'd been ambushed after he was betrayed by a woman, who had passed details of the fleet's movements to the enemy. Morgan himself survived, but he was forced to secretly carry forward into subsequent commands the guilt of that betrayal and the loss of most of his crew. This is another reason why as Frank, the bomber pilot, he fought so hard to save his air crew.

Through his awareness of Ismuth and from his own studies, Jeremy is bringing his newly acquired energy skills to planet Earth by greater conscious awareness. He is also changing old patterns of being exclusively caught up in the physical existence of earthly lives. These days, Jeremy travels the world playing his music. Having explored his purpose through LBL, he uses energy more consciously. For example, there have been times during concert setups when he has asked for more aisles to be created in the seating area to enable the music to flow better to the audience. On one occasion, he played at one of the most prestigious concert venues in Europe, in which Mozart himself had performed. The piano had sat in a particular place on stage for decades, but Jeremy felt it was in the wrong place. Against all expectation, he found he was able to have the staff move the piano to a new position. Even the somewhat austere conductor admitted he felt this was much, much better and decided to leave it there permanently. Once again, Jeremy had left them all feeling warmer...

For Jeremy, body selection and also geographical location had been important. A life as a Tibetan monk and an American politician had been rejected in favor of the life as Jeremy, living in Australia as a musician.

Ismuth put it this way:

> People need to identify with you more as Jeremy. Australia is a
> good choice...you can quietly get ready there. (5)

I sense that "getting ready" refers to preparation for pending Earth changes. Since Australia is not torn by strife, famine, and war, I feel this is probably the reason Jeremy chose to live in the land "down under."

Two years after the LBL experience, Jeremy and I caught up at a café in the eastern suburbs of Sydney to talk about how his session had made a difference in his life.

Jeremy had recently been telling his teenage son about life purpose and planning—even about soul connections that he had understood from his own session. His son was able to paraphrase the lesson well:

"So, Dad, this girl I like. If she is my soul mate, then we will likely be together anyway. If we don't get together, chances are we aren't supposed to be. So either way, I really shouldn't worry too much about it, right?"

Jeremy used an analogy to summarize his view on life following his LBL experience. The beautiful city of Perth is on the west coast of Australia and is separated from the east coast by thousands of miles of desert, called the Nullarbor Plain.

> LBL gives you a different perspective. Life is now like you are driving across the Nullarbor at night. You can see about a hundred meters ahead, as that is all your headlights reveal. However, it's like you have visited Perth on a virtual tour on the Internet. You have done your research and know how beautiful it is. As you sit in the car and travel across the desert, you know that something amazing waits for you at the end of it. It makes you think and feel differently during the trip.

So there is something about two perspectives in parallel that become part of the outcomes of LBL hypnotherapy. As we maintain our dual existence, part immortal and part physical being, we must stay grounded and integrated. Jeremy's way of doing that is very practical, as he states:

> So I believe I'm here to work on evolving global consciousness, which really sounds very important... but then isn't that why everyone's here anyway? It sounds very ordinary as well.

This expanded view of life is typical of those who undertake the LBL exploration. Jeremy's story is not uncommon, though the real power of these explorations comes from that new perspective back in day-to-day life. It's the shifting belief systems and the ability to live life with greater energy and purpose that make the outcome of LBL really profound.

As Jeremy and I left the café and went our separate ways, I realized something: I was warmer than when I had arrived...

---

(1) Souls often leave their bodies just before the impact of a dramatic termination of life; see JS 10.

(2) Spiritual beings can assume any shape they wish, and our guides may choose to appear in some form that relates to a soul's latest life or the circumstances surrounding its death. Perhaps Phineus assumed the small figure of a gnome because of their earthly reputations for secret knowledge combined with dry humor.

(3) We often hear about how souls practice the use of energy in the spirit world, in other dimensions, and on both mental and physical worlds. This is the first time I have heard about the use of Ganymede, the largest satellite in our solar system at 3,800 miles in diameter. It is exotic that this moon of Jupiter, whose surface is like a washboard of ice and rock involving complex systems of plate tectonics, should be mentioned by the soul, Ismuth, as a place where he can manipulate light and energy. Of course, Jupiter itself, our largest planet, does take in a massive amount of electrically charged particles from the sun into its powerful magnetic whirlpool of energy. See galactic energy, DS 339, and interdimensional exploration, DS 344–345.

(4) On Earth, music soothes the mind, and as such is a vehicle for peace, harmony, and comfort. In the afterlife, there are many references by souls to a universal harmonic resonance and musical vibrational energy; see JS 21–22, 43–44 and DS 99, 307.

(5) For an example of a soul who deliberately chose a body with potential musical talent in a particular geographic location, see JS case 25, 214–217.

17

A Volunteer
for
Murder

Lynn McGonagill
(Sarasota, Florida)
Works to bring people's lives into
alignment with their soul intentions.

Memories from childhood illustrate wonderfully how our early years groom us for our adult challenges. Many people seem to feel their childhood was difficult and even painful. When they realize we choose our parents, siblings, and earthly environment, they exclaim, "Oh, no! Not me! I would never have chosen that for myself." Yet, when placed into the context of their life's work—their soul's plan for their life—each person's unique childhood is the perfect preparation for that work.

So it is for Kia, who is being prepared for the central purpose of her life: for doing what's right regardless of criticism. She discovers during her LBL how it also prepared her for the death of her son.

KIA, A LOVING grandmother and kindergarten teacher, came to me roughly one year after her son Evan's death. Evan, a twenty-six-year-old taxi driver in the Tampa Bay area, was brutally murdered by a total stranger, a passenger in his cab. Almost immediately after his passing, Kia felt his presence around her, confirming that he was okay. Although she was most grateful for these visits, they didn't fully satisfy her. She was still deeply grieving and having difficulty accepting his body's death.

As it is for everyone, Kia's guides directed much of her soul experience during the life-between-lives (LBL) process. The events her superconsciousness mind delivered for her review were perfectly selected to heal her deep wounds. Even in the beginning phase of regression, in which the client revisits events from their current life's childhood, one finds the start of the healing process. The first glimpse of Kia's childhood at age fourteen targets the very heart of Kia's pain. She receives insight that she must find sources of comfort in other people and other places, exactly what we must do to survive the death of a loved one. We need to find solace in everyday occurrences to overcome such a life-changing event. Here, at the very start of the process, her soul is already opening up to healing.

KIA (AGE 14): I am with my sister. We are in the woods, and it looks like we are carving on a tree. I am feeling anxious.

LYNN: What is it that is making you feel anxious right now?

K: Our parents are fighting again.

L: Are you in the woods because your parents are fighting or is there another reason?

K: I go to the woods for solitude.

L: Does it help you get peaceful to be in the woods?

K: Yes.

L: What is important for us to understand about this moment right now?

K: To find sources of comfort in other people and other places.

L: Is this the time in your life when you are learning how to do this—at age fourteen—learning how to find sources of comfort where they show themselves, or is this a skill you already know quite well?

K: I am already learning it.

L: Learning and practicing, is that it?

K: Yes.

Let's go a bit further back in time with Kia for another example:

KIA (AGE 5): I am in class, talking with the teacher.

L: And how are you feeling: happy, sad, or some other way?

K: There are kids who break the rules. I want to see what it's like to break the rules, because I won't break the rules.

L: Yes. And what is your teacher saying about this—about breaking the rules?

K: That you shouldn't break the rules. She says stand in the corner to see how it feels, but I didn't break the rules.

L: Are you seeing how it feels?

K: Yes. The bad boy is making fun of me. It is making me mad, because I didn't do anything, and he is still making fun of me, and he breaks all the rules.

L: Yes. What is important to understand about this?

K: People will say stuff about you even if you do what's right.

Only later in the process of Kia's life-between-lives visualization do we discover how relevant this message is: Kia's elders tell her what her soul's mission is, and how Evan's death plays a crucial role in her life plan. They tell her she will have to overcome her fears, and that she will have to overcome rejection and criticism. Here, at this very early stage of the experience, they give her a preview of that central message. At age five, Kia was already beginning to understand that people will form their own opinions and judge you even if you haven't done anything wrong.

Just as our childhoods prepare us for our main purpose, we prepare ourselves over many lifetimes. And just as our souls show us applicable glimpses
into childhood, they show us relevant snippets of other lives during the LBL
experience. Kia prepares for the challenge of a murdered son in at least
three other lifetimes, which she views during our work together. First, Kia
reviews a past life as Sara, who left a comfortable, pampered life in Europe
to immigrate with her new husband to the New World. She has already seen
that her life in the colonies has loneliness and some disappointment in it.

KIA/SARA: I am tired. I have to do a lot of things that I did not have to do
   before. Washing, cooking, sewing, cleaning...

L: What else is important for us to understand about this period in your
   life, Sara?

K/S: I miss my family and friends. It's very lonely.

L: Move forward to the most important event in this life as Sara, the most
   significant event in Sara's lifetime. How are you feeling now?

K/S: I am full of joy... I learned to make the best of what I had and be
   happy. We choose to be happy or not in life.

L: That is beautiful—happiness is our choice, is that it?

K/S: Yes.

L: And have you made the choice, Sara, to be happy?

K/S: Yes.

L: Is this the most significant event of your life—having made the choice
   to be happy?

K/S: Yes!

This illustrates something else that is often seen when working with insightful clients: the most significant event in a lifetime isn't necessarily an external occurrence. It can be, as it was for Sara long ago, a choice, an internal
happening: a choice to be happy regardless of circumstance.

   This message and preparation for Evan's passing in Kia's current life is
echoed in the manner of Sara's death. In this past life, she dies as a young

mother, leaving behind four children and a husband who loves her deeply. On her deathbed, she has another epiphany, this time about the people she is leaving behind:

K/S: I am very, very sick and in bed. I am exhausted and weak.

L: What do you think is going to happen?

K/S: I am going to go on (to die).

L: How are you feeling about that?

K/S: I don't want to leave my children, and I am pregnant.

L: Oh, I am sorry. Do you have any awareness of what is significant about this, other than your health situation?

K/S: They will all need to choose to be happy, won't they. Death is hard, no matter when or how it comes, for the people left behind.

This is true for all of us. We can choose to be happy in bad traffic, when we don't get the raise we want, or when our husband leaves us. And it is certainly true for Kia in her current life: she can choose to be happy even though her only son was murdered. How healing it is for Kia to receive this vital reminder during her LBL: to choose to be happy.

Still later in the session, Kia reviews an earlier lifetime as Elizabeth, in which she herself is murdered. Here she is given an entirely different viewpoint. The story begins as Kia admires her reflection:

KIA/ELIZABETH: I think I must be vain; I am enjoying how attractive I think I look. I have very thick, long golden hair, wavy at the ends, very slender, very, very beautiful in this pretty dress.

L: Where are you?

K/E: It is like a big empty castle with this incredible stream of light and only me ... There was a fight. It was here at the castle. (surprised) I think I am already dead!

L: And do you know that you are dead, or are you confused about it?

K/E: I think I was confused. The castle is empty. I think it must have been a little while (since the fight). I think I was carrying on like nothing happened but it did. I think I died as a result of the fighting. I was raped and stabbed.

L: I'm sorry. How long has it been since then?

K/E: Two, maybe three years. Many died that day, and those who were left said the castle was haunted. There used to be others (who had died) too, but I am the only one left.

L: What are your plans now, Elizabeth?

K/E: Well, I think maybe I should see about this light.

Interestingly, the deepest insight about this lifetime was not experienced as we worked together, but instead it came to Kia four and a half months later in an episode of spontaneous recall. Kia wrote it down at the time and shared it with me recently:

> I sensed the real importance of this life was for me to realize the manner of death was insignificant, that though I had been raped and murdered, I felt nothing and was unscathed when I returned home (to the spirit world). It was important for me to realize that this was so for Evan too; that despite how horrific his whole death scene was, he did not feel it and returned to heaven unscathed, whole and clean. It did not matter.

This beautiful and significant insight that came to Kia months after her official LBL session illustrates a wonderful facet of experiencing the LBL state. There is something about the process itself that opens doors between the higher self and the incarnated personality. These doors tend to stay open afterward, so deeper messages can continue to be received months and years later. Some clients describe themselves as having a much higher degree of psychic or intuitive awareness following their LBL journey. As a result, they feel more in tune with their life's purpose and that their life experiences have meaning.

Still in deep trance, Kia's insights grow more profound after the murdered Elizabeth goes into the light. By following the light, the soul of Kia/

Elizabeth moves into the spirit world. There, she is drawn at the speed of thought into a room where all time is in stop action.

K: It's round, and there are three people, elders. I see purple, everywhere purple. (1)

L: Can you ask them what is important for Kia to know? Why is it important for her to be here in this situation with them?

K: The one in the middle (2) says I must stop doubting what I get intuitively—to accept it as truth—to not let others diminish what I hear—what I see—what I know in my soul is real. The one on the right says my higher purpose here has not been accomplished yet—that it ties in with Evan somehow, with Evan being taken from me.

L: Yes, go on.

K: It has to do with spiritual pursuits and helping others, beliefs that are unorthodox compared to how I was raised. It's going to raise eyebrows where I am, you know... (starts crying) They brought Evan in... I can hug him for real! I feel so good. I miss him so much. I can feel him, and I hear him (in my normal life), but this is better! (long pause and sniffles) The one on the left says this is for strength and courage.

L: To help you to build strength and courage by having this visit with Evan, is that it?

K: Yes.

L: Is there anything that Evan wants to say?

K: That he loves me, that he is helping me, that we agreed to this a long time ago, that it's important... He's still here, but I knew that. They are showing me how it was all arranged. Evan went in someone else's place; someone else was going to die that day.

L: Evan took that spot? (3)

K: Yes, because it would serve dual purposes. It wasn't exactly as we had talked about before we incarnated, but by taking someone else's place, he saved five people. (4)

L: Does that bring a balance to the situation somehow? What was Evan's motivation?

K: Evan has a sense of humor; he says, "Brownie points in heaven!" You have to know him; he's a wise guy.

L: Does he have anything else to say about this or about any other aspect of this life?

K: He says he is sorry he was such a difficult teenager. Silly boy.

L: Anything else?

K: That today is only for reassurance. (laughs) He says, "Tune in next week for the rest of the adventure." I told you he's a wise guy. And he is singing a commercial—"After these messages, we'll be right back!"

L: So this brief visit with him is for reassurance, and the next time we come to the higher planes, there will be more. Is that what he means?

K: Yes.

L: Do you feel that is true?

K: Yes.

This beautiful exchange between a loving mother and son is a great example of how real these interactions feel. In an email to me years later, Kia expressed that her meeting with Evan, standing in front of the elders, was more real than being in my office. She went on to say, "I felt the sensation of physical embrace, even though we were both in spiritual form. The feeling of all-encompassing love is truly one that words cannot adequately convey. It was bliss and peace and joy and hope and renewal and understanding all in a fraction of a second. It was awesome."

In Kia's second visit to the between-lives state the following week, she once again finds herself in front of the three elders. She asks them what the true purpose of Evan's murder was and why she had to go through such pain from losing him.

K: They say it was a means to become more spiritual.

L: What is your purpose in the future?

K: That avenues (of psychic awareness) are opening for me since Evan died. The elders say I should get out the word to the world that life doesn't end at death. Not only life, but also personality. That we don't need to fear it (death) ... People need to know it's not harps and angels; it's different than what the church teaches. We don't cease to exist. There's comfort in knowing that you are still you. Not a new message, of course, but many still don't listen.

L: And your overall psychic development: how does that fit in to the process?

K: The one in the middle says it's always been there but I didn't use it, and now it's necessary to use it.

L: Would that one in the middle say that most if not all people have latent psychic power, latent psychic potential?

K: Absolutely ... The one on the right wants me to know that one person can make a difference, and we all own that power.

L: Do they have anything else they feel it would be important or helpful for you to know right now?

K: The one in the middle says as hard as it is to acknowledge, Evan's death truly was a gift. And that without that gift, I would not be able to do what I came to do.

L: Does that feel true to you?

K: Yes, but I still don't like it.

L: Do we have to like it?

K: No, standing here with them it makes sense, but sometimes standing at the cemetery it doesn't make sense.

L: I understand this situation. Is there anything they can do to help with that?

K: By being more spiritual.

It is during the most painful and challenging parts of our lives that we tend to question what the plan for our life is, and if there *is* a plan. It is so hard, in those moments of pain, to make sense of events, to find meaning inside the anguish. And yet it is often the agony that drives us to fulfill the central purpose of our life. Many people looking back on the effects of tragedy in their lives conclude that there was nothing else that would have been a strong enough motivation to change—that the most extreme suffering was needed to drive them toward their soul's mission. This is especially so for Kia and for others who have lost the person most dear to them.

After Kia's meeting with her elders, she is left alone with her personal spirit guide, Miguel. He continues the process of supporting her movement into acceptance of the unacceptable.

L: What does Miguel have to say right now—what is his important message to you now?

KIA/MIGUEL: Don't be afraid of what's to come.

L: Do you understand what he is referring to?

K: I think so.

L: Can he clarify it so you have no doubt whatsoever?

K/M: There are going to be changes coming, changes in career, changes in outlook, changes in priorities, and some people are not going to like it, some people are going to criticize, and some people will turn and walk away because it doesn't fit with their beliefs and what they thought in this lifetime.

L: How are you to deal with that?

K/M: Don't be afraid.

Three years later, Kia tells me that she felt complete understanding when she was with the elders, even though she couldn't fully put it into words at the time. She reports that although she could not bring that full level of realization back with her to the physical plane, much of it did stay with her. She explains that before her LBL sessions, she had felt compelled to visit Evan's grave two to three times a week. Afterwards, she knew he wasn't there in his grave. She still visits once or twice a month, just to make sure the grave is tidy and well-maintained, but the quality of the experiences are much different, less painful and more peaceful.

During our work together, Kia was able to find much satisfaction and answers to the questions that had been haunting her since Evan's passing. Her elders and guide telepathically explained much, all in kind and loving tones. She could feel the love and compassion they directed to her. She was allowed to review her life selection, her plan for her current life. Best of all, she was able to visit with Evan for real in the spirit world. The entire process brought her peace of mind that still remains, three years later.

---

(1) Purple is the color most often seen around highly advanced beings who have completed their incarnations; see LBLH 126.

(2) Frequently during a council meeting, the elder in the middle is visualized as the moderator, or chairman, directing the meeting; see DS 214 and LBLH 151.

(3) Notice the similarity here to the case in chapter 3 in terms of untimely death. In choosing a life where the probability for an early death in the next life's body is high, souls must consider carefully if they want to attach to such a body. The karmic patterns for learning in this case bridge more than one soul experience and may, as Kia states, "serve dual purposes." Also, consider that Evan tells us that he is going to get "brownie points in heaven" for taking such a short-term assignment. As I have said, some souls call this a "filler life," which is considered in the afterlife to be a very unselfish, generous act. Further references here can be found under karmic debt, JS 70; karmic choices, JS 228; probability of dying young, JS 235, 359, 372–373; filler lives, JS 220, DS 384; and timelines in body selection, LBLH 176–177.

(4) The saving of five people through Evan's actions that cost him his life was brought about by Evan sensing that a male passenger in his car had evil intent. This man was on his way to murder a storekeeper and his wife and three young children over an earlier altercation. By stalling, Evan did not take the killer to his destination, and an intense fight ensued where Evan was stabbed and his cab set on fire. The police subsequently arrested the murderer. Thus, we can see that not only was a courageous soul (JS 142) chosen for this assignment, but a strong and tenacious human body was working in concert with the soul as well. While it is true that much evil in the world is not prevented in this way, the karmic influences of our misdeeds do follow us in one form or another.

18

Manipulating Energy
for
Healing

Lauren Pohn
(Delavan, Wisconsin, and Chicago, Illinois)
Master hypnotherapist, Reiki Master, NLP
trainer, yoga/meditation instructor,
and past registrar for TNI training.

My client Savana, age thirty-four, was a lovely young woman who seemed to have it all in life yet was confused about herself in many ways. She came to me for an LBL session because she felt her spirit guide had sent her mental messages to get in touch with her inner self. The top three things she wanted from the session were: Who am I here to help the most, what are the major lessons I am here to learn in this life, and who is my soul mate?

IN OUR DISCUSSION leading into the session, Savana revealed that she had a lot of excess mental energy. There were times when she actually wondered if she was mentally ill. She had a great deal of pent-up extra energy and had to run four to six miles a day to even sleep at night! She rated the severity of this excess mental energy as a nine out of ten and remembered having it her entire life, even as a little girl. She never saw a doctor about this, as she thought that there was nothing she could do about it. Exercise was a stopgap measure, and she tried a little meditation from time to time. It became clear that her excess mental energy overlaid other issues.

Savana related that a few times in her life, situations would arise in which she believed she could help someone, and when she did, it made her wonder if she had a gift. She would focus on a good outcome for the situation and meditate on it to assist in problem solving. Savana gave me an example of one of these situations. Her boyfriend had a golf outing scheduled with his boss, and it was important for him to do well. An hour before the outing, Savana focused and meditated, and visualized her boyfriend hitting straight down the fairway on each and every hole, then sinking each putt effortlessly. That day, her boyfriend, Trevor, played the best round of golf he had ever shot in his entire life.

As we began the LBL session, it was evident that Savana was comfortable with hypnosis. She easily moved back through time. During her time in her mother's womb, the first interesting clue arose. I questioned her from her soul's perspective. She was very responsive, so I asked her many questions. She affirmed that both her body and brain in Savana's life were easy to integrate with her soul, and that Savana had a very sharp mind. She said she brought 80 percent of her energy into this life, which is rather on the high side.

SAVANA: I think I needed the energy to accomplish the things I want to do, but oftentimes it's way too much.

LAUREN: Is there a way you could help this body deal with this excess energy when it's not busy accomplishing things?

S: Through meditation ... learning to focus my energy more. Through meditation, I can help other people. It will accelerate my growth ... but I don't do it enough.

L: Is there anything you can do to help accomplish this?

S: To get better at meditating ... to do it more often. To spend less time with random thinking ... just pick one thought and focus on that.

Her past-life regression was clear and distinct. Savana was an African-American man, Brian Curtis, with a large nose, mustache, very tall and awkward. It was 1924 in Detroit. Brian was poor, in his fifties, in money trouble, and near the end of his life. When he was fifty-eight, Brian was walking along the lakeside, was shot, and fell in.

Savana moved very quickly out of Brian's body with much relief.

S: I'm moving up ... pretty fast ... I know where I'm going ... toward a light like the sun.

L: Can you describe what you are seeing and experiencing?

S: One spirit ... energy ... Celeste.

Celeste's aura becomes red and takes Savana's hand and is taking her someplace.

L: Is Celeste your guide?

S: No, I don't think so ... I feel like it's a friend that met me.

L: Ask your guide to come forward.

S: It's a female, Orida ... there are a multitude of souls behind her. She has a dark blue aura. She reaches out to me, and we join hands. I feel comfort and deep peace.

Orida then takes Savana to the place of rejuvenation to heal the violence of dying of a gunshot wound as Brian in the life just ended.

At this point, Savana reveals her immortal spiritual name: Gret. Gret's aura is red with some green. Orida is helping her process her last life and then leads Gret to a school building with books everywhere. (1) Gret opens a book in another language, which doesn't make sense to her, though she seems to understand what it means. When questioned further, Gret says

"It's about souls, from different countries and cultures. It's a way to study people and their energy." She then notices that there is a group of ten souls with her, also studying. She agrees that this is her working group, and she feels good about them. When asked further about the work they do, Gret replies, "It's hard work." She finds it difficult to describe. "It's like studying people in their mind to help them … so you can better communicate with them through your mind. You can do it on Earth, but most people don't know how to do it … communicate without language. All I can say is it helps people through your mind—pushing energy around, I guess."

Asked if she's been at it for a long time, Gret replies, "A very long time, actually. It's hard work! I'm supposed to learn to do it while I'm incarnated (on Earth), and it's very hard. Some souls in this group are really good, and I want to be like them. Some aren't so good either." The group sends her the message to lighten up. Looking around, Gret sees Trevor. Trevor turns out to be Celeste, the soul who greeted her at the gate to the spirit world. He is also red. It's a totally red group. (2) Trevor/Celeste turns out to be her primary soul mate.

I ask Gret to expound a bit more on her group's work. She has much hesitancy and gropes for the right words to describe it. "Adjust energy to align them (incarnate beings) with spirit energy … to make them faster … to make their energy faster. Because when they vibrate more intensely, they feel better. They become open to more knowledge to learn more. It helps them move forward as both a human and as a soul. It brings soul energy into human form." At one point, Gret feels a lot of concentrated energy in her head that is beyond words and explanations. I ask her to focus on it and breathe with it. Then I ask if this is one of those moments when she is receiving a shift in energy—this higher vibration. (3)

With laughter, "I think so … it's kind of cool." I then suggest that she really focus on it and to notice that it intensifies in a delightful way. Savana becomes very alert and aware of these shifts in energy that Gret is experiencing, as a sign and signal so that she understands what she's doing and how to use it. The following dialog demonstrates a therapeutic spiritual communication between Savana's human ego and that of her soul mind, Gret:

S (AS GRET): Savana gets scared ... afraid of what others may think, it's kind of strange. (laughing) So she's always hesitant to talk about things like this with people.

L: What's useful to do with the intensification of the energy in her head?

S (AS GRET): I think this is a sign that I'm on the right track ... it freaks me out! Savana is trying to get in the act, but she is tensing up and closing the energy down.

L: So, Gret, take a breath ... and I want you, as Savana's higher soul self, to communicate with her and direct Savana in a way where she can stay open and listen so she can utilize her energy in a positive manner. (pause) What are you communicating with Savana at this moment?

S (AS GRET): Stay focused.

L: And the meaning?

S (AS GRET): Savana has too much on her plate for her current brain to stay focused and do the work I need to do through her by her meditation.

L: Can you elaborate?

S (AS GRET): For Savana, having too much on her plate is a way of trying to help people in ways that may not be as conducive as what I can do with my (soul) mind. Savana needs to meditate every single day ... this will take many years. She'll have to learn more, too, so she can continue to work and help people for longer periods. (4)

L: And what does your guide, Orida, say about all this?

S: Orida says I will be better able to help people and their spirits some day, but I have to go through this training first. It's just a lot of demanding work!

L: Gret, what can Savana do on Earth to help Trevor, her partner?

S (RESPONDING AS GRET): He's very protective of his mind, so it is good for Savana to learn patience in communicating with him. You can't make changes overnight; it takes a long time.

I have also learned from this dialog with my client's immortal soul that Gret has the opportunity to eventually become a junior guide in training with spirits of her own to help and guide. However, she must get through her own training first in the use of energy communication and become much better at it. In closing with the topic of Savana's soul mate, Trevor/Celeste, Gret has the following information to share with me:

> I have to learn that everybody is different. Each has their own way of using their mental energy, and the more time I spend with Trevor, the more I will learn about how his mind works in this life. Here in the spirit world, he's asking me to get to know him better mentally and take it step by step and not slam him with too much information at once. He wants me to be more gentle and nurturing of his mental needs before I start to teach him. Be patient, slow down. Get to know him better, and stick with it.

As we near the end of this theme, I see that greater spiritual understanding is helping Savana learn that she is not mentally ill. She is able to tell me, "I'm not crazy. I'm able to use my mind so much and to do so many things...and I see the results of what I do, and I sometimes think that I'm the only one that can do this, and it's good to know that it's part of a bigger plan."

Gret is now finished with her working group, and I touch her forehead and suggest she find herself in another aspect of the spirit world. I ask her to tell me where she is.

> I'm near a flowing river...a river of energy. It's a big open space with colored energy flowing by me. You can reach your hand out, touch it, and feel it go into you. You can learn how to manipulate the energy by touching it as it goes by. The river contains the emotions of souls...other souls' energy. Their energy flows into me. I'm not sure how they got it into a river. It's about waist high. You put your hands in this, and you can control how much energy comes into you, and then you can feel the change within. If you put your hand in for a long time, you get an overwhelming sense of it. (5) When you are in a room with people on Earth, energy comes into you, and you can either let it overwhelm you or you just

can take it for what it is ... to figure out that's who they are. I think
when I do this river thing that I am practicing how to organize
their energy in a positive way and give it back to them.

I enlist the help of Orida and Gret so Savana can do this in a crowded
room comfortably and not get overwhelmed by the variety of human energy.
This conversation is enhanced by the integration of Savana's human and
soul egos. (6)

I ask if this process of energy manipulation accelerates with touch. Absolutely, these higher spirits tell me: "Savana has to be mindful about those she
chooses to touch. Actually, it's more about being in someone's space."

I bring up the concept of people who suck your energy and whether she
should avoid them. "They are a challenge. You learn how to channel that
energy, to cleanse and heal it ... but only if they are receptive. It can be very
difficult to do, because you can't do it all for them."

In conversation with Gret, we ask for a signal so Savana will know when
to do her energy work and when to move away. "When Savana feels a tight-
ness on her right side (she often thinks she is sick when she feels that, but
she's not), it signals that the incoming energy is too much ... that there's
nothing that she can do at that time ... she has to let it go. Savana will be better able to handle this in time, with practice. Learning this signal is part of
the reason she came for our session."

Gret then moves on to "a group of older souls with higher energies."
Orida and Trevor/Celeste accompany Savana/Gret. From an LBL perspective, this would be her Council of Wise Elders. "They're teaching us how to
make everyone on Earth more connected. When you get an idea of where
things are going on Earth and where they will go in the future, it makes your
work more enjoyable and more worthwhile. What they're telling Celeste
and me is that you have to have faith that connection can change everyone,
that it will help generations in the future. That's good, because one of the
main issues Savana has is that it's so overwhelming, you can't fix everything
overnight. Trust!"

When the group of older souls tries to take Gret somewhere else, Savana
asks me if she should go. "Of course, remember trust!" We both laugh. She

is taken to the place of the current life's body selection. In this place, there are big movie screens. With millions and millions of people to choose from, Gret was certain she had made the right choice to do this energy work as Savana. She also saw big cities and commented that people compacted tightly would have a lot more stress than people who live in the countryside. It's important to do her work in big cities, where it's more needed.

Gret now returns to her Council of Wise Elders, and there are four members seated at a long table. She says, "I am told a little about how I select the bodies I am offered before each life and how to take better care of them." Then a council member shows her a locket with a picture of her mother in Savana's current life. The message was to use her work to help her mother. Gret likes this idea, because Savana's mother is receptive, and Savana can get instant results. They say there's time for play, fun, and joy, but also time for quiet and meditation.

Gret recalls her first incarnation and remembers, "It was on a much easier planet. It was all mental. We just all understood each other. This was a much easier place than Earth. It makes sense. Savana gets frustrated at how hard Earth is. I think I'm using skills that I learned on another planet." (7)

At this point, Gret felt complete with her session, and I brought her back to consciousness as Savana.

When I contacted Savana eight months later, I asked her how this LBL session had changed her life. Here is a synopsis of her experience:

> What has helped me the most was learning what work I have been sent to do in this lifetime. Even before my LBL session, I knew I was skilled at manipulating mental energy, though I couldn't put my finger exactly on what I was doing. Visiting my soul group left such a strong impression on me that I continue to think about it constantly—especially about the river of mental, colored energy of real souls. We would practice putting our hands in and try to identify the energy—such as confused, happy, sad, guilty—then to understand and learn about it. The biggest challenge was to heal it in a way that would not affect the true makeup and character of the soul or change it in any way. We would have to be both quick

and subtle as the energy continued to flow down the river. In my life on Earth, I use these skills when I am in the presence of someone whose negative energy I feel. It allows me to send them healing energy that harmonizes their being without overwhelming them. I am glad to use my skills to help humanity, even if in small ways.

My LBL session has changed my life. I now meditate a minimum of thirty minutes a day and practice sending healing energy to help others and myself. I feel like I'm just getting started with this and will get better over years of practice. Meditating has allowed me to be more focused at work and when interacting with friends and family. Meditation is a mental outlet for me. The more I meditate, the better I sleep at night.

I've also become a hospice volunteer and lead bereavement support groups as well. I am able to very subtly heal people's grieving minds. I believe this is a continuation of my soul work. I used to feel pulled to do something and wasn't clear on how it would help others. Since my LBL session, I am better able to trust my instincts. I know that there are more intelligent beings who have confidence in me and are leading me in the right direction. I also know that there are more advanced souls who are guiding and teaching me how to help others. Thinking about my LBL session on a regular basis definitely keeps me motivated to continue the work I am supposed to be doing in this lifetime. It was an unforgettable experience!

---

(1) The spiritual library of life books. See DS 150–152 and LBLH 105, 119.

(2) The author tells us that both Trevor/Celeste and Savana/Gret are soul mates who display a core color of red. Normally, this means they are most likely level II souls in development with a vibrational energy character representation indicating intensity and passion. Gret, Savana's soul, also has a color tint of green, which indicates a soul with developing healing capabilities. Her spirit guide, Orida, displays the deep blue of an advanced soul with knowledge and experience. See DS 170–174 and LBLH 126.

(3) Areas of soul specialization training in the spirit world depend upon talent, interest, motivation, and experience. The soul, Gret, in this story as the client Savana, appears to be preparing over the long term to be a harmonizer

soul. These souls are essentially communicators who balance the energy of both human relationships and events on Earth. See DS 330–334.

(4) Notice how the facilitator allows the client to respond to questions as her own soul. When we disengage from our human ego in this fashion during LBL therapy, soul responses become more enlightened and allow for increased cognition from the inner ego of our minds. See the dual roles of observer and participant under therapeutic opportunities for clients in LBLH 156.

(5) The imagery here regarding a river of energy in the spirit world is a training procedure under the direction of the client's guide, Orida. Indications here are that this is a space of transformation where souls learn to integrate their energy with animate and inanimate objects. Rivers and pools of water are very symbolic of liquid energy that can be manipulated by souls in training; see JS 168, 218 and DS 302–304.

(6) For more elaboration involving the spiritual integration of the dual egos each of us has between the soul and our human brain, see LBLH 80–81, 163, 181–189.

(7) Hybrid souls on Earth with prior experience on other planets often bring skills learned there to Earth in one form or another. See DS 100 and LBLH 22.

19

A
renegotiated
Soul Contract

Andy Tomlinson
(Corfe Mullen, Dorset, England)
Psychotherapist, author of articles and
books on LBL, and training director
for Past Life Regression Academy.

This chapter illustrates quite clearly that through the experiences of past-life and life-between-lives regressions, clients can experience many levels of healing and deep understanding. This story demonstrates that it is possible to gain freedom from physical pain and fear as soul lessons are recognized and accepted. It also underlines how we can learn to compare and contrast the perspectives of the human mind and the immortal soul.

WHEN I FIRST met Dean, I was impressed with his bright, cheerful nature and broad smile. He was a senior marketing manager for an international bank and had just joined one of my past-life-regression therapy training workshops to discover more about the subject. He explained that he first started experiencing a pain in his left testicle, groin, and lower abdomen early in 1998, shortly after starting an extramarital affair. In his words:

> The pain was strong to excruciating, and I would experience it
> for one to two weeks, then it would disappear for a few months.
> During 2000, the pain became constant and would at times have
> me doubled over. One testicle shrank in size, and this is what
> finally made me see the doctor. I was referred to an urologist
> and underwent an MRI, two CT scans, an IVP (intravenous
> pyelogram), and three ultrasounds over the course of the year.
> They couldn't find anything wrong with me and told me to take
> Advil (medication for pain relief) for thirty days. The pain in my
> groin and testicle came and went, but generally there has been a
> low level of discomfort with the occasional flare-up. I described it
> to my wife as being like someone driving a nail through my testicle.
> These past couple of years, it has been much more manageable but
> elevated to the extreme for some minutes as the workshop drew
> closer. On the days of the workshop, it was very painful.

During the workshop, Dean asked for a regression to discover if a past life was contributing to his pain. He regressed quickly into the life of a Roman centurion during the time of a civil war, and after the session, this is how he described what happened:

> I entered the past life at the point of death, where I was being held
> down by a few of my men. One had his foot on my neck, another a
> foot on my right arm, and one was standing over me and had just
> plunged a sword into my groin. Previously, the one with the sword
> had cut off my genitals and held them up to me and had said, "You
> can't do much without these, can you?" He threw them to the
> ground and stamped on them.
>   During the healing process within the regression, I experienced
> body therapy from you (Dean is referring to Andy, the facilitator)
> so that I could use my hands to experience pulling out the sword
> and bring my body pieces back together. (1) Doing this felt

wonderful, as if my body was being made whole again. Later, I experienced meeting my spirit guide, who explained that in that life, I had raped and pillaged. Those wounds had been carried over into this life and had been activated by the energy I was putting into my sex life outside marriage. It also acted as a reminder of when I'm doing things that take a whole lot of my time and focus away from achieving my life purpose.

Understandably, Dean was quick to book a personal LBL session to discover his life purpose. In deep hypnosis, he first regressed into a past life, that of a nineteenth-century merchant who had just received disastrous news of the loss of his ship in Africa. Previously, he had signed a business contract, and this news meant that his family business would be taken from him. Drinking heavily in a tavern to console himself, the merchant was set upon by four thugs and killed in the ensuing fight. The LBL regression is picked up at the point at which he first meets his spirit guide:

DEAN: He's asking me if I am ready to learn.

ANDY: And what do you say?

D: I say yes, because I don't understand. He says that I am here because this is where I am meant to be, and while things may not make sense, I will one day have understanding. This life was to learn that hard work does not always have a reward—that you are not always rewarded for the things you do, and what may seem unfair is just a perception. He's asking me to think about that statement, because he senses I still don't understand.

A: Ask how you get that understanding.

D: He's telling me to look at that life and the things that happened... He's showing me my life...

A: In what sort of way is this being shown to you?

D: The view is a living room, but I am not in my body. I am watching myself sitting at the table with the contract, and he's asking me to isolate a single point of that evening when I originally signed the business contract, which showed where good intent was rewarded or had a good outcome.

A: And what do you say?

D: I'm starting to understand. At the time, I was young and looking to please. I was pleased to sign the piece of paper and take possession of a person. My father-in-law was quite happy to bargain for his daughter. Each step along the way and each moment during that evening—the word seems harsh, but "atrocities" were committed.

A: Can you explain what "atrocities" means?

D: In the context of my father-in-law trading his daughter for what he perceived was a financial gain through a manipulative contract. It gave him certain controls at certain points in time over my family's company, and ultimately their fortune and hard work. The atrocity is that a human life could be bargained for that—the atrocities that I committed. I was prepared to walk in and enter that contract, together with the possession of a human life, and not really know the extent of the potential damage I could do to my family, to myself, to the people around me. Also the family that I was going to create and I hadn't even thought about at the time. But now my signing that paper made my children's life conditional. It made my family's independence cut in half. It signed away people's work, people's livelihoods, and people's lives, and I had no authority to do so. I understand. I understand the message now.

This past-life review illustrates how we are our own judge and jury of our lives' events. The role of a personal spirit guide is to help us understand the events and what happens when things go wrong, because this forms the basis of future life planning.

It's worth considering the statement of the spirit guide that hard work and good intent are not always rewarded. From our earthly perspective, this may be a surprise. From a soul perspective, our earthly decisions and the consequences are seen as learning. (2)

We now move to the point when Dean, accompanied by his spirit guide, is about to meet his soul group, whom he calls his counciling group:

D: I'm sensing a large room.

A: Describe this room.

D: It has no walls, no ceiling, and has a table that is carved into the bottom. It has chairs lined up on either side of the table, and at the head is a larger chair and also at the other end. The chairs are pulled back quite a distance from the table, except for the two at either end.

A: Do you know what this place is?

D: A counseling room. (3)

A: Are you by yourself?

D: No, I am sitting in the small chair, and my spirit guide is at the tall chair.

A: And what else is happening?

D: I am experiencing fear (this concern is coming from Dean's mind) (4) ... This is the point that we have been waiting for. My spirit guide is communicating with me telepathically, very patiently, and saying that I am the one that must make the first call. It is time for me to bring the plan in.

A: What's this plan your spirit guide has referred to?

D: This is my current life plan. I am asking why I am feeling this fear.

A: And what are you told?

D: This is the fear I have felt for so long and I have felt for many lives ... I can sense this mischievous nature that I have sensed before. I've brought fear into this realm ... because this is the fear that I have kept on experiencing and using as a crutch and avoiding it at all costs. I brought it in to show how silly it is.

A: Is anyone else with you?

D: My mother ... my son ... oh, there's a friend, she is Gloria now ... it's my father, oh god, that's my wife, that's my wife's ex-boyfriend. That's one side of the table complete.

A: And the other side?

D: My grandmother, two of my aunts, there's an ex-colleague of mine— it's Maurice, and there are three that I just don't recognize.

A: Tell me what happens.

D: They are all smiling. There is the increasing sense of the mischievous towards me. I say, "Why can't I catch up?" My mother's saying, "We have all been very patient, and you can take as long as you like. While you are learning to take this step, we are off doing other things. It is of no consequence, but we will have to move on. This is the plan that you said would be best suited to bring us all close to you. You wanted us all to be there to touch you, to be close to your life, and in that way you would be able to do it." They really are laughing at me ... She is referring to the fact that so many of my current soul group are close relations so that they would be there to pop in and pop out of my life as I grew ... My aunt just stood up and said, "Each of us has given you a message in this life. You seem to understand each of these messages, yet you look at the message (Dean nods his head in agreement) and you insist on more." She says I am not going to get any more messages.

A: Do they remind you what those messages are?

D: They laugh at me again. My spirit guide says, "You know the messages—why go through this?"

A: What happens next?

D: One of the souls that I am not familiar with is pushing across a jigsaw that is completed and says, "Solve the puzzle."

A: What does this mean?

D: They continue to make fun of me. The puzzle is solved—there are no missing pieces ... My spirit guide has told me to make sure that I am well entrenched in my earthly body, as I am not advancing. Everyone at the table here is ready to move on without me.

A: And is there something that you have to do?

D: It is my writing, and particularly it is the method that I intend to write books they are calling "a back door into the subconscious."

A: Tell me a little more about them.

D: I have all the stories within, and I have the skill to bring the stories out ... My goal is to assist in the increasing of awareness, because a lot of energy on Earth is getting stuck—just as I am, by continually looking for the easy way for everything... There is no one shift in awareness that is going to happen. It is a gradual process, and I need to write stories for the people to pick up the awareness.

So now Dean understands his life purpose and its importance. It is interesting to note that this session switched from the soul memories of the events between lives to a real-time interactive review of his current life and his difficulty in engaging his life purpose. This is one of the powerful ways in which LBL regression can help clients. Rather than waiting until the end of the life to have this sort of review, it can take place in the middle of a life. Doing so can bring soul awareness to the conscious mind and accelerate the possibility of soul advancement. For Dean, this was an opportunity to understand the fear that had its origins in the merchant past life and was diverting him from his current life plan. As the session continues with his spirit guide, we will see that some of the obstacles to achieving his life plan are discussed:

A: How are you going to be able to recognize your soul group?

D: There will be an eventual awareness. It will take me a long time; that's why they pop in and out of my life, and that's why they are part of my family. I will recognize them as symbolic of the issues I see at different times of my life... There's my brother—he will show me very clearly at one point that a lack of money doesn't mean a lack of contentment or a lack of purpose—that he finds a way regardless. My son—he will show me the unmistakable image of the love that I seek.

A: Is there anything more that is discussed at this point?

D: My earthly obligations to my family—keeping them clothed, fed, educated, and housed in a manner that I dreamed of is something I must consider. It may or may not happen the way I planned. My spirit guide is aware that my conscious mind has difficulty processing what I can perceive now as an abandonment of my obligations to my family. I can see from a higher awareness within me that achieving my purpose in life can get in the way of my primary obligations... I understand, I understand, I understand...

A: And is anything discussed at all about what happens if you aren't able to follow your purpose?

D: Yeah, I know. Someone else will do it. I will be left behind with another spirit group, and once again, that really is of no consequence, though I do have a strong urgency to catch up … My spirit guide is saying there is a benefit to me to associate some earthbound emotion with not staying with this group. Apparently, it's part of my relatively low level of spiritual advancement that I want to continue with this group, and it is conveyed to me via my Earth emotions (fear) and missing out. I don't really get it. (5) Hang on, it seems there is a time limit on Earth for the message to get out, and he says collectively, right now, there are many individuals who are seeking to form a web across the planet, and it is people like me who want to be part of that web, to touch as many souls as possible before the next wave.

A: Perhaps ask your spirit guide about these pains in various bodily parts. Are these any form of reminder for you?

D: Yes, but the reminder is going to be removed. I'm not going to be given a reminder anymore. It's all in my hands; it's my decision now.

This is an immensely important point about the physical pain in his testicles and groin being removed. Recall that this was originally a reminder of the energy Dean was misplacing away from his life purpose through sexual pursuits outside marriage. (6) It had its origins in the Roman centurion past life. The past-life-regression transformation work removed the symptoms, but Dean needed to integrate this learning into his current life for a permanent result. It appears that with Dean's deeper understanding of his life plan from the LBL regression, the need for this physical pain reminder has been taken away, whatever Dean chooses to do. This is soul purpose replanning with the consent of Dean's spiritual and conscious self. However, the fear at some level will remain until Dean makes the decision to leave his current career and write the spiritual books in his plan.

The other interesting insight was the spirit guide's comments about earthly obligations. Of course we all have responsibilities to others, particularly our family, but at times they can get in the way of our life purpose. We are being reminded that all souls know each other's life purpose before incarnation, so when we make difficult decisions not to follow our life purpose, the earthly consequences are not a concern from a soul perspective.

This is what Dean had to say about his LBL regression and change in his life:

> The most surprising thing about the LBL session was the clarity of the information I received. I was left with no doubt of what my purpose here is and what lessons I must learn in order to achieve it. The insight I received about obligations helped give me the courage to prepare for the very difficult step that I needed to take. I have progressively discussed my intentions with my family and others to whom I felt obligated, and while I wasn't particularly seeking support from anyone except my wife, they offered it encouragingly. Since I tended my resignation from the bank, things just seem to be falling nicely into place. The pain in my groin has subsided, and I have a strong sense it will not be back. The understanding I have gained from spending time with my soul group has brought a sense of calm. I have reached a turning point in my life, and I have chosen the right direction.

---

(1) This author believes that transformational body movement in a past-life regression is useful by some therapists to assist healing, because movement often goes deeper than words or visualizations and is very empowering for a client. This technique may be used when trauma or recurring unexplainable pain occurs.

(2) There might be some confusion with readers over the use of good "intent" in this case. While taking a man's daughter in a barter arrangement for business advantages is not good intent on Dean's part in a past life, the author explains that trying to make one's business and personal life successful is good intent from Dean's viewpoint. The larger issue mentioned here is that "hard work and good intent are not always rewarded" in the life of anyone. This, of course, is true because one must consider karmic influences from our deeds over multiple past lives and not just our current one.

(3) Not to be confused with a Council of Elders meeting room, in a different, nonthreatening setting in the spirit world, in which soul evaluation by a

group of highly advanced wise beings takes place. In the case of this client, what we have here could be described as an intervention group of Dean's soul companions brought spontaneously into a current timeline to discuss Dean's life contract. This is a very effective technique sometimes used by elders or spirit guides in life-between-lives regressions to give a more profound understanding. Readers should be advised that while guides and elders are very benevolent in their relations with incarnating souls, our soul group companions are not above teasing and criticizing our shortcomings while also praising us for a good performance in life; see soul group systems, DS 190–194.

(4) In a pure soul state of light energy, we don't see the sort of emotion generated by the central nervous system of the human body. Thus, when a hypnosis client such as Dean is visualizing being in a soul state and expresses strong emotion such as fear, this is an interpretation based on human feeling of the action and involves human emotional transference. All of our research indicates that such negative sensations as fear do not truly exist in the afterlife.

(5) Dean is told there is "an earthbound emotion" (fear) connected with his concern about not staying with his soul group because of slow development. Dean's comment that being left behind is "of no consequence" demonstrates a bit of bravado on his part. While it is true that the better learners in a basic soul cluster group do accelerate more quickly into new, specialized soul groups of similar interests, motivation, and talent at the intermediate levels, all our evidence involving thousands of cases suggests that the slower souls are not shifted elsewhere. Dean may fear this on a conscious level, but the story indicates he does not really believe it. This is because the formation of new cluster groups after creation are not randomly designed. One sees a common denominator of goals in every soul group, and they spend eons helping each other. At the same time, we must always be aware in our work that anomalies may occur in our spiritual conclusions. See placement, JS 105; soul group integrity, JS 88; and formation of soul groups, LBLH 139–142.

(6) With the multitude of host bodies souls have had during many incarnations, some have involved painful injuries, mutilations, and murderous death blows. We do see cases of a past-life body imprint in current bodies. In this case, Dean's groin pain was a reminder of past transgressions against women linked to his current infidelity. See JS 223–229; DS 136, 267, 272; and LBLH 167–168.

THE
downloading
SPIRIT GUIDE

Christine Pearson
(SURREY, ENGLAND)
LBL FACILITATOR, ACCREDITED
PSYCHOTHERAPIST AND HYPNOTHERAPIST.

There are no guarantees in LBL regression. While it is possible to have profound, life-changing contact with our own souls and the souls of loved ones, it could be that our guides block this contact because the time is not right for us to access this information. The following case turned out to be an experience that went way beyond the expectations of both client and therapist.

THE FIRST CONTACT I had with Marcus took place nine months after I'd trained with Dr. Michael Newton and his team. My first impression: here was a very intelligent, articulate, confident person working in the logical, factual world of computers. He might not have developed any interest in spiritual matters had he and his wife not spent some time living in a haunted house. This gave him direct experience of "weird" goings-on that didn't fit into the standard model of a rational, material world.

Marcus gave me wonderfully detailed background information on the main people in his life and clearly had thought deeply about the many questions to which he wanted to find answers as part of his LBL session. These questions covered broad issues such as the meaning of life and the workings of the various planes of existence, as well as personal issues relating to his own life purpose and how better to get his human personality working harmoniously with his soul.

We spoke on the phone and communicated by email several times before we met. Marcus had previously read the LBL books by Dr. Newton, so he had a basic understanding of what might happen.

At first, I found it difficult to guide Marcus into trance. The left side of his body was extremely relaxed, but the right side felt tense. I concluded from this that the right hemisphere of his brain, which controls the left side of the body, was happy to go into trance, but the left hemisphere was reluctant. I invited the two hemispheres to have a dialog and air their concerns. Marcus told me that his soul, which was operating the right hemisphere, was excited and enthusiastic about this journey, but that his human ego, which was operating the left hemisphere, didn't want to cooperate because it knew this would mean confronting the reality of its mortality. (1) This dialog had a successful outcome, and Marcus went fully into trance.

He went back to a past life in the nineteenth century, in which he was cheated by a business partner. In the scene we visited, Marcus was extremely angry and forcefully accusing the man, but his partner wouldn't apologize and refused to accept responsibility. He recognized this man as someone he'd also had difficulties with during his current life. From the soul perspective, he saw that the karmic lesson was in learning to let go and forgive.

He moved very rapidly through the death scene, rising up and away from Earth at breathtaking speed. He saw a tunnel and moved toward it and into it. The speed of the movement and the many colors that surrounded him, plus the completely different way of thinking here, were mind-blowing. Instead of the expected lightness, it was warm and thick, almost like a liquid, but it was pure love. As he experienced this, he commented: "Time isn't linear here. It's so thick around you. There's a shield around time. Outside, you experience linear time; inside, everything is accessible all at once." (2)

He spent a few moments experimenting by moving himself in and out, wholly in and then half out of this amazing space, in order to experience and understand the different realities. He commented that it felt like half of his body was in the spirit world, while the other half remained in the physical:

> The source is so powerful you can't join until you're ready, otherwise you'd be blown apart. I'm not close to the source, but I feel very connected. As a soul, I've been here before. I think there are things I generally have to attend to before meeting my guide. The speed is incredible. There are no limits. If you have the awareness, there is no limit, but it's easy to get lost. You learn. The younger ones have to be watched. They are such children; mischievous, like little monkeys! They get lost and frightened if they're not careful, and someone has to go and fetch them back. (3) I am an old soul—I don't know how old. I keep an eye on them. I can go very fast; it feels fantastic. There's no time. You have wonderful control over your environment and your ability to move around in it.

After spending some time with his young charges, Marcus was ready to meet his guide, Peter. He made a strong telepathic connection, imagining a beam of light going from his heart to Peter's heart, and then he asked to be given information one stage above the level for which Peter thought he was ready. Peter asked if he was sure, and Marcus replied, "Yes, give it to me." What happened next was a shock to both of us.

Marcus jolted violently in his reclining chair. There then followed loud exclamations of "Oh my god! Oh my god!" This went on for some minutes. Marcus had received a massive download of information from his guide, resulting in a change to his energy body around the heart and solar plexus chakras. He gasped:

> My god! There's so much going on! I can't put it into words. Communication is phenomenally fast. I've just been told 10 million things. Here's *x, y, z* for you to consume. It will take me a long time, maybe years, to process this. To process this information, I have to learn to meditate. I love physical sensation and passion, but I have to learn to switch off the human mind and meditate.

In the weeks following this session, Marcus did meditate regularly. He was now able to see energy around him, to hear tones, and generally be more open and receptive to energies around him. Along with this, however, came some unwelcome activity in the house. There would be loud bangs and knocks, and Marcus would see spirits in his energy field. He was worried about the effect this could be having on his son and therefore decided to reduce the meditation and concentrate on finding out more by reading widely on spiritual research and attending the College of Psychic Studies in London.

We had a second session the following year that involved, amongst other things, a meeting with his soul group and his council, and an exploration into the various planes of existence in which energy vibrates at different frequencies. In addition, Marcus connected to his soul energy still in residence within the spirit world, his higher self (4), resulting in a clearer understanding of how karma operates in relation to positive and negative energy. We were quite keen to learn to discriminate between the various energies that approached him—to know if they might be benign or malign. His guide said he would be recognizable because he would touch the back of Marcus's neck when he wanted to communicate with him, and beyond that, he should trust his gut feelings. However, apart from the download, Peter has proved to be quite a hands-off guide, who doesn't get involved in much direct communication. (5) When he does communicate, however, he can be quite blunt, making comments such as "Don't be daft, you don't need my help for that!" We asked the meaning of a green light that Marcus sometimes sees; and we were told that it simply means "go." He often sees a kind of energy static around him, a little like the transporter effect in *Star Trek* as it's beaming up Captain Kirk. He was told that his guide had switched off some of the filters in his brain in order to expand his perception, so he can now begin to see more of the many dimensions that exist here:

> The human brain is actually a simple organ at a basic level, and it has difficulty coping with different types of information, or communication streams. There are loads of filters in place. If you had a fully open doorway back home, your human brain wouldn't be able to take it. The level of energy overload would drive you insane. For example, people who practice working with kundalini (6) without knowing what they're doing are potentially playing with fire, because they're opening up, aligning their energy and removing filters. It can lead to insanity. They see demons where none exist. There are so many different types of filters that perform so many functions. Autistic children—some children's filters are damaged. But other filters are changed so that they are very high functioning. So many filters performing so many things, so we use a small amount of brain power. These filters are being switched on and off. That's being changed, opening up just a little bit more.

It's two years later, and the changes in Marcus's life that have resulted from his LBL session are profound. He has met his guide, his soul group, and his council. He has directly experienced different planes of existence and has expanded his consciousness. Healing energy is transmitted spontaneously through his hands. He hasn't been handed all this knowledge on a plate, though. His ability to perceive has been greatly enhanced, but to some degree he is still exploring uncharted territory, and this takes courage. There have been times when he has blocked out perceptions for fear of losing his sanity. At one time, during meditation, he became aware of a spirit scanning his body. Another time, again during a meditation, an apparently angry spirit began to tear at the energy around his heart center, and he rapidly shook himself back to full alertness. (7)

Despite this, however, the changes have been overwhelmingly positive. His guide has shown him various images during meditations—for instance, the birth of his own soul. This was a beautiful, profound witnessing of himself as a fragment of energy breaking away from the source amid a kaleidoscope of colors and an intense feeling of love. In addition, he has seen inside his physical body, watched it emit high levels of light energy, and witnessed the healing power of the light from above.

Marcus is a teacher soul, and part of his purpose during this lifetime is to make enlightenment available to others—to offer insights into the reality of our spiritual existence. Alongside his day job, he has been carrying out healing and charity work in shelters for the homeless. He plans to offer help in hospices, to ease the passing of those who are frightened of death simply because they don't know that they are more than their human personality. One of his best discoveries, though, is simply to know at a deep level who he is: a multidimensional soul, interconnected with all that is.

Marcus is planning to write a film script depicting the spirit world and the various activities in which souls participate—again, in order to play his part in making the knowledge of these spiritual realities available to as many people as possible. This is a very capable, dynamic person with great passion and great talent, and I look forward to his plans becoming reality. It was a real joy and a privilege for me to be able to work with him.

---

(1) It is not standard practice for the soul to operate solely from the right hemisphere of the brain, although that is our creative, intuitive side. It is just what was reported in this instance. For an account of a soul's balanced entry and engagement with the entire brain, see DS 386. For human hemispheric imbalances that affect souls, see DS, case 37, 208–209.

(2) Spiritual versus linear time: see JS 212, DS 164, and LBLH 161.

(3) White light characteristics of child souls: see LBLH 97. Teachers of child souls: LBLH 143.

(4) Soul division: see DS 62, 108, 116–119 and LBLH 135–137.

(5) With our first assignment to a newly formed soul cluster group after creation, an advanced nonincarnating personal guide is chosen for us and other members of our group. This is not a haphazard appointment. While the

immortal character of every teacher guide is different, it has been apparently determined by even higher beings that specific qualities of character and experience in guides are matched with our own soul character to produce the best results for our advancement. See guide assignments to souls, JS 110–111, and teaching characteristics of spirit guides, JS 118.

(6) Kundalini is a concentrated form of universal life force involving both yoga and meditative discipline to create communication between the spiritual and physical planes.

(7) We are told that Marcus has had to "block out perceptions" for fear of losing his sanity. Psychologically, this statement is very revealing in light of what follows in terms of meditations, long after his sessions, where this client was frightened by "angry spirits" who were ready to take over his body. There are people who are terrified of the idea that meditation, hypnosis, sleep, being in a coma, etc., let down the mental barriers of the conscious mind and leave us open to demonic spirits. A whole cottage industry has emerged in recent years over this false belief system. The misuse of "energy cleansing" therapy in some quarters under the title of "spiritual attachment release" is a good example. This smacks of exorcism and attracts people in certain religious circles. Every concept in our conscious mind has its own psychic associations that vary in intensity depending on life circumstances and belief systems. The notion that evil spirits are waiting to attach themselves to our soul creates unnecessary fear with susceptible people who are attracted to medieval superstition, because many feel they deserve to be punished for their transgressions on Earth.

While there are discarnated souls who are not ready to go into the light after death, and even extraterrestrial souls (souls who have never been incarnated in human form), or simply curious or mischievous souls, there are not "dark forces" involving evil or demonic entities ready to attach or steal the souls of the incarnated. Why? Because evil does not exist in the spirit world—a sphere of love, compassion, and kindness. The idea of dangerous spirits ready to inhabit the human mind is not something the highly advanced, benevolent beings of the spirit world would permit. Many of us working in the field of spiritual integration involving the soul and human brain believe that the notion of spirit attachments are fragments of one's own self that require healing. Suppressing aspects of the self may create a phenomenon that resembles possession as an aspect of the unintregated self. Psychologically, such negative energy in fearful people often involves feelings of guilt, unworthiness, personal inadequacy, and a variety of unresolved issues in life.

It is relevant for readers to know that if Marcus had experienced a troublesome and unaccounted spirit during his session, the LBL facilitator in this story would have dealt with it promptly. Such disturbing visualizations are rare in our work, but they do occur. As an example, the therapist in this case worked with a lady who visualized something similar to Marcus, and the facilitator immediately called on this woman's personal spirit guide for assistance. The guide explained that the dark, sinister figure who came "to steal" this hypnosis subject's soul was actually a member of her own soul group on a mission to shake her out of her depression and learn to value her life more. Not all spirits are advanced or skillful enough to engage the human mind smoothly during the first try. See communication skills of souls, DS 37; displaced souls, JS 45–47; client belief systems, LBLH 3–6; and spirit attachment, LBLH 70–71.

21

Jingle Bells

Nancy Hajek
(Nashville, Tennessee)
Case-study reviewer for TNI certification
committee; performs clinical hypnosis,
past-life and between-lives regression.

This case illustrates how people may play similar roles in both our past and current lives, and how present relationships can be colored by the nature of these past associations. It also reveals a direct correlation between physical symptoms manifesting in the current life and the circumstances of death in the former life, linked by feelings of guilt and helplessness.

James learns that his feelings of anger and self-loathing, carried over from the past, are causing a block to his evolution. Upon retrieving his between-lives memories, he learns that it is up to him to let go of the wounds of the past in order to fulfill his life's purpose.

This case also demonstrates how our guides use images that are important to us as metaphors in illustrating our strengths and weaknesses.

JAMES CAME TO my office a man on a mission. A psychotherapist, he devoted himself to helping others burdened with anxiety and depression while suffering privately with the very same conditions. He explained that on the outside, his life appeared idyllic: a beautiful family, nice home, and an ambitious career with a thriving practice. But at forty-five, he had already experienced a long history of inner turmoil, escalating into migraines, paralyzing panic attacks, and agoraphobia. Medication and traditional therapy had mediated his unease for short periods, but an undercurrent of anxiety continued to surface, and the damage to his family life, career, and own self-image was increasing. James told me that he'd had enough; he intended to get to the source of his condition, heal himself, and live free of fear and medication.

As a child, James lived with his mom and grandparents, never knowing his father. When he was four years old, his mother introduced him to Bill, a man she was dating. "No, not him!" was the boy's first response. As Bill became a permanent fixture, so did his emotional and verbal abuse. James's attachment to his mom turned into a constant fear of losing her, and his dislike of Bill turned into anger and resentment. The day he graduated from high school, he came home to find his stepfather violently shaking his mother. James punched him in the face, and Bill went down. That night, James was told to leave.

We began our investigation with past-life regression, looking to a lifetime significant to James's anxiety. He recalled being a black slave, Albert, in the American South—1800s Georgia. Due to his position as overseer of the field slaves, he was callously whipped and humiliated by his master, and forced to whip his own people when instructed. Albert grew to hate his master but held his anger in check to stay alive. His wife was often raped and beaten by the master, and succumbed to wounds and a broken spirit, dying early in life. Albert lived the remainder of his life angry, resentful, and lonely. As he died, he felt his soul shoot upward, coming to rest in the presence of a vibrant being. He reported that his body began to shiver up the spine with excitement. He recognizes the being as his guide and calls him George.

NANCY: How does George greet you?

JAMES: He tells me it was my lack of faith in myself that made me lonely as Albert. And now, he asks, why do I worry? Everything will be taken care of; if I had more faith, I would know this and not have the anxiety. When I waver, he has to bring me back; he grows tired of it.

N: Is he truly tired of working with you in this manner?

J: (hesitating) No, not really...he just says that for effect...he waits patiently for me to come back to faith...to trust in his presence. He's telling me he's proud of me...I never got that from anyone in this life. And I see now that my wife in the past is my mother today, and the slave master is the same soul as that of my stepfather, Bill.

N: Will we work with George in the spirit world during our next session?

J: (chuckle) He says if you must...I think he says that to me often. He says that when he wants to imply there is a more direct route, if I would have faith and connect with him internally. Sometimes I go about things in a particular way...circuitously. He says it will come out the same in the end...he's patient...and amused.

A few weeks passed, and James was back for his life-between-lives regression; he felt he had become more relaxed after his last visit and was looking forward to further revelations. Recounting his life as Albert had brought great insight into the dynamics between himself and his mother and stepfather. The baffling panic he often felt before going to work became comprehensible. He confessed he was so excited about his LBL that he felt like there was a Santa Claus, and today was going to be like opening up presents on Christmas morning. His objective was to find relief for his headaches and continue defusing his anxiety, particularly the anxiety that originated in his stomach. We began the journey by going to my client's most recent past life as a German soldier in World War II.

The scene opens in the cold woods; my client finds himself as Klaus, preparing for night watch. He inventories his weapons: rifle in right hand, ammunition box on left, pistol on right, canteen on left, grenades in back, all attached to a big belt, "like a Santa Claus belt," he explains. He's lonely;

he thinks of his wife and children. He does not want to be here; he never wanted to come. He says he was forced to come; the Nazis threatened his family. The next day, the enemy is engaged. He says tensely:

> I'm at the front of the pack, behind a dirt bank. I'm stationed as a sniper... I shoot them when they move for position between the trees. I shoot for the head, as I'm told... we have the advantage... we kill them all. I don't feel good about it. We march forward, dead Americans everywhere, it makes me sick. Later, the others celebrate, drink. I separate myself... I want to throw up. I'm torn up inside. I like to be the best... I like the praise from my commander... but I hate myself for the killing.

Another battle follows. Klaus is moving across an open field when he is shot in the stomach. He feels the hot, burning pain as he drifts in and out of consciousness. He slips from his body, sees a light in the distance, and feels peace. Moving closer, he sees the light is a tunnel. He enters, and as he glides through the tunnel, the earthly pain gradually disappears. George is behind him; they exit the tunnel and move through layers of fog:

N: What is the purpose of the fog?

J: Contemplation... I process the past life... my guide has his hand on the small of my back, calming me, allowing me to do this.

N: By what name does he call you?

J: Theos.

> *After a warm welcome by familiar souls, Theos is taken to a small enclosure he calls a 4 x 8-foot room to think. (1)*

N: What do you think about in this place?

J: (sadly) I'm thinking about the emotions I felt as Klaus—the regret I have now... the pain I caused... the fear of those I killed... the loss to their families... the burning of their gunshot wounds.

N: Where do you feel the burning?

J: In my head... I aimed for the head.

N: Is this related to the migraines experienced in the present time?

J: Yes ... directly.

N: Is the sense of anxiety in the stomach related to these past events?

J: Yes ... to my fatal wound.

N: What triggers these symptoms to manifest in the current time?

J: (Theos is absorbed in strong feelings of disappointment in himself, and then he answers the question.) I am condemning myself more than anyone around me is ... but I am responsible for a lot of misery ... being the best meant killing many ... why couldn't I have been more like Jesus ... he let himself be killed before he would harm another ... it is wrong to kill ... I am not proud of myself.

N: Is your guide able to help you work through these feelings?

J: (pause) Yes ... but it seems that there are others as well ... sending thoughts into this space. It's very peaceful in this small room.

N: Who are these others?

J: (searching) I'm not sure ...

N: Will those who are helping you suggest how to remedy the headache and anxiety in your life as James? (2)

J: (quietly) I hold this against the self ... I need to release the self-loathing in order to truly love others ... forgive myself so that I can forgive others.

As my client tentatively ponders this advice, another being appears; James says it is Jesus and is somewhat unnerved, but as he looks more closely, he reports the figure changes in appearance, now wearing gold track shoes and a toga!

N: Who is this being?

J: (a bit relieved) Oh, it's Donovan. He helps me as well, more of a junior guide working under George. He appeared as Jesus to get my attention ... it worked! (3)

N: Why would he appear as Jesus to get your attention?

J: In my life as Albert, I tried hard to follow Jesus's example ... I was taught to read. The one book I had was a bible. I see myself clinging to his words when things were hard to bear.

N: Does Donovan remind you of this for a reason?

J: He wants me to remember how well I used this ... how I could have lashed out in anger many times but instead controlled myself in the wake of great provocation.

N: Is this knowledge important in your life as James?

J: (reflective) Yes ... Donovan is showing me a common theme. As Albert, I hated being afraid, humiliated ... the fear turned into anger ... I was angry at being powerless ... I even envied the master's position. While I did well to control impulsive acts, focusing on the message of Jesus ... I did not take it into my heart. The feelings return to me now as James ... anger at being disrespected, fear when I am not on top of the heap. The anxiety comes from this ... and is a signal that I'm going off-message ... I wanted to resolve all this as James. Donovan shows me how these feelings surfaced recently ... he was stimulating them ... he knew I wanted to face them and was helping me.

Donovan escorts Theos to a group of souls he collaborates with, both in the spirit world and on Earth. He says they work on a shared lesson: to express great amounts of love when faced with great challenge on Earth. He is reminded that both his need for recognition and the self-condemnation when he pursues recognition pose a block to his mission. Interestingly, the group members position themselves in the shape of a triangle—one of several triangles presented to Theos during his journey through the spirit world. Here he finds himself in the center of the formation:

N: Why the triangles, Theos? What is the importance of this shape?

J: They are using this shape to describe the importance I place on reaching the apex ... my need to be on top ... that I feel I have to be the best.

N: Why do they place you in the center?

J: They surround me with their love ... it feels good ... they want me to know the love I can feel by being in the center of the triangle ... I don't have to be at the top to be loved.

Later, Theos is escorted into what appears to be a courtroom and finds himself standing before a council of elder beings. Their configuration is created by a raised platform, highest in the center while descending in steps on either side, giving the presentation of a triangle. Theos peers intensely at the figures, trying to answer my inquiries. Frustrated, he says they are white statues; the highest one, in the middle, looks like a white Santa Claus statue.

N: (after deepening) I'd like you to relax your gaze and glance softly toward the center figure.

J: (excitedly) He becomes animated ... like a jolly Saint Nick ... red and green come to life in his clothes ... he wears a necklace with a round pendant ... the peace sign. (4)

N: And the significance of this symbol?

J: (pause) Peace within myself ... peace with what I've done ... peace with the anxiety ... it's everything that I yearn for ... I put out my hand ... he laughs ... ho-ho-ho ... I get the message ... I'll prosper more if I attain it for myself.

Theos describes the other figures; each time he strains to see them clearly, they become white statues. When I ask Theos to discern the purpose of this effect, he discovers it demonstrates the effect of straining. He sees this is generated when he becomes fearful and forces things to happen, rendering his aspirations lifeless and beyond reach. The elders convey that his goals will come easier if he will relax his grip and have faith in the inner workings of his life. They tell him to lighten up and have some fun along the way and enjoy life. The council members continue to display the attitudes that revivify fears of the past and generate anxiety in the present:

J: Another of the elders is dressed as Rameses (an Egyptian pharaoh) ... his extravagant gold headdress implies fancy nothingness ... I should not be preoccupied with being head man ... the words of Jesus come: "The first shall be last, the last shall be first." Next to him is another ... a crow sits on his right shoulder. Being critical comes to mind. The crow implies my impulse to pick at things ... I become consumed in critical thought when I fear failure. He shows me a bird sitting quietly ... I don't have to get rid of it, simply tame it ... rely more on my intuition. When I forget this, the anxiety comes in my stomach ... when I get it right, I feel the shiver up my spine.

N: Your council members seem like an imaginative bunch. Do they always appear as these characters?

J: (laughs) No, they use whatever suits the lesson best ... and my state of mind. They knew the Santa would get my attention today ... very clever. I feel now they were the ones sending thoughts into the box when I first arrived, helping me to start figuring things out for myself.

N: Theos, it seems you have learned much about the origins of your desire for esteem and position, and the anxiety that comes when you fear losing these. The connection between your lives as Albert and James is becoming clearer, but how does your life as Klaus fit into the plan? We know that period left you deeply conflicted and forlorn.

J: (pensive) I see now ... it was an ambitious idea, but I wanted it. Just coming out of my time as Albert, it would be very tempting to choose the path offered to Klaus ... being important ... praise for my marksman-ship, respect from others ... I really messed up. I had intended to resist the offer, to go with my heart, stay with my family. Instead I fell for it. I see why I could not stomach the killing ... I was not there in any sense of service or moral conviction ... it was all about personal recognition. Donovan, the council ... they knew it would be challenging ... they fig-ured in several ways out of this path, but I was so hungry for acclaim, I missed them all.

N: How does it feel to be aware of these intents and choices?

J: Oh, very helpful ... I know what I need to do ... I want to get a handle on this and achieve what I intended ... rather than seek rank and power (as in his German life) to remedy my wounds, I want to respect myself for the love and forgiveness I can offer.

In the year following his LBL, James took to heart the advice of his guide and elders, and came up with a new way to excel. He learned to quiet himself, listen to inner counsel, to trust his intuition and the shivers up his spine. A man inspired, James says it best:

> This experience has changed my entire worldview, my perspective. Knowing of the life of my soul, I know this life isn't final—it's a process. The goals of my daily life have changed; my self-esteem had been determined by my material accomplishments. Now I am smelling the roses for the first time in my life, and I feel emotionally connected to life again. My work ethic is back, and my anxiety is completely gone. My eldest son is showing signs of being just like I was ... angry, frustrated, anxious ... he was a fellow slave in my time as Albert ... now I can show him the things that are important and those that are not. I also feel more normal ... when I did not understand myself so well, I felt odd for having these thoughts and feelings inside. Now it just seems reasonable! Things just pop out into my consciousness now ... realizations about what I recalled in session and sometimes totally new information. I feel I can communicate with my guides whenever I choose. I think what I hold most dear is the humor, playfulness, patient demeanor, and creativity of my guides and elders; I believe they have rubbed off on me.

Being human, we blanket ourselves from our greater purpose and prior intention. Our lives on Earth tend to separate us from the body of our work as souls and leave us grappling not only with the angst of the moment but with its resonant mumbling from the past. Sometimes I think it remarkable that we glean as much as we do from a lifetime! For James, recalling his immortality was like shaking off sleep, and with it the blunders that can come with drowsiness. His sense of himself has shifted; he is now aware of his courageously inventive soul and at home in a universe supported by wisdom, suffused with light, and surrounded by love.

(1) It may appear to the reader that this soul has been delegated to solitary confinement for transgressions in life as a kind of purgatory. Actually, nothing of the sort is happening here. Souls often require a place of solitude and reflection right after a physical life, before rejoining their spirit group. These small spaces have been described as enclosures of high energy vibrations to facilitate thought and sometimes are portrayed as crystalline caves in nature. See souls in seclusion, DS 67–68, 105, and soul solitude before returning to cluster groups, LBLH 106.

(2) While it seems as though the hypnotherapist here is "leading the client" in their exchanges, I want to stress that when writers of dialog in past-life and afterlife cases construct their stories for books, we have a dilemma due to the space condensations that this sort of writing requires. If we wrote about all the nuances connecting our open-ended questions, the average case would be double in length on the written page. For example, the writer in this section probably began her inquiry with something like, "What can you tell me about those around you?" Typically, there would be a number of questions before "Who is helping you with how to remedy the headache and anxiety in your life?" We don't have the space for all the questions leading up to the one on the printed page.

However, having said that, I should also add that there are clients who occasionally will require a leading, or directive, question by the hypnosis facilitator to jolt them into a response. There are clients who are so in awe of the afterlife that they don't want to speak of the divine revelations that they are visualizing and hearing. The experience is almost sacred to them, and they must almost be given permission to affirm what they already know or are learning about during the session. This is what makes our work so challenging. See phrasing questions, LBLH 74–78 and also encouraging verbal responses from clients, LBLH 146.

(3) During the earlier alpha stages of hypnosis in LBL sessions, there are subjects who may mention known historical religious figures on Earth whom they relate to on a conscious level. This is what is known as preconditioned conscious interference. But once the deeper theta state of hypnosis is achieved, usually after mentally crossing into the spirit world, symbolic religious figures disappear in favor of the recognition of a personal spirit guide. See LBLH 4, 5, and 108.

(4) Signs and symbols are often presented in one form or another to souls appearing before a council. They are designed to have specific meaning to the developing soul. Medallions worn by the elders add to a soul's learning about events and actions in their physical lives. See DS 224–242.

22

THE
reluctant
SOUL MATE

David Allen

(TONBRIDGE, ENGLAND)
A REGISTERED HYPNOTHERAPIST, LBL THERAPIST,
AND EMOTIONAL FREEDOM TECHNIQUES
(EFT) TRAINER SPECIALIZING IN SPIRITUAL
INTEGRATION AND ALCOHOL DEPENDENCY ISSUES.

In Jacqueline's story, the timely discovery of Dr. Michael Newton's book Destiny of Souls *and one lengthy phone call preceded the LBL experience that would lead to the life changes and understanding she so desperately sought. An honest, trustworthy, hardworking individual who hated her body and herself, Jacqueline couldn't begin to form the relationship she so desperately wanted, had issues with jealousy, commitment, and trust, and just felt her life was going nowhere. Her revelations in LBL led her to the discovery of her soul mate and a whole new perspective on her life and its purpose.*

THIS FASCINATING STORY began one quiet afternoon when, from out of the blue, I received a telephone call that was almost panicky in nature. The caller was a forty-nine-year-old woman, Jacqueline, in the midst of an experience she didn't understand, and she was clearly concerned about how it was affecting her life and her sanity.

We spent over an hour on the telephone, in part so I could help her anxiety subside, but also because I found myself listening with mounting interest and excitement. There was something missing from her story—and I had the overwhelming sensation that I knew what it might be. I couldn't know the details, of course, but I knew how we might fill that gap. I offered possible explanations, answered some questions, and listened a lot, and finally we agreed that the LBL process could be a way to bring her life and afterlife into perspective.

Jacqueline's life has had its share of difficulties, both financial and emotional, with a particularly low point exactly one year before, symbolized by the now-faded lines on her right forearm, the result of a desperate sawing action with a kitchen knife. She told me that over time and with a history of unsatisfactory relationships, it was just getting harder and harder for her to trust and commit to anyone. What she said she wanted just seemed to be more and more difficult to achieve:

> For much of my adult life I've been single. Even in the
> relationships I've had, I have often felt single. One twelve-year
> commitment to the father of my daughters perhaps was the
> highlight. That ended because he just didn't care anymore, and I
> couldn't understand why. I really want an adult, loving relationship.
> I like sex and I love people and I work hard in my job and at
> home. It isn't easy spending most of your life as a single parent, and
> my parents, bless them, have been on many rescue missions during
> that time to their poor, underachieving single daughter.

While things haven't gone particularly well for her, she freely acknowledges that there are others who have it far harder, and she is frequently self-deprecating for wanting more from her own life. She is courageous and can make rational decisions for practical purposes. In the absence of a loving sexual relationship and the emotional stability to form one, a practical approach is to perhaps pursue the sexual aspect alone. Because her emotional barriers are firmly in place, they have to be suppressed with alcohol for her to be able to engage in short-term sexual congress. But to be capable of such an approach does demonstrate the rational, practical edge that is so much a part of Jacqueline and her life experiences to date.

Six months before she felt the urge to call me, Jacqueline had made contact with Paul on a dating website. This had a significant impact; she said, "When I saw his picture for the first time, my entire chest tingled with excitement. He was so beautiful."

Paul and Jacqueline began a relationship within a dimension involving distance of which few people are capable. Their communications, both verbal and cognitive, were and still are spiritual and telepathic. They have never met in person, and the only "real" contact they have experienced is by phone.

> Paul and I have spoken only four times on the phone and exchanged a few texts but have never met physically in person. In the metaphysical world, we have spent many nights together, spoken at length in the language of the mind; I've felt his body sexually and lovingly, cuddling in those early hours just before I have to go work; he has taken me on wondrous journeys to many places and is truly my soul mate and guide, yet amongst all this, we cannot meet and cannot fulfill those most necessary of adult human needs. He cannot come into my life, because he is damaged and will damage me, but he is there.

Their interdimensional closeness occurred at all levels and felt to her as real as life. He took her to wondrous places and supported her when the need arose:

> Paul showed me who he was. At first, I saw an Indian medicine man standing in front of his tepee and looking over his people. He was a good man and a proud man and in return, he was well-respected and loved. Then there was a woman next to him, and she was so proud to be there. She loved her man; he might have been the medicine man, but she was the strength behind him. That woman was me.

Jacqueline and Paul's relationship started well but began to unravel in a disturbing way.

> The closeness and loving all too often were followed by periods when he became spiteful and hurtful. For some reason, he pushed me away with aggression, and by this time, his presence had become an intrusion in my life that I couldn't stop. It was in this climate and at this time that I opened and began to read *Destiny of Souls*.
>
> As I turned the pages, I could hardly believe what I was reading. Here was someone explaining in detail things that were happening to me—in black and white, it described exactly what was happening to me, and I couldn't even begin to understand how anyone else could know that. I had been to a crystal recovery center, experienced a healing shower, and saw that my spiritual home is a beautiful garden, as described in the book where newly arrived souls are oriented.
>
> These discoveries haunted me, because they also raised questions that seemingly couldn't be answered. I spent some days wondering what to do and looked up the author of this book and the Newton Institute website and made that life-changing telephone call.

Spiritual memories are discovered during deep hypnosis. The way to achieve the necessary level of trance is in two stages, induction and deepening. In essence, I have to establish a trance state and then improve on it until this deep level is reached. Inductions can be of varying length, depending on the client, but my preference is "slowly does it." This stage usually takes around half an hour.

About ten minutes into Jacqueline's induction, the following happened:

> Oh god this feeling of love, I've got this feeling of sitting in the sunshine. Oh this heat and love. There are some people in the distance, I'm getting a bit nervous and they have backed off a bit, I'm going to try and calm myself down.
>
> Oh my god. It's, it's ... they are there, these people. I'm in almost like a playground and there's all these people and they're so happy to see me, oh I'm going to cry, oh, the emotion is just

overwhelming, they are so happy to see me. It's so physical, I'm in a playground with physical people, they are still standing back but they are there, they are getting closer, they are standing behind a barrier, a barrier coming up to their knees, this happened last night as well and this morning... then they were in my room, god, I've never felt such emotion from so many people, who are these people?

They are all different ages, I've got one woman with gray hair and glasses... that's my nan, there's a few people huddled in a group about five feet away but she is my great nan, I don't know her name, she is smiling. She wants me to come forward so that she can hug me.

There's a little boy about nine years old near her, and I don't know who he is, I don't recognize him... he is just standing there smiling, he's small for his age, my nan has just got hold of his hand.

I've gone to someone else, she's pushing her way through the crowd and I don't know who she is, she is about thirty and a bit taller than me, very confident, she's got hold of my hand and it's like she's known me all of her life but I don't know who she is.

Oh, it's my granddad, oh my god, it's Bill. Bill was never my granddad, he was my nan's second husband, and I absolutely loved him, really loved him. Oh my god, he's here, it's very emotional, this, I'm just going to cry again.

They've gone now with love, sorry, sorry. (1)

After this jumping-ahead interlude, we continued at a slower progression. Jacqueline went to a past life as a woman named Beth who had an unhappy, unfulfilled life with a miserable marriage. On the last day of her life, she was so tired, and it just seemed to be an appropriate and ordinary end:

My spiritual name is Sanu, and I'm now home in my garden. The grass is as green as it could be, though it does need cutting. When I breathe in, I can breathe the colors of the flowers and take on the energy that the garden can give me. I have to stay here for a while, for at the moment, I'm not ready to move on.

Sanu asks me if I would like a tour of her house, and she describes to me the décor and ornaments until she feels tired again. We have to wait until her energy has been restored fully. There is a pause in proceedings, and she takes a shower to cleanse her of the last life.

I ask Sanu if she would like to meet her guide, but even before I had uttered all the words, she says:

> He is here, and it is Paul, I didn't expect that; oh, why am I
> surprised? He is lovely and so beautiful. His spirit name is
> Treymar. He is really happy to see me and presents himself as I see
> him on Earth so that I can recognize him. It's a little odd because
> I'm not as I am here. He is also in my garden, holding my hand,
> and he hugs me.

Jacqueline goes on to describe an intense connection she can actually feel in her physical body. She is telling Paul to behave himself because she doesn't want to be embarrassed. This physical connection is sexual as well as loving, and she is as overwhelmed by his beauty in spirit as she is with his earthly incarnation. He is her soul mate and her guide, and an eternal love binds them together.

Her guide and her soul mate exist in two places. The energy of this being is divided into two approximately equal parts, one part pure and complete and the other entwined and linked with the physical human being who is Paul. The spiritual energy within Paul is no longer pure; it has been damaged by his life experiences and is strangely separate from the purity of Treymar. Because of the change to the energy, it is no longer the same, and that has practical ramifications. The energy cannot be rejoined as it stands, and to become as one again, the part that is in Paul will need to be repaired when his life is ended. Although this is one spiritual energy entity, its aspects are not able to connect in any meaningful way while Paul's physical body and brain has possession. If Paul's energy is insufficient to cope, nothing can be done. Treymar is aware but is effectively just an onlooker; he cannot alter or supplement the part of his energy that is in use, and he cannot influence Paul's actions and decisions. Once the energy has been allocated and installed, as it were, the resultant being—which could be you or me or anyone else—lives with independence, and how we fare in this existence can dramatically alter the structure of the spiritual energy. (2)

Jacqueline is now dating but not clinging. She has developed an entirely new perspective on herself, physically and emotionally. Her daughters have observed and commented on the change in her demeanor and confidence. It seems that the inner person has finally arisen.

Jacqueline sums up her new perspective with clarity and understanding:

> I've met my soul mate and guide in true spiritual form. I
> understand now so much of what scared me, and the knowledge
> and experience of my everlasting role in the universe and
> knowingly being loved so completely by so many has changed my
> entire perspective about my own being on this earth, my life, and
> my expectations. I am truly at one now with my body and soul.

---

(1) In a spiritual regression session, the hypnosis subject will usually move from an alpha state past-life death scene to a deeper theta state as they reach the spiritual gateway and eventually their soul group. What has happened here is that Jacqueline has moved past the pace of the facilitator and more rapidly regressed herself in order to see her soul companions. Following this scene with her soul group, the facilitator takes this subject back to finish the past-life recall so he can move Jacqueline forward again in a more orderly manner for the interaction with her soul companions. For a more typical LBL progression, see homecoming, JS 27–44. For diagrams of soul group positions at the greeting time for incoming souls, see DS figures 2 and 3, page 143.

(2) In the spirit world, there are senior and sometime junior guides assigned to souls. The junior (less developed) guides may still choose to incarnate on vary rare occasions to complete some unfinished business in their own karmic path that involves a still-incarnating soul. To have a soul even of junior-guide status in your life is quite extraordinary; see guides, JS 107–122. In such cases where a client states that someone in their life who is close to them is actually a spirit guide, I initially suspect conscious interference and wishful thinking is at work on the part of the client. In Jacqueline's case, for a junior guide such as Paul to have damaged energy from any physical source indicates either a very tentative new guide or a misstatement by the client from a lack of true perception. In my experience, all guides are too advanced to be walking around with damaged energy. For a review of energy damage and restoration, see DS 85–95.

23

FINDING THE
courage
TO CHANGE

Catherina Severin
(SCOTTSDALE, ARIZONA)
CERTIFIED CLINICAL HYPNOTHERAPIST
SPECIALIZING IN REGRESSION AND SELF-
HELP TECHNIQUES; REIKI TEACHER
AND THOUGHT FIELD THERAPIST.

When people realize that they are unhappy with their lives, they search for answers. In this LBL session, we see how answers and advice for change is given. Our guides can help us to remember things we did not even know were important, thus making our purpose in life even more fulfilling. Here, Howard discovers far more than he was looking for, which ultimately leads to a healthy life change.

HOWARD, A SUCCESSFUL businessman in his fifties, scheduled his life-between-lives session for a late summer day. Though he was not familiar with the literature about spiritual regression, he had great interest in spirituality and working with aspects of healing. He was happily married, the father of two grown daughters, and working in a very well-paid senior management job. However, his prestigious job brought about unwanted negative emotions. Anger and frustration would regularly overtake any kind of reasoned approach to a problem, and one colleague in particular made Howard fly off the handle regularly. Meanwhile, his wife's job was stressing her to the point of exhaustion. A further complication for Howard and his wife was the geographic location of their home, which inhibited regular sailing on their sailboat, a beloved hobby for them both. His own lack of fulfillment and the high level of stress his wife was experiencing prompted him to take action and seek answers. So the most important question on Howard's list was how to resolve these increasingly challenging issues. He also wanted to know about his mission, his evolution, his guides, his karmic relationship with his wife, and how to make the best of his life.

Shortly into the LBL session, Howard easily went into a deep trance state and soon found himself going through his most immediate past life as a German Jew in 1933. He was a man of twenty-five years when he got laid off because of being Jewish, and shortly afterwards, he was killed in the streets for the same reason. He left that lifetime without understanding the reason for this experience. From the moment of death in that life, he made an easy and swift transition into the spirit world:

HOWARD: I am moving slowly, and it is getting lighter and lighter, it's as if I am coming out of the clouds, and someone in light-colored clothing is welcoming me. It is so white and light that I can hardly see. But I can tell it is a male, bigger than me, and he is smiling. He tells me to forget what just happened because now I am somewhere else.

CATHERINA: Who is this? Is it someone you recognize?

H: He is the one who welcomes me. He brings me to a place I know from my current lifetime—it is by a creek. This is a peaceful place. From here, he leads me through the woods to the beach. I am surprised. He wants to show me something peaceful from this lifetime.

C: What happens next?

H: He asks me if I want to meet others ... I see my father, though he seems to show himself in a younger version, and he asks me to come with him, to join them. But I would rather go with the welcoming spirit. I am pulled in different directions.

Howard chooses to go with the welcoming spirit and reports that together they move into a light.

C: Who is this welcoming spirit? What is his role?

H: I don't know him. But he tells me his name is Herman, and he is the one to show me around. He says if I want to find my friends, I have to do so myself. (1)

After a pause, Howard has found his group.

H: There are many others gathered here, but I cannot clearly see them, they are only shadows in the light. (pause) After a while, the first one comes forward to greet me ... Oh, it is my wife (in his current life), Jane. (pause) She is holding me.

C: Have you had many incarnations together?

H: Yes, so many she is laughing at the question. We have incarnated together all along, ever since the Stone Age. I see stone axes.

C: Is there a specific karmic relation between the two of you?

H: We like to be man and wife, and together our mission is to find work with all aspects of love.

The others to come forward from Howard's soul group include his brother in this lifetime, whose condemning behavior is to teach Howard by making him aware of how *not* to be. Howard also meets his two daughters and finds his role is to be teaching them independence and giving them freedom. This rather serious spirit group seems to be headed by Howard and Jane. (2)

From here, Howard moves on to another area to discover his and Jane's specialty in the spirit world. It turns out they are teachers. Through story-telling, they teach a group of twelve to fourteen souls about incarnating for spiritual advancement. The emphasis is on issues of happiness, enthusiasm, and love, qualities and understandings they need for their next incarnation.

Finding out about being a teacher is humbling to Howard, and from this experience he discovers that he has come quite far in his own development as a spirit.

C: Are your own incarnations primarily for the purpose of teaching others?

H: No, in that case it would be a waste to incarnate. I still need to learn myself. I have had one hundred or more incarnations. (3) My previous life as a Jew in Germany was to learn tolerance, but not for the sake of teaching about it. I am being taught myself here in the spirit world as preparation for the next incarnation.

C: What were you taught before this lifetime as Howard?

H: I have to learn about anger by being angry. Anger and emotional temperament are aspects of this lifetime.

C: What are you learning, then?

H: That I mustn't restrain these emotions by damaging myself. That is what I am doing now at work—not saying what I mean. I can't keep doing that. It is better to give my opinion. If that isn't possible, I must take the consequences and find another job somewhere else. The main message here is that I mustn't forget myself.

C: Are you being taught anything else?

H: There is a wise man, one of the ones who doesn't incarnate anymore. He is a teacher in the spirit world and knows about karma. He tells me the last thing I need to learn is not to spread bad karma, and that I will need more incarnations to do that. He says we need to come back as long as we create bad karma. It is very complicated, and it is not in this lifetime that I will learn how to overcome this particular karma. I am learning about anger and temperament. That is my mission in this lifetime.

After visiting the area of the guides, Howard meets Aron. Aron is a superior guide who has always been with Howard. Aron also emphasizes the importance of taming anger and a high-strung temperament without forgetting himself. He refers to the Jewish lifetime, saying, "You learned it the hard way. And now you have your brother to remind you to be tolerant in your current incarnation. And remember not to be arrogant and proud. You have done well."

Howard's session came to an end, and he felt he had achieved the answers he was looking for. It was interesting how the Jewish past life was related to understanding tolerance, and that this lifetime as Howard was dedicated to anger and temperamental outbursts without any vital karmic issues to resolve. Howard was clearly on a mission to get insights on a personal emotional level.

Most of his questions were answered without prompting, and the answers seemed quite natural and obvious to him. The meeting with the guides and Aron held a great confirmation for him, and as he reported later, this meeting would turn out to be of great importance.

One year later, Howard shared the outcome of his experience with me:

> As you may remember, I was in the quagmire of a very well-paid job which bored me tremendously, and my wife had an extremely stressful job which was literally killing her. After my LBL session, we made a plan: in order to get to a place where we could relax and sail our boat, I needed to find a job in a different area of the country. We would then sell our house and find a spot for the boat and a house in the vicinity. Then my wife would quit her job and pack our belongings and look for another job. This was the way we envisaged our transformation to work out, and we made it happen.
>
> All in all, we have a much better life now than before, and my LBL session played a very important role in finding the courage to make the change. The LBL session has been important in bringing me further in my present incarnation. The greatest impact was that not only did I get confirmation that it was advisable for us to change our life, but it was necessary. We had already considered the possibility of major changes in order to get on the right track, but the actual confirmation was very important. The way everything has unfolded proves to me that our guides were with us all the way. Despite making drastic and fast changes, everything fell into place beautifully. And, I might add, by following the advice I was given, the issues of anger and temperament have dissolved.
>
> The grandest emotional experience in the regression was, however, in another area: I was overwhelmed, happy, and humbled by the role Jane and I have in spirit, where we help others by teaching them to get the best out of their incarnations. (4)

(1) For a soul reentering the spirit world after a life to be told they must find their soul companions themselves is highly uncommon. Normally, joyful reunions are staged by our friends, usually with guides nearby. Newly arrived souls typically are ushered into these events from the gateway or after orientation. However, it should be said that every guide has their own character traits, and they don't all follow the same standard procedures. For more perspective on this aspect of the spirit world, see homecoming, JS 27–44, and LBLH 100–101.

(2) We have seen the dual capacity of souls to divide their energy before with other cases in this book. A soul never brings in 100 percent of their energy into any single physical body on Earth because the human brain could not tolerate this high concentration of energy. What is left behind in the spirit world is an exact duplicate of identity as the incarnated portion, although less potent, to be sure. There are two ways in which a subject in deep hypnosis can see relatives and friends from their lives. A) As in this case, with Howard seeing his wife, brother, and two daughters who are still living in his current lifetime. We do this through now-time techniques that have been previously illustrated with council meeting discussions about current problems in the subject's life. B) Contact with one's soul group members and other important souls, such as parents, who have died in current time and may or may not have moved into a new incarnation. This is because a portion of their soul has not left the spirit world.

  A word of warning: in our LBL work, there are no guarantees that a hypnosis subject will see any particular soul in category A or B. The client may not have reached a point of development in their current life where they should see them. Certain karmic cross roads might not have been reached yet, or there could be other karmic reasons that a particular being may not wish to appear, or they might simply be engaged somewhere else in another spiritual space. See soul division, DS 2, 45, 62, 116–120, and LBLH 101, 135–137.

(3) The figure of a hundred lives is probably quite low for an estimate in terms of total incarnations. Clients recalling their past lives basically remember only the most significant ones.

(4) This case illustrates how each of our lives involves choices. The forks in the road often involve the opportunities for positive change in terms of improvement and positive change, both in this life and from the karmic carryovers in former lives. Confronting our karmic influences gives us the opportunity to progress, but it is not fatalistic or predetermined, because our life decisions must involve free will. Karma involves the sum of our deeds from all our past lives, not just the last one. Free will is caught in the events of cause and effect. What we strive to be is as important as who we are at the moment. See LBLH 141.

24

AN
emerging
SPIRITUAL HEALER

Madeline Stringer
(DUBLIN, IRELAND)
HOMEOPATH, AUTHOR, HYPNOSIS REGRESSION
THERAPIST, AND MEMBER OF THE NATIONAL
SOCIETY OF PROFESSIONAL HYPNOTHERAPISTS.

When Marguerite first visited her LBL therapist, she was fifty-four years of age, a tall woman with a cheery smile, who had great understanding of what made her tick. But, she said, she still felt stuck. She had spent ten years of her youth in a Catholic religious order, but left after she felt she no longer believed in the church's perceived wisdom. She had been sent as a missionary to a developing country and while there had been asked wise and searching questions by the local people she was teaching. In the end, their questions taught Marguerite that there were other ways of looking at things, and she started her search.

Marguerite returned home and over the years trained in theology and psychotherapy. She retained a great interest in spirituality in its widest sense and considered setting down her ideas in a book but was finding it very difficult to get started. Something was blocking her. The following account shows clearly how past-life and LBL sessions enabled her to remove her blocks and gain freedom and clarity.

BEFORE DOING THE life-between-lives session, we started with a past-life regression to get Marguerite used to being under hypnosis and to allow any issues from the past to surface. She saw two lives: one from prehistoric times, which showed what was perhaps her first experience of living in a community, on this occasion a village; and the other showing her, at some time between 500 and 1 BC, living in a community with shamanic practices, joining in with energy work and healing. Both these lives resonated with Marguerite in terms of healing. She still remembers with pleasure living in the religious community. But neither past life gave her any answers to her query as to why she felt stuck.

We started the journey into the life-between-lives state with another past-life visit, this time to a pioneer life in Australia, where my client was pregnant with her sixth child. Married to an abusive husband, Peter, she died young in this life. She immediately lifted out of her body and was met by the part of her husband's soul that had not gone to Earth. He hugged her with a pleasant energy and encouraged her to move on. Marguerite knows Peter as Adabba in the spirit world, where he has a different energy to that which he had in the Australian life, even though he is still dealing with issues of anger. (1) They had taken the life together for mutual support and learning. Adabba brought Marguerite to meet her soul group (2), where she recognized about seven people, none of whom were significant in her current life. But during the visit with this group of souls, she became aware of a bigger, dark blue/purple soul, who she felt was helping her to go deeper into the experience. This spirit was totally trustworthy, and because it was so big, it felt more male than female in nature. They stayed quietly together for a while, until he put out a hand, which Marguerite took. It took her awhile to recognize him as her guide Banonda, even after he "put on" a face to help her. But she remembered him and realized that he does not come to Earth anymore. He has been closely relating to her over the past five or six lifetimes only, since she is moving to a more advanced group where he is the lead guide.

Banonda's main role for Marguerite is to help her let go of some relationships. He told her that it was time for her to let go of this soul group, with whom she has been working for forty to fifty lifetimes. Marguerite has progressed a little faster than her group and needs the stimulus of a group of friends more at her own level. In other words, she is to move up a grade! (3)

Banonda brought Marguerite to her other group. When she arrived with them, she remembered that she had already met and worked with them. There were about six members of this group, which is a specialized advanced study group rather than a primary soul cluster group. She recognized several of these souls as people she knows in present-day Ireland, with whom she has work in common. This group's area of study is about "the articulation of the divine." Marguerite said that her group was particularly involved in disseminating images of the divine and working with several other groups who "birthed" the images and ideas. Her group was helping people to notice the divine within themselves and to let go of old images that did not help them. Marguerite noticed the difference between her work on Earth, which is about healing, and her spirit work, which is simply about noticing the divine and letting go of old fears that prevent such awareness.

Marguerite found that helping people in this way is her primary reason to be on Earth in this life, and it gave her encouragement to make another attempt to write her book. She is also meant to contact like-minded people, but she was sad to realize that having a personal relationship in her present life is of secondary importance. The relationship of the souls in the study group was very close; almost, at times, like a mind-merge, and they all had a very deep sense of the divine. They also enjoyed playing with light, throwing beams around themselves and creating light shows a bit like the aurora borealis. (4)

Banonda then encouraged Marguerite to visit her Council of Elders. She felt her consciousness greatly expanding as she met with six androgynous beings who sat on chaise longues in a semicircle. Marguerite was only a little apart from them, and Banonda was to one side. As the visit progressed, Marguerite felt more and more as one of them. They were very supportive and said she had made good choices and was on the right track for this life. There was a discussion about her sadness at having to make the break from her soul group and how hard her life was, as her lack of a partner causes a sense of aloneness. The council members nodded—that is not what this life is about. Marguerite felt a bit overwhelmed at realizing her primary purpose but also a sense of joy at the intense synergy between herself and her council.

With her guide, Marguerite was then able to review all her past lives. Her first incarnations were 100,000 years ago, sometimes in places other than Earth, where matter was less dense. She added that she likes the colors here on Earth! Her soul energy has usually won through during her incarnations, and she has carried "a sense of presence" with her from life to life. Many but not all her lives have been spent in "pursuit of the divine," though she has had to develop other skills too. She has spent about 20 percent of her lives in Europe, the rest divided between Africa and Asia, and has mostly taken male bodies as a balance to her soul's energy, which is quite female. (5) After looking at her past lives, she went quickly back to the council to express her thanks, because she realized she likes this life, as she is on the edge of something new.

As a break from their work about the divine, she and her group spent leisure time in water activities such as canoeing and diving. They find the water refreshing, as dealing with divine energy all the time is very taxing; it's not an easy energy to hold.

When she looked at why she had chosen to take this life, Marguerite realized that she had been very keen to incarnate, even though she knew her early years would be difficult but she wanted to avoid "falling back into myself and having victim energy." Her sense of isolation by working alone was to balance the need to be either victim or aggressor. (6)

When Marguerite finished her session, she was pleased to have confirmed that her instinct to become involved in disseminating information about the divine was the correct one, although she would have preferred to discover that she was going to find a life partner the next day! She told me that she would now be able to start writing her book, and she left quite content and even a little excited.

Three months later, Marguerite phoned me requesting another past-life session. When she arrived, she explained that she had been unable to get started on her writing, as it made her anxious each time she tried. She had been discussing things with her psychotherapist and wanted to look into issues of personal power.

She quickly found herself in Roman times, maybe even in Rome itself, as a senator called Stentorius. She and another man were going to a meeting, to discuss "a clash between the gods." There were many factions amongst the people. Stentorius was in favor of a rational approach, as Marguerite said, "to the whole gods business." He felt that the old gods were too whimsical, flighty, and unpredictable. He thought there should be some way of looking at the gods so that the people would be less fearful and less easily manipulated by some unscrupulous priests. He made a speech advocating more clarity and that the auguries should be downplayed. The priests were unhappy, but other leaders agreed that the republic should not be at the mercy of irrational gods.

A rabble-rouser priest then spoke and put the blame for a recent earthquake on the other side for inadequately communicating with the gods. The crowd became very upset, and some of the leaders, including Stentorius, were chased through the town before soldiers restored order.

Stentorius then lived a precarious existence with a bodyguard, but priests bribed one of his servants to put poison in his food, so he died a painful death.

Looking back at this life from just after its end, Marguerite expressed frustration at having been intimidated by the priests. She could not see what she could have done differently, except not speak out at all, or speak out only in some way that was not a public challenge to the priests, even though they were making it difficult for the republic to function. She was upset that she had the courage to speak out and had died as a result, even though she had gained a new sense of the divine. In her modern persona, she told me she felt some people were still behaving like the ancient priests, and she still felt victimized by that. So I suggested we look at another past life to see if we could get a different angle on things.

When Marguerite found herself as a healer in ancient West Africa, she was initially delighted. "At last," she thought, "I am working with the divine and getting recognition for it." She was a woman wearing feathers and a raffia skirt and waving a fly whisk. She was treating her sister, who had just come through a difficult childbirth, but her treatment was ineffective, and her sister died. This was devastating, not the least because it was rare for her patients to die, and she began to worry about the efficacy of her approach. Marguerite (we never discovered her African name) had learned the techniques from a healer a few villages away, where she had been told that humans are not in control of the spirits. However, Marguerite became cynical about the vagaries of the spirits and the fact they were not biddable, and she wanted to find a way to be in control and provide an effective way of making things happen.

She became involved with darker practices. A young child from another village was kidnapped and sacrificed. Marguerite did not admit immediately who had carried out the sacrifice. After seeing several lives in which she had been the victim, it was such a shock to become aware that this time, she herself had nothing to be proud of, for it was Marguerite's ancient African embodiment who performed the child sacrifice. In this way, she thought she gained the child's life force and therefore more power in the eyes of the villagers, particularly with her skill against disease. She did become more effective and became much more respected. As a powerful spirit healer, life went very well for a while. But eventually she began to feel fearful within herself, presumably because she had overstepped the boundaries, and at last, she killed herself with a knife to her own throat. (7)

After she died and returned to the spirit world, Marguerite looked back over the life and realized that wanting to be effective had gotten totally out of hand, as she had been unable to realize or accept that her sister's life was unfolding as it should. She realized she was right that her issues were about personal power and the need to make things happen: "It's hard to watch people suffer, but I have to be patient with the healing process."

Then Marguerite talked again to her guide, Banonda. He told her that in this session she had resolved many imbalances. It was now time to manifest a nonmanipulative, noninterfering, nonviolent personal power and to experiment with being effective and being heard. Banonda was encouraging and was enjoying the conversation. He told Marguerite to overcome her own fear, as people need to hear her this time and that "it is appropriate now." He told her to let things unfold at their own pace—"it's all about timing." He said that if things go off-track, he will give a warning sign so that Marguerite can slow the pace. If she is on the right track, there will be a positive response. He also told her that she does not have to fight the battle with the opposition this time—that others will do it.

Marguerite left after this session feeling much more upbeat and also much calmer and less worried about the outcome. At the time of this writing, she has almost finished her book about her own take on spirituality and has taught her material to many interested people.

I feel that she needed to see herself in a "bad" light as the perpetrator of a crime, in addition to experiencing herself as the victim, in order to break her inner fear about facing opposition. When we realize that we ourselves can choose to act either for good or for bad, this reduces the power of any opposition. We become aware that the people on the opposing side may hold their opinions just as honestly as we hold our own, and that mostly they are not inherently evil.

It is often difficult to allow oneself the unpleasant experience of "being the villain." We can become accustomed to seeing ourselves as victims in many aspects of our lives, assuming everyone from the traffic cop to the tax man is out to get us! It was easier for Marguerite to see herself in a "wicked" role once she had visited the spirit world, in which we all see ourselves as equal and gain a clearer understanding of the swings and roundabouts of karma—that it is all planned and chosen, and that we are generally on the right path.

---

(1) The immortal character of that portion of a soul remaining in the spirit world in a pure state is not altered by the melding of the other portion with a human being on Earth. However, the Earth portion of this energy can be contaminated by a disturbed human brain combined with a harsh life of trauma. In this sense, for the period of incarnation, the two parts of the soul may indeed be not quite the same as we see between Peter and Adabba. See soul contamination, LBLH 107, 182. Also, in this case, it would seem that

Adabba is not a companion soul from Marguerite's primary group but an affiliated soul from a secondary spirit group selected to work out his anger issues in the Australian life with her. See DS 265.

(2) Adabba appears to be an affiliated soul from a secondary group rather than the client's own primary soul group. Adabba also is quite active conducting Marguerite around with only part of his soul energy since Peter has the balance on Earth. Readers should know that the amount of activity a soul engages in within the spirit world during those periods when part of its energy is incarnating depends upon the volume left behind. Naturally, a soul in a pure energy state operating in the afterlife with only 25 percent or less is not going to be as active as a soul with 50 percent or more of pure energy. As has been said, a typical soul brings 50–70 percent of its entire energy into the new human body. However, the soul's state of advancement is another variable to consider. Advanced souls at level III and above can be more active in the spirit world with less energy.

(3) For a detailed analysis about the advancement of individual companion souls to higher levels, see DS 265, 320–323.

(4) For descriptions of spiritual games using energy bolts, see DS 310–311. For other types of spiritual recreation in the afterlife, see DS 304–315.

(5) Typically, incarnating souls advancing to the intermediate levels will choose one gender over another about 75 percent or more times in their lives on Earth. One of the indicators of reaching level III is that gender choices are more balanced; see DS 263.

(6) The differences between a soul mate versus our associations with companion and affiliated souls in our existence are complex in human society. In some lives, we may have little or no association with our true soul mate for specific karmic reasons. See community dynamics, DS 259–266. For information as to why we might have the "wrong" mate in life who is not a soul mate, specifically see DS 261 and LBLH 129–132.

(7) Some people have the mistaken impression that we advance forward in every life with our karmic development. Sometimes learning involves our slipping backwards from one life to the next. For a graphic example of long-term slippage in one area, see DS 215–216 and case 38, 216–218.

25

EVOLUTION
of a
SPIRITUAL PARTNERSHIP

Jonathan Yorks
(BOSTON, MASSACHUSETTS)
PSYCHOTHERAPIST, LBL TRAINING ASSISTANT
FOR TNI, SOUL SELF PSYCHOLOGY, AND CLINICAL
AND SPIRITUAL REGRESSION HYPNOSIS THERAPY.

This story shows how seemingly opposite personalities on Earth can really be complementary souls who have connections in the same soul group in the spirit world with the same lessons. Ron and Sharon find that they have been helping each other meet their own personal goals through past lifetimes and spiritual time together, and that they have significant effects today as they assist each other toward understanding their life purpose. While this couple must take responsibility for their own problems individually to avoid self-defeating behavior, by working together as a couple these tasks become less burdensome and more productive. Outward goals must satisfy internal needs as an essential element for living and long-term growth. From this case, we will see the beauty of having a compassionate relationship in the spirit world before physical life begins between two souls working in unison, and why nontraditional therapeutic methods of exposing this fact can be of great value in couples counseling on Earth.

WHEN RON AND Sharon came to me, they knew they had met each other for a reason, but it was not specific, and they felt stuck in their relationship. They had met late in their lives, Ron in his fifties, Sharon in her early forties, both after second marriages. Ron was working as a CEO of a small health care organization and Sharon as contracted help. They wondered about the direction of their relationship. What came out of their LBL experience was a deepened understanding of how souls evolve through spiritual partnership.

Ron admitted feeling most comfortable in positions where he has power over situations and people. We found the resonance for this characteristic in his most recent incarnation as a woman who had died tragically in Yugoslavia after being raped and shot by German soldiers during World War II. Sharon was not in this life with Ron, and indeed we will see that their past lives together are intermittent. Apparently, this practice allows both to grow individually before coming together again in other lives. All souls within soul groups have their own formulas for working together or apart in their incarnations to achieve goals.

Ron left this past life with a feeling of helplessness and powerlessness that he counterbalances today by doing his best to be in positions of authority in both his professional and personal lives. He illustrates this in his relationship with Sharon when he becomes highly agitated, inflexible, and argumentative during disagreements. Sharon is a self-described soft soul with openly loving energy who complies to avoid power struggles and keep the peace, and yet I sensed elements of passive aggression in Sharon's relationship with Ron that was causing her conflict.

I took Sharon first into her past-life and afterlife experiences. Entering the spiritual gateway might not always be from an immediate past life if we are working with other past lives in session. In this case, generally I like the client to choose the past life they want in experiencing a death scene in order to avoid a very traumatic one. Sharon found there was an earlier past life with Ron as general store owners on the American plains in the last century. Here, their gender roles were reversed from today. Sharon described a life filled with frustration as a husband unable to placate the dissatisfactions of a wife (Ron) who resented being a homemaker raising children. Today, Sharon now tends to acquiesce when challenged with Ron's dissatisfactions. We would later find out that Sharon and Ron had a soul agreement to help each other intermittently over long time periods to advance their understanding of the use of free will in terms of being themselves while still advancing together.

Sharon was also the first to go through the life-between-lives process. She became aware of her journey in the use of free will on her first stop in the spirit world, while meeting with her Council of Elders. Her spiritual name is Ioplex—Plex for short. She saw herself as more feminine in her energy, having a medium-blue core with a pink edge. (1) This was useful information for Sharon. She described her soul's character as stubborn, sensitive, brave, and the one who strives for eternal balanced wisdom. There are two guides in the soul group where Sharon and Ron are members. The guide that works chiefly with Sharon is called Ryo, who is deep blue in color throughout his form. Ryo was waiting for her at the council meeting. She called him a wise mentor and friend. Plex also reported that her council was made up of four members, chaired by a deep purple light being called Ila, who had a very businesslike approach. I will pick up on our dialog at this point in the LBL session.

JONATHAN: Plex, what can Ila tell us about what you are working on as a soul?

SHARON: She says I have been trying to understand the use of free will as it relates to authority over others.

J: How are you doing with this?

S: I struggle with it. I have had many lives in leadership positions, but I would overpower (doing this in order to overcompensate for this soul's more natural disposition). I finally came to understand my use of free will within a role of authority in my life in Africa.

J: What can you tell me about that life?

S: My name was Tirtha. I was a tribal princess around 1000 BC. It was a life that also involved compassion. I set up what would be considered educational programs about food and shelter for women in the tribe who had lost their husbands to battle.

J: Tell me something about why you would go about doing that?

S: In this tribe, the men were responsible for food and shelter. There was a big battle with a rival tribe, and many men were killed. Women and children were left on their own after this battle, and I did something about it. (Sharon obviously felt good relating this aspect of her story.)

By experiencing empathy in the life as Tirtha, where she was more comfortable in the use of compassion over power, Plex was able to develop her understanding of free will in positions of authority so her own natural inclinations would surface. Ron, we would later discover, had rather the same lesson to learn himself. There was also an interesting lesson for Plex about the choice of life bodies. Up to the incarnation of Tirtha, Plex had chosen mostly male lives with strong bodies because of the belief it would increase the likelihood of surviving the hardships of human life, including the domination of women then prevalent on Earth. When she finally chose a life with a strong female form, she discovered an emotional system that she felt was more advanced than human males and better suited to her natural immortal character as a soul. (2)

While Sharon evidently had associations with Ron in other cultural areas of the world, such as China and Egypt, she reported in her trance state about her most recent past life with Ron, which had occurred in England in the late nineteenth century. This was a life with Ron after their earlier past life together on the Western plains. She described being a woman named Amelia married to a man named Stanley (Ron) with money and power. Stanley had died running into a burning stable to save his prized horses. She admitted in our pre-session discussion that in her present life, when she and Ron would argue, she would experience an overwhelming feeling of dread that he would suddenly leave her and not return. Because of this past-life imprint on her current body, during contentious arguments Sharon would subsequently back down. Yet, it was not until she encountered Ron in her soul group during our session that she began to understand the opportunity their relationship today offered her for the growth of her soul.

After the council, Plex met with her soul group. Ron was the first to come forward, and she called him Rahia. His energy was male, with a green core color and a lavender halo rather like her own halo tone. She described his soul character as filled with compassion. It is this quality of Rahia's character that Plex now likes to be in a relationship with since her life as the African princess, where she learned much about herself, although she was not with Rahia in that life. During our session, there was a point when Plex and Rahia exchanged an embrace within their soul group, emanating a feeling of deep love between them. I then asked:

J: As you and Rahia embrace, tell me—was there a life of real significance that might give us insight into your current relationship together?

S: Yes.

J: Which life was it?

S: It was our last life together in England—my life as Amelia.

J: How does that life give us insight into your relationship with Ron today?

S: I had chosen a role of submissiveness during a culture of oppression, where men controlled women like property.

J: (continuing to press the client) And how does this give us insight into Sharon and Ron's relationship?

S: I have chosen to continue the lessons which I must learn as Plex in our current life together. I work for him, and he is my boss. I am working through the feelings of opposition I had with him in my life as Amelia, and Rahia is working through his impulsivity and need to dominate others.

J: What is significant about this?

S: This is something we also work on as a couple. The roles we have in our work relationship are necessary so we can maneuver through it in our personal relationship. We are both exploring the use of free will, and this helps us in our individual way of learning about it.

J: In what way?

S: Because, as Sharon, I have a tendency to submit to aggressive energy, and Rahia (Ron's soul) is working through not controlling others (but so far has been unsuccessful in this life). We unconsciously draw out from each other the issues we are working on.

J: What issue are you both working on specifically?

S: I am trying to understand the use of free will as it is paired with feelings of oppression, and Rahia is trying to understand how to be in positions of power without the need to control. I am a good pairing for Rahia, because I have already gone through this understanding (with the same issues). I can be compassionate with his struggles, reminding him of his spiritual nature and also as a healing, compassionate soul.

Sharon left her session with a deepened awareness of her relationship with Ron that she was committed to fulfill. Now it was time for Ron to explore his past-life and LBL experiences.

Ron first became aware of his journey with free will issues in his past-life regression, not in England but rather in western China's Sun Chi province in the eighteenth century as a man named Machii. Working with couples in LBL, one finds that, although their souls were together in a number of past lives, certain significant lesson learning may not take place in the same life together. Partly it is the human body they occupy, and partly it is what is going on environmentally in the life. Each soul is impacted in a different way, depending upon a variety of conditions. The soul of Rahia, in the body of Machii, lived as a field worker on a feudal lord's land who took much and gave little back, just enough to survive.

Machii angrily struggled with his feelings of mistreatment and subjugation until he married a loving and compassionate woman, Xian (Sharon), to whom he could dedicate his life. Her kind dedication ignited in him a peace that he could not provide for himself. After his wife died, he became angry once again and eventually willed himself to death. Ron's experience of oppression was meant to advance his understanding of the use of free will in relation to powerlessness. This past-life-regression session would be a wonderful precursor to his LBL session that followed.

Upon crossing into the afterlife, Ron was greeted by his spirit guide, Gypsum, a purple light being with masculine energy. He is apparently a senior guide to Ryo, who is working with Sharon in their spirit group. As Rahia, Ron described Gypsum as patient, nurturing, and somewhat overprotective—a real hands-on guide. (Keep in mind that our guides are assigned to us for specific reasons of immortal character associations.) Among other things, Gypsum reminded Rahia of a very early life in ancient Egypt where he was a slave. While treated well by his master, Rahia found his social role difficult, and it was here that he began his current lesson. We found that Rahia was meant to internalize the message that powerlessness did not equate to loss of self. I had the feeling that Sharon was in later Egyptian lives with Ron, but not in this very early life. We found that Ron and Sharon had shared loving lifetimes with each other only to lose one another early in their relationships on Earth. One or both would die rather young. I wondered what we would find in the life selection room in terms of Ron's body choices.

Ron described the life selection area, an environment where he would review potential life bodies, as a place that projected life-sized holographic images all around him. This holographic field would alter its form depending on the life shown. This environment was attended by two silver light beings whose purpose was to assist in the selection process. (3) His guide Gypsum was there as well. Ron was shown three potential bodies for his current life: a woman in modern Pakistan, an Asian man who lived in the Orient, and a Caucasian man living in the United States. He rejected the life body of the woman and also the Asian because he did not want to live another life of social oppression, especially in that part of the world. In viewing the life of Ron, Rahia would come to find a good fit for his purpose. I will pick up on our dialog at this stage of the session, while we are still linked to the life selection area:

J: Why did you choose this life?

R: It was an opportunity to fulfill what I have not yet fully accomplished in my other lives.

J: What is it that you are seeking to accomplish?

R: To bring compassion into a framework of unconditional love, to genuinely connect with people.

J: If this occurs, how will it affect you?

R: It opens me, releasing my ego-centered sense of self that interferes with my ability to connect with others. I have a tendency to personalize things.

J: What is it about connection with others that you are uncomfortable with?

R: How to be an individual and yet be part of a group without requiring others to think as I do. It also has to do with definitions of self—how one defines their self in relation to an environment of interdependence for collective well-being. It's very tricky.

J: What is especially tricky about it for you?

R: Because I identify with the harmony and selflessness of group consciousness. I struggle with being an individual within a group, but I'm getting better at it.

J: Are you shown anything that might help in your current life selection that addresses this?

R: Yes, I can see that there will be opportunities both personally and professionally where I will be challenged to connect with groups in a compassionate way, where my sense of self will be threatened.

J: Is there anything more that is specific about what you are being shown?

R: I see a series of jobs where I seek to connect institutions to people, and depending on my sense of self, I will either use my free will to try and control them or find the uniqueness within them and bring that forward.

J: So, free will is a test for you here. What happens if you try to control them?

R: I fracture the bonds (energetically) that nurture connection.

J: Are you given a signal or impression when you are in alignment with self and others, when you bring their uniqueness forward?

R: I am given a feeling. It is a feeling of harmony (with his compassionate nature as a soul), an internal sense of peace.

J: What must take place for this to occur?

R: When egos are respected but not emphasized—for the fulfillment of all, not just the agenda of one.

J: As you look at this life as Ron in the United States, are you shown anyone else who may be part of this journey?

R: (pause and then in a tone of astonishment) Someone of significance is entering my life...it's...it's Sharon! I know it's her!

J: What gives you that impression?

R: It's the feeling I have for her in my life as Ron. It just came to me. (pause) I think I get it.

J: What are you getting?

R: She will be a catalyst to help me release my ego and do things outside of my own needs. I have the tendency to take on too much and personalize things and then force others to go along with what I want. She will teach me patience and balance. She will soften me; we are partners.

I can say with pleasure that this couple both showed the immediate benefits from their respective LBL sessions because they discovered their spiritual partnership. This may or may not happen right away with clients. Ron and Sharon have since left my area for another state, where they work together in a remote, wooded place in their own holistic center. In my last correspondence with them, they describe being in their eighth month of business together and say their relationship is filled with love, compassion, balance, and peace.

(1) With spiritual (not human) auras, the primary core, or main body, of a soul's color represents the stage of development, while the halo effect around the edges demonstrates attitudes, beliefs, and aspirations. See DS 170–176 and LBLH 125–127.

(2) The immortal character of a soul may be in opposition to, or conjunction with, the biological mind of a human being. For more details about ego duality in our body, see LBLH 184.

(3) The life selection room is sometimes also called "the ring" by clients to indicate a sphere surrounded by screens. This is what Ron called the holographic effect. During the experience of choosing our next body, our guide is often in attendance, as he was with Ron. However, always there are other highly advanced specialized beings in charge of this spiritual area, who may appear only as shadow figures. Some have called these specialized beings Timemasters (DS 355–370) or Planners (DS 387–388).

26

UNBLOCKING
a
SPIRITUAL GOAL

Dorothea Fuckert
(GERMANY)
MEDICAL TEAM, STIFTUNG AUSWEGE; DIRECTOR,
AKADEMIE FUER HEILUNG; WILHELM REICH
INSTITUT; HOLISTIC PSYCHOTHERAPIST.

Benjamin is the subject of this remarkable story. He is a tall, thin, pale and seemingly physically weak man. Shy, withdrawn, and lacking drive, nonetheless he is gentle, kind, and very intelligent. Benjamin's LBL session enabled his profound, transforming release from life-restraining physical blockages in the head. There is a chronic and painful blockage of energy in his sinuses and in the brow region of his third eye, the junction of his optic nerve and the area of his pituitary. What was hidden behind these blocks, and where would removing them lead?

BENJAMIN'S EMOTIONAL PROBLEMS led to a generally reserved demeanor; he was even emotionally and sexually restrained toward his wife. At the core of his suffering was the unfulfilled search for his life purpose. For a period of four years I worked with him intermittently and then for two more years I saw him for regular psychotherapy, using various skills including talk therapy, hypnotherapy, and regressions into several past lives. There was a focus on his severe childhood traumas, and over time these sessions provided deep healing, but it was an astounding discovery during his life-between-lives session that finally dissolved his blocks and set him onto a fulfilling new life path.

Benjamin is now thirty years old. When I first met him, I noticed the extraordinary expression in his eyes; in my thirty years in this profession, I had never before seen a client with such dark, deep, soulful eyes. I was reminded of artists' portraits of the eyes of Jesus Christ. I never told him this, but later in this chapter, you will read about his own Christ experience.

Benjamin studied film at his university. Frustrated by academic life and disoriented in general, he came for psychotherapy. Having made some progress, Benjamin was inspired to become a healing practitioner; he went to college to learn osteopathy and naturopathy.

However, even there he couldn't find his professional niche. Despite achieving his certification, he didn't begin work in a healing profession but instead worked as a driver, delivering health foods. I found it hard to understand and accept this, especially as by now he was married and had two small children. He was responsible for his growing family, but he was blocked, stuck. Eight years after completing regular therapy, Benjamin made an appointment to experience LBL.

Benjamin brought many important questions to the LBL session: Which part of me restrains me from my own destiny? What blocks me from focusing my energies upon my goals? What is the root cause of my fear to use all my skills and energy for myself and others? What can I do to reach this core understanding and to overcome my blocks? How can I communicate with the earth in order to understand what's going on here? Is there a specific task for my family in our rapidly changing world? Why can I not fully feel and express love toward my wife and others?

Benjamin went into deep trance easily and quickly. Despite his early severe traumas, he could remember pleasant childhood experiences. In the womb, he felt his body as physically weak but enduring. His soul "slipped into his body" during the second month of pregnancy because, in his own words, "my body needed me for survival." (1) He had chosen his body as a good channelling instrument for connection with the spiritual world; there was a "fascination with sensuous perception and the beauty of the earth." The moment of incarnation—when his soul entered his tiny body—was very painful for his extremely sensitive brain and nervous system, especially at the nape of the neck, the base of the skull and brain. When his mother was stressed during the pregnancy, he helped her by sending out light, expanding his strong soul. He received insight that he had come into this incarnation with 85 percent of his soul energy and there are times when he feels he is not utilizing all of it properly. (2)

I guided him into a past life where he recognized himself as a young man called Agathos living within a temple community in an early Mediterranean culture. He could designate neither time nor region, but he knew that many people made a pilgrimage to this temple, seeking cures and knowledge. His work focused on techniques for creating expanded awareness in others; his task was to enhance therapeutic effects simply by concentrating his thoughts. He reexperienced and was touched by the happiness of community life and his love for his wife and children. He was amazed at all the events within the temple, and he was joyful as he participated in the precious knowledge that allowed him to do so much good for so many people. In his own simple words: "It's a blessing."

Suddenly, he saw a scene of horror: Roman soldiers attacking the temple, killing people. Virtually the whole community was murdered, including his family. Though frightened and shocked, he escaped. He carried a papyrus scroll with him—something precious that he was able to save. His trance consciousness could not remember its exact contents, only that it dealt with sacred knowledge for humankind. During his escape, he feared the scroll could get into the hands of the wrong people, so, reluctantly, he hid it in a mountain cave. Then he moved on to the north, eventually settling in a small village where he tried to preserve and pass on to selected people the knowledge he'd learned from his temple life. However, he felt lonely, sorrowful, and fearful. Later, he was captured by his enemies and then tortured, finally dying in prison. He could not remember the exact events, just that he did not reveal the secret of the scroll. All these memories came from deep within, and he observed the agonizing experiences from a secure distance, as if in a movie. Then his soul left his body, and we join him as he begins his LBL journey.

He sees innumerable hovering light beings around him, each of different shapes, sizes, and qualities. He perceives them as "angelic" beings. (3) There is a memory that in former times he was one of them, and he feels their ancient and intensive bond. They take care of the balance of power in the universe and even intervene if someone on Earth calls on them for help. The being next to him is light blue-violet, pulsating in form; his unpronounceable name means "welcome with bubbly joy"! Another being appears as a masculine-looking giant of pure reddish energy. He especially senses the upper body and that this is an aspect of the archangel Uriel, who criticizes Benjamin kindly but sternly.

Despite all of Uriel's efforts—over many incarnations—to send him energy, Benjamin is still refusing to accept and use that energy. It is high time for this to change, for it is a gift. A long time ago, this wonderful being had placed a switch behind Benjamin's third eye, which had become jammed in the "off" position. (4) Superficially, this jamming had been triggered by an experience in his present life, during which Benjamin had fixed an aggressive boy with a "hateful look" powered by his third eye after receiving harassment from the youngster. Frightened silly, the little bully ran away, having certainly glimpsed in Benjamin's eyes the power of his spiritual energy. Scared of his own power, however, Benjamin had decided he would no longer use it in this life. How often have we heard the phrase "be careful what you wish for, for you will surely get it"?

But was this the whole story? The revelations continue as we rejoin Benjamin in his LBL experience.

He perceives his own soul as light, forming a drop-shape and containing the colors violet, blue, silver, and gold. (5) He feels truly exhausted, old, and scarred by his human incarnations. As he becomes aware of this, he immediately receives revitalization within a bath of liquid white light, a treatment from a team whose members resemble bearded Greek philosophers. This team then urges him to look closely at a particular experience in-depth. During an incarnation ages ago as a wise woman, she and other like-minded people experimented, with the best of intentions, to preserve our planet from being vandalized by destructive people. This group tried to focus their mental power in unison, but apparently the experiment backfired. The telekinetic energy imploded and settled behind their third eyes and at the bases of their brains, resulting in mental breakdowns. Benjamin's deep fear of becoming mentally nonfunctional jammed his own switch in the "off" position. This specific fear had already appeared countless times during psychotherapy, and at last, amazing as it sounds, the cause was now uncovered.

Benjamin then receives instruction from his "treatment team" for the removal of his blockage. They advise him to train his third eye; to consciously cultivate contact with his spirit guide, maintaining his spiritual power at a productive level and enabling him to receive regular instructions. It is time to open his heart and, above all, to forgive himself—to give and to accept love. At this moment, he catches sight of a brightly lit form with loving eyes, an image he perceives as Jesus Christ—or, perhaps, a projection of his own Christ aspect. (6) His instructions continue: he must regularly put a rock crystal onto his third eye and drink crystal-infused water. Moreover, it is beneficial for him to link with nature using the "sensory perception of the moment." He can tune in by singing a specific tone, and he receives a recipe for an herbal ointment to put on his neck, lips, third eye, and heart chakra.

The healing team tells him that his task in life is to use his eyes to detect the causes of his patients' diseases—to remove negative pathological energy with his left hand and to transfer healing energy onto the sick body with his right hand. From now on, he will receive healing recipes from his spiritual guide. He must leave behind his fear of Earth's destruction and should develop more self-confidence and trust in the spiritual world. From this focus and trust, helpful forces may assist humankind. Most importantly, he will be able to put all this into action right after the session.

Then came the promise of a visit to South American shamans, a network of like-minded people who, as a result of his connection with them, will spread their healing work. The mission of his soul is to enrich the universe with his thirst for knowledge, inquisitiveness, learning, and integration. He and his family are lights in the dark, and his soul name, Azurol (or Azorel), links with the light blue, silvery water element. He is then given a glimpse of his very first incarnation and experiences rocks in a different solar system outside our galaxy. He incarnated there to experience the consciousness of dense matter, and he gained great pleasure from the awareness that he was united with the whole. His first earthly incarnation as a human being was in the early Stone Age, and he experienced a divine spark in the center of his body. Thus, this amazing and cosmic LBL session drew to its close.

Benjamin told me:

> Some days after the session, I participated in a parent-teacher meeting. During this meeting, I could see, quite distinctly, an angelic figure standing in the corner. The phenomenon was so clear and unequivocal that I almost had the impression that I could touch him, as if he were a material entity. After a while, this being revealed the reason for his appearance in this group; he told me he wanted to ensure the evening's success in order to strengthen the harmony and community of the school. In addition, he wanted the attendees to be consciously aware of the love of children. This event reinforced within me an acceptance of the omnipresence of spirits. I now know we are never really alone or isolated in life. I feel waves of joy about the possibility of interdimensional communication opening up for me.
>
> Now I know where my life task is leading me. If I can overcome my fear of the very strong Uriel energy of my soul guide and let it flow freely through my physical body, this energy will act directly on my own body and on the bodies of those I am treating. With

the energies from my hands, I will start to shift my clients' blocked feelings. Above all, I will receive information that will measure and support the treatments, resulting in an immediate improvement of symptoms and conditions.

It seemed that Benjamin was ultimately led to his mission as seer and healer by the blockage in his third eye. The eye has gradually opened, and he now experiences enhanced psychic perception and healing abilities. At times, he has experienced rational doubts about all this, but eventually he has come to accept his "seeing" talents as a healing gift. The painful, built-up energy in his head has softened and gradually dissolved.

Since his LBL session, upon awakening each morning Benjamin receives healing energy and naturopathic prescriptions from Uriel and other spiritual guides. They obviously act for him, his family members, and for clients he is treating. He wrote to tell me that it is not easy for him to get used to the powerful Uriel energy—that he had to learn to let it flow through him. Benjamin is well on his way in his business and practice as an osteopath.

From his past history, I know that Benjamin had little to do with angels or with the spiritual world, and that he was never religious. When I met him again, months after our session, he had a more lively and open personality and, in great contrast to his earlier demeanor, he could laugh heartily. He now experiences a close connection with nature.

This story shows, on many different levels, both the causes and the results of a single, unresolved spiritual trauma—namely, in this case, the unfathomable backlash of focused personal power. Deep healing was accomplished throughout the physical body, the emotional and mental fields, and on the energetic, karmic, and spiritual planes. Benjamin became aware of the emotional backdrop of his present life—the power of playing around with destructive thought forces and the resultant feelings of guilt. He remembered past-life imprints of violence, which led to an unconscious, physically repressed fear of using his power in his current life task to aid, heal, learn, and enlighten. In the spiritual world, Benjamin accessed the probable karmic background of his blockage: his headstrong and immature experimentation with creative power, albeit with good intentions, that was followed by a disastrous implosion and mental breakdown. On the physical plane, in his brain and nervous system, this theme appeared as an intolerance or reluctance to accept his own strong soul energy (quite high at 85 percent). Energetically, the blockage had manifested in the area of his third eye as a deep emotional fear—a fear of being overwhelmed by his own psychic power, which could be used to ruin himself. It's no surprise that originally, his third-eye vision spurred him into studying film, but now he has other visions.

I imagine him working with his patients as they look into those deep, dark, soulful eyes.

We still know very little about how unresolved ancient issues are transferred into other incarnations. In any case, Benjamin revealed, in a single LBL session, complete insight and spiritual help to solve his central blockage. The factors contributing to his remarkable healing were openness, knowledge, understanding, integration, self-forgiveness, love, and blessing of and from the spiritual world. All these factors came together and formed a healing crescendo in this single session.

I was given the pleasure and inner satisfaction of helping this young man to find his life task—to accept his gifts and attune to the power of his soul energy, and to use it for the benefit of others. One might argue that the changes I have described would have occurred anyway, as an after-effect of long-standing psychotherapy or even spontaneously. However, there is an unequivocal chronological and contextual connection between the LBL session and Benjamin's ensuing changes two years after the end of the regular psychotherapeutic sessions and right after the single session. One could even conclude that the LBL session acted as an ignition spark for Benjamin's accumulated insights and breakthroughs. After all, transformation and healing are rarely the linear results of one single cause; they depend on complex interactions as well as grace. And certainly not every LBL session would lead to such major changes and development. Benjamin's breakthrough experience was definitely an eye-opener on many levels, but primarily together we had removed the blocks to his spiritual goal.

(1) Typically, souls join the fetus between the fourth and ninth month, because apparently in the first trimester there is not enough brain tissue for soul integration with a human brain; see DS 382–386. To appreciate the highly complex manner of a soul joining with a host brain of a developing fetus, see LBLH 51.

(2) For more information on soul energy transfer, see LBLH 135–136.

(3) Many people believe in the religious mythology of angels. Thus, conscious interference from a prior belief system is always a consideration when a client in trance exclaims they see angels, usually at the gateway into the spirit world after death. Jung believed that comforting myths were expressions of the basic needs of humankind. I feel that from our earliest beginnings, human beings have had a yearning for spiritual guardians to provide self-protection in a difficult and often cruel world. My belief is that the concept of angels as religious symbols evolved into a mental archetype for what is actually personal spirit guides. In the early stages of our mental crossing into the afterlife, spirit guides are sometimes visually misinterpreted at first as angels with wings because they float and have radiant light around an ethereal head and shoulders as they come toward the newly discarnate soul; see DS 38–39.

(4) Some subjects in the unconscious state do carry conscious memories, ideas, and concepts into the early stages of their spiritual regression. The third eye chakra is symbolically considered by believers to be the gate that leads to the inner spiritual realms through a higher consciousness.

(5) The meaning of soul colors is described in JS and DS, but I would start with the color (souls) entry in the index of LBLH, 219, and also see the diagram in the appendix, 216.

(6) Conscious feedback in this case indicates enlightenment from a divine spirit that is more metaphysically spiritual than religious.

27

A JOURNEY
toward
FREEDOM

Clare Albinson

(FRODSHAM, CHESHIRE, ENGLAND)
LAWYER, ARTIST, AUTHOR, AND REIKI MASTER
SPECIALIZING IN THERAPEUTIC REGRESSION.

Jodie's life was at a very low ebb. His beginning had been less than auspicious. He was mildly autistic and suffered from a condition called nystagmus, which caused uncontrolled movement in his eyes. Later, he was found to be dyslexic. Then a hernia operation left him in grievous pain and greatly depleted his previously high energy levels. The pain and lack of energy caused detrimental changes in his life, and this led to severe depression. He attempted suicide. Despite his autism and dyslexia, Jodie was highly intelligent in many spheres of life, most particularly in music and art, but because of his problems he was perceived by others to be thick, or stupid. He even felt that his own mother was embarrassed and ashamed of him, and his conditions and his grandfather's cruel attitude toward him had added to the upset and humiliation that she had already felt. He was confused, unhappy, and often frustrated with life, the contrast between what was going on in his brain and what he was able to express was a source of constant frustration to him.

JODIE'S TWO LBL regression sessions allowed him to find the acceptance that he needed for his body's limitations. It allowed him the freedom to be happy.

Jodie's life so far had been challenging. The hardest part had been the resentment that he felt for his own body and the many ways in which it had let him down. He could find no acceptance of the limitations that his body and its many disabilities had placed on him. This lack of acceptance had probably been compounded or perhaps even created by the shame that his mother had felt about his condition. Not surprisingly, his self-esteem was very low, and he wanted to change this. He needed to understand himself and wanted to know what his life purpose was within this seemingly useless body. He wanted release from his dreadful depression. He wanted to be happy.

During regression in hypnosis, Jodie relaxed easily and soon began to visualize pictures of a pretty nineteen-year-old girl who, he said, was "full of confidence and tarty (sexually provocative)." She was making a mess of her life through prostitution and low-life connections and had become pregnant, with nowhere to go and no one to turn to. Finally, he watched her commit suicide by walking into the sea. He heard himself saying to her, "Don't do it! Don't do it!"—but she did. Though he was watching the action, it seems very likely that he was, in fact, watching himself in a past life, and it is interesting to note that, in this life, Jodie had himself felt desperate enough to attempt suicide, just as this girl had. Very often when someone gets it wrong in one life, such as committing suicide, the soul seeks another similar situation in a further life to test itself again. So, Jodie was being tested again—and in his suicide attempt, getting it wrong again—but the attempt had been unsuccessful; he had given himself another chance.

Having gone through the death process to the life beyond, he went on to be with his own guide, Galcien. Because of his very low energy levels, his guide was asked, through Jodie, if he had incarnated with enough energy for the tasks he was to accomplish in this life. The answer was no, he hadn't, so it was agreed that he could briefly receive more. For the next five or so minutes, Jodie was the receiver of an incredible flow of energy. During this, he said that it felt as if he were plugged into a sizeable electricity supply, leaving him greatly energized. It was easy to see from looking at and listening to him that the change had been substantial. Such energy boosts can only be temporary, but it must have remained with him long enough for his needs, because Jodie reported that he had four days of feeling fantastic. (1)

Shortly after our first session, a bombshell hit when he was arrested on suspicion of rape. He was held in the cells, questioned, and charged by police. After his release, he was forced to leave his house and live away from his home area. His world was turned upside down. The woman who was his accuser not only denied her consent to the sexual act, she also denied their previous relationship. It was a harrowing time for Jodie, but he told me that thanks to the regression and temporary energy boost, he had the courage to cope with it, emerging stronger that he would ever have expected. The work he had done helped him to understand his accuser was a sick lady for whom he was able to feel pity. She would have to live with her conscience, while his was clear. Jodie would have to wait for many months for the opportunity to prove his innocence, and that waiting was an ordeal for him.

It was during this time of high uncertainty that Jodie experienced a formal life-between-lives regression as a follow-up from the therapeutic session that had preceded it. He had no knowledge of Dr. Newton's books, but despite this, he encountered much that had been experienced by others, lending a powerful authenticity to the process. Time and again during regression, Jodie expressed extreme dissatisfaction with his body. His less-than-perfect physicality was at the core of everything that was wrong with his life. He went back to being a child, where he remembered sitting in his highchair, unable to speak clearly even though his autism was a mild form. He described the feeling of frustration because the words were formed in his mind but wouldn't come out. It felt to him as if he had been gagged. Then he went back even further to the time before his birth, when he was in the womb. Here, it was even worse for him because he felt trapped, uncomfortable, and cramped. He was frustrated with his body, feeling that it wasn't the one that he had chosen, and in his frustration, he kicked so hard that he broke his mother's coccyx. He had no doubt that his body wasn't a good match for his soul and didn't like it at all. It didn't work the way he wanted it to, and everything about it felt stiff. He never felt properly integrated with it, and everything was a struggle for him. Overcoming this disdain that he felt for his body was going to be difficult for him, but until he did, he would be trapped forever in his unhappiness. We then visited another past life where again he was unhappy with his body. After his death in that life, his most immediate past life, he found himself looking down at his body and feeling indifferent to it, as if it, too, didn't feel like it had been the right one. By now, though, he was dead and free of the heaviness and tiredness of that life; he felt fine. Here, again, there was a strong evidence of karmic planning because of the great disappointment felt with his body in both lives. Leaving that previous body, he was pulled forward by highly condensed, magnetic energy. He saw a light ahead, which became stronger as he neared it. A life-force energy pulled him closer, allowing his initial fear of the unknown to succumb to a loving energy, lifting his mood to one of bliss. He was now elevated to a place where he would have the opportunity to overcome the negative emotions brought about by his malfunctioning body, though even here it would be hard.

His guide, Galcien, a warm and confident character, appeared to him as an androgynous being of pure love. He gave him high marks for his performance in his last life and told him that his rate of development in the current one with physical challenges had been tremendous, which is why it had been such a struggle. Jodie, whose soul name was Yos, had often known his guide to be with him and reckoned that he'd saved him from death numerous times. When he visited his soul group, he described them as "jollity and laughter," all of them operating on a harmonious wavelength. Next he met with his bearded seniors (often called the Council of Elders by LBL clients) in a small chapel that seemed more like a schoolroom with chairs and desks, with his guide sitting behind him. They gave him advice about his accuser of the so-called rape, saying that she was providing him with yet another opportunity for advancement. (2)

After leaving his meeting with the council, Yos made a decision to meet the soul who had been his grandfather. Jodie had hated him when he was alive because of his arrogance and cruelty, and he called him "a bastard" for upsetting and embarrassing his mother about Jodie's disabilities. Yet again he was drawn back to this theme of his disappointment with his body. He took a few moments of quiet contemplation, after which he announced that he could now allow himself to feel differently about this man who had caused him so much hurt. They became friends, and Jodie told him that he loved him and was sorry he had hated him, because he had now gained a sense of the man's love and humility.

Jodie's main goal in his LBL was to discover a route to happiness, so I suggested he ask his guide for help with this. Galcien told him he had been putting too much energy into personal relationships and this was wrong for him, because that was not his plan. His purpose was to travel and to help others. Then there was another moment of inner transformation when Jodie announced that if he saw things globally, the fact that he came in with body infirmities didn't matter. However, he still felt dissatisfied that he would never achieve his human goals. Along with letting go of some of his dissatisfaction with his body, there were still hurdles for him to overcome. At the next point in our work together, Jodie saw himself in a mirror:

> I see myself in the mirror. I'm going into the mirror. (3) There's a bright light there, as if I've gone beyond me and I'm the light. It's beautiful, comforting. My heart is crying ... It's as if I'm not allowed the fruits of it—the warmth and love. I'm there to observe ... It feels like I have to be dead to be there ... I have to go through this to the trial for rape, and then I can move on ... there's a contentment to know that there's something more within me to connect to, even though it is hard.

In the place of life selection, he realized that he had chosen his parents more than his body. He was able to try out the body, but only when it was static. (4) Then he felt confident about it and it felt all right, but when it was too late—when he had incarnated into his body, when he started to move— he felt pain. He still had difficulty in accepting that he had agreed to take it on: "It was almost as if I was tricked into accepting it." After taking time to reflect, in an almost miraculous change of mind, he decided that, after all, he was quite happy with his body, realizing that whatever his incarnated form, he can still learn valuable lessons. (5)

During regression, Jodie became aware of a negative emotion in his body. The effect of this negative emotion was a feeling of heaviness, and this heaviness, he believed, was self-punishment for his guilt at being a difficult teenager and for not helping his parents as much as he could. His parents then joined Jodie, and his father had his arms stretched out to him. They hugged each other, and Jodie said he was sorry to his mother, who told him it was okay. Despite their forgiveness, Jodie still felt guilty, saying that as a teenager, he was rebelling against the world and was confused. This led him to feel morose and dejected, the experience taking him toward more pain rather than away from it. Then, again after another few moments' reflection, he experienced yet another miraculous change of heart. Sounding so happy, he announced: "They chose me! I feel so much better. I almost want to cry. Thank you, Mum and Dad, thank you for having me, for being my parents... It feels wonderful saying that."

Now I knew there was a deep healing taking place. He had accepted that being him was okay despite its limitations. He now had a better understanding of himself; "I feel more complete, and there's an inner feeling of knowing that everything is going to be okay." A couple of days later, Jodie told me that the LBL had "healed his heart."

Unfortunately, despite much emotional and financial cost, Jodie was unable to prove his innocence in court, resulting in his imprisonment in one of Her Majesty's prisons. This was a dreadfully difficult time for him, firstly being unable to prove his innocence and most particularly being surrounded by men of a violent and disturbed nature. Despite the terror of this confinement, he has told me that he has been able to come to terms with what happened and accept it in a way that he would never have been able to had it not been for his regressions and the strength he gained during his life-between-lives experiences. He was also sure that if it hadn't been for this work, he would have had great difficulty in resisting the desire to end his life. He has now left jail and is in the process of rebuilding his life.

I recently heard from Jodie when he wrote these heartwarming words to me:

> I now feel more complete in myself... my pilot light is lit; a warm, glowing light which will never leave me now, warming my heart and mind. My journey hasn't finished yet. All that has happened to me will become clear in my next episode, which I'm not shunning away from.

As you can imagine, facilitating Jodie's life-between-lives experience has been my privilege and pleasure.

---

(1) Soul energy is homogenous, so the portion that is left behind in the spirit world during an incarnation is no different in composition from what we bring to Earth. The differences are in energy volume. What is important to know here is that we cannot receive more on a permanent basis during a life. Jodie's boost was temporary. The decision to bring a certain amount of energy is made in the spirit world based on a number of decisions by the soul, primarily the type of body that has been selected as the host in the next life. The reason an energy boost can only be temporary is that when we join the human brain in the fetal state, it is a delicate operation of melding, and in the process the brain has adapted itself to a given amount of energy. To increase it very high temporarily or increase it at all permanently would, as one client told me, "blow the circuits." It would disrupt and even damage brain tissue.

　　However, we may receive a brief, temporary boost either by ourselves or with the help of a guide during periods of trauma such as a car accident, being in a coma, during sleep, or in an emotional crisis. Some people are capable of tapping into their own stored immortal energy in the spirit world, but personal guides often do this for us of their own volition while we are praying for temporary sustenance, during physical exercise such as yoga, or in deep meditation. See energy restoration, DS 107–108, 116–120.

(2) One of the most powerful therapeutic tools in LBL therapy is the ability of the facilitator to suspend time and engage in the now-time of the spirit world in order to better recognize client problems. The open mind of the soul in a superconscious state has more conceptual differentiation, with less rigid human boundaries than when we are in a conscious state. We are also not locked into linear time during an LBL session. Although we may take a client into the council chamber after a past life, a skillful facilitator is quite capable of reviewing current life trauma in front of the elders

to gain answers to client questions, as our other cases have demonstrated. Much positive therapy is achieved with both guides and elders participating in current human reality. See therapeutic opportunities during council visitations, LBLH 161.

(3) The mirror is probably symbolic of Jodie's mentally passing into the spirit world.

(4) In the space of life selection, souls may take a participating role involving live action or that of an observer simply watching scenes unfold in the life to come. Occasionally, we hear, as in this client's case, of an observer who sees future bodies they might occupy only as static, inert, or suspended human forms. See JS 216, DS 164, and LBLH 175.

(5) Body matches between the immortal character of a soul combined with the temperament of a temporary human brain to produce one personality for one lifetime is highly complex. We have only scratched the surface of this procedure. Understanding the process of how our spiritual planners select certain bodies for particular lives in the future during the karmic development of the soul seems to be beyond the comprehension of a still-incarnating soul. See choosing a new body, JS 221–248; life and body selection, DS 385–394, and LBLH 50, 175–189. For the characterization of a "poor quality" body, see DS 387.

28

I
am
HOME

Scott DeTamble

(CLAREMONT, CALIFORNIA)
PL AND LBL HYPNOTHERAPIST, TRAINING
ASSISTANT AND CASE REVIEWER FOR
THE NEWTON INSTITUTE.

Cast out into the cold, naked and alone... Some souls feel this sense of banishment upon entering the earthly plane from the communal hearth of the spirit realm. Yet their exile is self-imposed, as souls come to realize they must venture forth into the physical to find the meat that brings sustenance and growth.

There are many challenges in the world. In Monique's case, fierce human emotions were the wild animals that nearly chased her back into the warm embrace of spirit before her ordeal was accomplished.

ON AN OVERCAST April morning, Monique sent me an email:

> I have a history of clinical depression, with two failed suicide
> attempts by drug overdose. I have received psychiatric treatment,
> which included the use of Prozac. I have attended psychological
> counseling. I've also participated in self-help groups and read
> many self-help books. These experiences have given me survival
> skills, but not one of them has taught me how to enjoy living.
>
> My depressive thoughts and feelings are best summarized as
> being "homesick." I long for my ethereal cosmic home. You might
> imagine how delighted I was to read about "home" in Michael
> Newton's books. It's time for me to have my own life-between-
> lives revelation. I want to avoid another clinical depressive episode
> that is looming over my head.

Monique was sinking into darkness, desperately reaching out for the
golden ray of a transcendent experience. I felt serious concern about the
gravity of her situation yet instinctively felt we would be guided.

We spoke by telephone, and Monique told me that yes, she was homesick
for spirit, but both of her suicide attempts had actually been precipitated by
turbulent and broken relationships with men. As we set a date for our meeting, there emerged from her voice a hopeful note. Soon, she sent me another
email: "I have begun my homework assignment for the session. My short list
of questions is not so short! Ultimately, I've decided to bring all of my questions and to keep an open mind."

Our session progressed smoothly. While Monique's soul may have felt
some reluctance to incarnate, she could not conceal a youthful curiosity and
excitement at the prospect of a new body and new adventure.

SCOTT: What are you sensing or feeling there in the womb?

MONIQUE: Well-being, very safe.

S: When did you first join the fetus?

M: Moments after conception. I needed to verify that it was indeed
happening. I can see cells splitting. I'm satisfied.

S: Wow! As your body develops—as time goes by—do you move in and
out, or do you stay put?

M: I don't return until the beginning of the second trimester. (1)

S: What do you find at that time?

M: I can feel the roundness of my fingers, attachment to Mother, the umbilical cord ... I begin to suck my thumb. It comforts me, reassuring.

S: Does your soul mind feel this body is a good match for you or not?

M: Yes, a good match. It will have fluid motion, like the freeness of my soul.

S: Is that why you chose this body, or are there other reasons?

M: I need a female body to have children and to be married to Thomas. Also, being female ... I will feel vulnerable.

Monique connected with her soul consciousness in the womb portion of the session, telling of soul agreements as wife and mother and a need to be vulnerable in her present incarnation. The past-life experience that formed the next part of her session introduced another range of emotional lessons. Monique's mind drifted back, not to her most immediate past life but to a much earlier lifetime where she was a young woman within a band of nomadic hunters who stalked game high in the Alps. (2)

S: Are you sitting, standing, or lying down in this past life we're exploring?

M: I'm kneeling.

S: Are you alone or with someone?

M: I'm with Jomor, who's dying.

S: What's happening?

M: I don't know what happened. He was injured—a puncture wound, a knife? I don't know what to do for him.

S: And you're kneeling? Where is he?

M: He's on the ground, lying down on his side.

S: Where is the wound, do you know?

M: I can't see at first, there's so much blood. I think it's on his side.

S: Are you in a city or out in the countryside?

M: We're high in the mountains. It's cold, but it's not snowing right now. There's a clearing of dirt. The trees have snow on them ... the rocks have snow on them.

S: Can you see Jomor's face?

M: I roll him onto his back and I can. He's in anguish, he hurts. Now I can see the wound is in his right side, in the ribs. He's dying, and he knows. He's not able to speak; too much blood in his mouth. I can see he's dying. I've come too late.

S: What was your relationship with Jomor?

M: Not his sister, but love him like a sister. He made us laugh at life.

S: All right now, let that fade, and let's move to the last day of your own life in this mountain life. Be there: last day. Describe what's happening.

M: I'm in a blizzard. I'm lost. My people can't find me, I can't find them. The coldness, I've gone beyond the coldness; it was very painful, but now it's numb. I'm very tired, and I'm just going to go to sleep. I know I'm not going to wake up. There's no struggle left.

S: How old are you on this last day of your life?

M: Twenty-one, a young woman.

S: What do you think about this life you've just lived?

M: It was curious to be dependent on land and animals. I'd not experienced that—to live like one of the animals, to understand them.

S: It's time to move to the moment just after death, and you can rise from your body, and you'll be able to continue to talk to me. Feel yourself expanding to the highest levels ... where are you in relation to your body?

M: I'm very close to my guide. I can still see my body. I regret that it's time to be leaving it. It's six weeks before they find my body and bring it back to the village. A long time, but the body was preserved because of the snow. There was some nibbling on my leg from the animals.

S: Is there a ritual for burial?

M: They wrap me in leathers, and they cremate me. My guide and I
watch.

S: Does your guide communicate with you while you're watching this?

M: No, it's just a silent reverence. We leave with my body burning.

> *In this past life of long ago, after becoming lost in a storm, Monique went to sleep to escape*
> *the pain of living. Yet, it was important during this session to remind her of the sad regret*
> *she felt at leaving a young, healthy body in the prime of life.*
>
> *Soon, her spirit guide spoke, telling her when and why he acted in the past life to stimu-*
> *late her to feel particular emotions.*

S: Is there a time when your guide communicates with you? What passes
between you?

M: He assures me that Jomor is well and fine. He has arrived home.

S: Tell me about your guide.

M: I call him Zion. He's tall, with a stern expression, stern posture. He
wears a black robe and hood.

S: What does he tell you next? What does he say about your spiritual
progress?

M: He asks me what I think about my own progress, and I'm kind of
indifferent to it. I don't really care if I made progress or not; that's why
he is stern with me. I didn't perform as well as I could, but he should
be happy that I agreed to be born at all! Ha, he's even stern with that
answer of mine! He thinks I should be more serious about all of this.

S: How does he feel about your performance in that lifetime?

M: He said that I certainly did learn how the animals live, and I did very
little to understand the feelings of my people in my village. The only
true concern I showed was the death of Jomor. There were other
deaths. My parents, I felt nothing when they died. He's asking me why
my answer is so flippant. I say because I know they got to go home.
But he wants me to feel more compassion.

S: Does he give you any advice about this?

M: Yes. He manipulated me to find Jomor, and he asks me, "How did you feel when you found Jomor?" And I was sad when I found him, I was upset at seeing his blood, I was sad that his life was ended. That he would not be able to hunt. It was a moment of compassion. And this is what Zion wants from me, this feeling.

S: Does he tell you anything else about that?

M: I actually go into a course of study on emotions, feelings. A lot of time is spent watching people, watching my peers.

S: Do you mean watching people on Earth?

M: No, watching my peers in spirit. Seeing when they laugh or the frustration when someone is struggling to understand a new concept. I'm given a lot of time to watch so that I can identify their feelings on sight.

S: So this course of study takes place in the spiritual realm?

M: Yes. (3)

S: Does your guide Zion help you on this course, or are there other instructors?

M: There are other people, like helpers or tutors. And they say, "Look and see, see why he's frustrated, do you see what he's reaching for, do you see why he can't reach his goal? Do you see why you need to know this?"

S: Why do you need to know this?

M: Zion tells me you cannot be a healer if you cannot identify what hurts.

In a pure state of energy, souls do not have a central nervous system as in their human form, but they are capable of study, either by themselves or in a classroom situation, about the complex human reactions to stimulus that causes love, hate, fear, anger, and so forth. Souls acquire this sensitivity during their incarnations and carry this experience to the spirit world between lives. I might describe this process as a form of sympathetic awareness toward the human state of capability about having feelings and what those emotions mean in terms of reaction to events.

For Monique, a clear pattern emerges about her need to understand the importance of human emotions. In her tribal hunter lifetime in the Alps, Monique was somewhat indifferent, even callous, although her guide began to induce feelings in her; then, in spirit between lives, she focused on a course of study in emotion; and finally, in the present, she chose a body that is much more sensitive and vulnerable.

She walks a tightrope in the present lifetime. She needs to feel, but the intense emotional struggles of her romantic relationships unbalance her and threaten to tip her over the edge. The heartbreak of her fractured marriage with Thomas and a recent tempestuous love affair with Jeremy were particularly difficult. She wrote of this latest stormy relationship:

> I know that love is eternal. With Jeremy, he smiles at me, and I
> know who he is and I love him fiercely, ferociously. But somehow
> my relationship with him has been full of hurt feelings, anger, and
> frustration. We turn toward each other until hurt feelings and
> anger lead to abandonment again.

In the soul group meeting, we learn how Monique's lessons are related to the souls of two of her great loves. We also find the ultimate reason for her studies in emotion.

S: You mentioned your soul group; would you like to check in with them?

M: It's a short distance; I can see it from here.

S: Describe the place for me.

M: It's circular. It's like light energy, domed. It provides a boundary. (4)

S: Be there now. Is there anything meaningful going on right now between you and your group?

M: Yes. Thomas and Jeremy (who was Jomor) and I are in studies of the emotions. On our next Earth visit, this visit, this incarnation, we'll do this.

S: This is a plan you three have? Is there a goal to these studies?

M: Compassion, they relate to compassion.

S: So you three are going to come and learn about emotion, live it, study it, really immerse yourselves?

M: Yes. We're gonna take it out on each other! Act it out, sound it out, lay it out.

S: Do you have a primary aspiration?

M: Yes. To care for those who come back from Earth.

S: I can see why compassion might be important.

The aches and pains of Monique's romantic entanglements in the present day are not random events. Her sufferings are not the result of bad karma, nor are they punishment from a spiteful creator. These circumstances were self-chosen and mapped out in concert with two dear soul group companions as part of a grand study of human emotion. All three have agreed to incarnate and interact in order to explore the intensity of human feelings. In Monique's case, these experiences will serve to advance empathy and compassion in preparation for her future work as a caretaker of souls returning from Earth.

Pieces of the puzzle come together; the larger picture begins to take shape. Deeper understandings of her emotional lessons are gained as Monique's spirit guide now leads her to appear before her Council of Elders.

S: Tell me where you go now.

M: It appears very much like a temple. I see us moving through archways; the elders are sitting straight across in a row, in thronelike chairs. There are seven.

S: Good. What position do you take up in relation to these wise ones?

M: In the center, I stand. I want to stand behind my guide Zion; I don't want to be in front of them. Zion's next to me, but I want to be behind him, like a child would hide behind your leg.

S: Do you sense any sort of feeling or emanation from the council members to make you feel that way?

M: Yes, and it's really weird. They are indifferent. It's not really indifference, it's not acceptance, it's not dissatisfaction... I can't tell what they expect from me.

S: Do they offer any criticism or encouragement?

M: They give me understanding of my defiance and my feeling of disappointment and hesitation in facing them. That in itself is a message to me.

S: How do you decipher that? What does it mean to you?

M: It means that you can't scold someone into learning something. The elders do not scold. Instead, they gave me understanding, and I was able to comprehend the lesson and see the necessity for progress.

S: What message is being given to you that can be useful in your current life as Monique?

M: Today I've learned compassion, but I need to learn forgiveness.

S: So the compassion is more from a past life, but forgiveness is the present life lesson?

M: Yes.

S: What is true forgiveness?

M: It is understanding that each creation has their own method of learning and producing, and they're entitled to mistakes, as I am. The growth process isn't perfect, and you must understand that so you don't always remember people for the hurt you imagined from them in the past.

S: "The hurt you imagined from them"—so this is something you create for yourself, this hurt?

M: Sometimes. Souls are not always on track with their purpose. But you have a choice.

S: You have a choice to protect yourself from getting hurt?

M: Well, you can, but then you don't benefit fully from your lesson. You don't have the scenario to have an imagined hurt to forgive!

S: It seems like a kind of game.

M: It is. These are parameters that we put up from which to learn.

In LBL trance, a wise friend once spoke to me of Earth as a testing ground:

> The spirit world's a resting place. You learn, you teach, you reevaluate, but then you have to test what you've learned. You test yourself through living different lives to see if it's really, truly become part of your essence. It's like ... when you've been hurt, do you have it deep within you to forgive? Do you have it deep within you to show compassion? Do you have unconditional love without demands? All of these things are tested in a life. That's like separating the wheat from the chaff.

Monique's session was winding down:

S: I would like you to ask the council some of your personal questions. What was the purpose to be gained from your past possessive relationships?

M: More scenarios for forgiveness.

S: What lesson are you to learn from your interaction with Jeremy in this incarnation?

M: Hmm. What it feels like *not* to be forgiven. It's the shoe on the other foot! Jeremy is a very close soul mate. Not my primary soul mate, but very close.

S: Are there any suggestions from the council or Zion about what you can actually do now in your life to progress?

M: I've been given ears to hear, to listen, to pay attention.

S: Are there any actions you can take?

M: I will be guided in actions, as I have been guided here to you.

As the session closed, Monique was granted a parting gift:

S: Take a last look around and see if there's anything we might have missed.

M: I'm receiving an energy adjustment of feeling less homesickness. They're aligning me that so I won't be affected by that so much.

S: Who is doing this?

M: Two healer workers. They are not strangers to me, but I do not feel them as intimately as I do my soul cluster. This is given to me to encourage my progress toward the very kind of work that I aspire to do myself.

S: What does that feel like?

M: I feel it in the solar plexus, right here. The homesickness is an extreme desire to just be at home. Like "I've had a hard day at work, I wanna go home and get in bed" kind of a feeling. Only I can't really go home and get in bed from Earth to the spiritual home.

S: What does this have to do with your suicide attempts?

M: It is the nature of this spirit to prefer home.

S: So they do something to you, making you feel how?

M: I can see them actually moving the energy of my aura around. They're mixing pink into my white and light blue, creating pale lavender. I can feel the lessening of the need to be home as they do that. (5)

S: What a blessing. Relax, breathe, take all the time you need. Just tell me when you're ready to move on.

M: I'm ready already!

Three years after her session, Monique is still with us, living, working, growing. She struggles at times but no longer feels cold, naked, or alone. She is excited about her new role as a grandmother. She continues to listen and to practice forgiveness as best she can. Here, she writes about some of the insights that she gained from her life-between-lives experience:

> I guess you could call the despair that gave me two suicide attempts, and thoughts of yet another attempt, "homesickness" —sick and needing to go home. But my LBL session has shown me that I *am* home. Earth is real, but it's only an extension of the heavenly classroom. There's no pass or fail; it's simply having an experience.
>
> Living isn't overwhelming anymore. In fact, my thoughts of suicide have taken a change. I'm now thinking that it might be wiser to live to be ninety years old, so I can get two lifetimes out of one.

(1) Souls permanently join the fetus of their human hosts between the fourth and ninth month. While the soul might visit the mother during the first three months, apparently during this early period there is too little brain tissue for a successful merger with the developing fetus; DS 382–384.

(2) Our LBL facilitators often ask clients something on the order of "go back in time to the past life that most significantly relates to your current problem." It is remarkable how quickly a subject in deep hypnosis can sort through their spiritual memory banks and lock on to the appropriate life to discuss. A client might even override a command by the facilitator to go to their immediate past life in order to reach the life they most need to review in terms of their karmic issues today. Apparently, this is what happened with Monique. For readers who wish more details regarding the initial questions asked when a hypnosis subject visualizes their first past-life scene, see LBLH 56.

(3) While the author has explained about soul capacity for studying human emotions from the spirit world, I should add that there is also a spiritual place for further study in private or in groups. I have mentioned this teaching tool before in connection with other cases. This area has been called the Space of Transformation, where a timeless energy field exists that allows soul energy to blend into the field and become amorphous, totally integrating into a particular human feeling or emotion to sharpen their sensitivity to beings on Earth. Souls can capture the essence and assimilate the energy from both living and non-living things within belts of concentrated energy. This space has other teaching capabilities for souls, such as working with substances on other physical and mental worlds. See JS 168, 218 and DS 302.

(4) With some souls, especially the younger ones, there is a sense of spiritual enclosures or boundaries separating their own soul group from others in the afterlife. See JS 83–84, 96.

(5) The receiving of an energy adjustment here is interesting because there is no actual infusion of new energy to upset the balance of volume initially brought into Monique's body. Rather, the existing vibrational frequency is altered in Monique's human aura form to advance the pink energy tones of passion with clarity of thought in white blended to the wisdom of the color blue. A new lavender aura from this mix is designed to assist Monique in her human emotion lesson-learning. Auras for souls actually in the spirit world are far more consistent and slow to change over time than human auras. People confuse these two auras, thinking they are the same, when they are not. See DS 170–179, LBLH 97, 126.

29

I Know
I am
Going to Hell

Tina Zion

(Fort Wayne, Indiana)
Certified hypnotherapist, internationally
known author, counselor, and intuitive.

This case study illustrates how a religious teaching can affect one's beliefs about life and death. What we are taught as children stays with us. Fear-based beliefs can be become a debilitating burden. Amy carried a burden of damnation through life that had severe effects on her. The fear of hell is common for people brought up in some religious structures and even for those who were not. As this case will show, hell is a construct of earthly teachings, not an experience found in the spirit world.

AMY SPOKE IN a soft voice as she sat down for the first time in my office. "I know that I am going to hell."

I was surprised to hear this statement from her. In spite of this declaration, Amy had no specific goals for an LBL, only a curiosity about what might happen. She was so matter-of-fact about her imminent damnation to hell that I realized she had already submitted to her fate. Amy stated that she knew deep within her heart that she would have an eternal life in hell.

Since childhood, Amy's family had attended a small, independent fundamental Christian church. Now twenty-six-years old, Amy's minister and family had convinced her that she was a sinner and was going to hell. While explaining her church life, she admitted to me that she was not yet baptized in her own church because she had failed as a Christian and was not worthy of baptism. Amy continued to explain that on her wedding day, her own minister refused to marry them. She had to hire a minister from a different church. When I questioned her about this arrangement, Amy quietly said that she is not a Christian because she has not been baptized. Amy cannot see any hope of ever meeting the standards of her church and minister in the future.

This young woman continued describing the heavy burden of guilt, shame, and responsibility that she carried with her:

> I agonize over a couple of people because they went to hell because of me. I have guilt because I did not read the Bible to them and didn't do my part to lead them to Christ before they died. I have always been told that it is my duty to tell people about the Bible and to teach them. You are obligated to do this for others.

When I asked her to explain this to me, Amy continued:

> The minister used me as an example in our church one time. He pointed me out to everyone in the church. When I was fourteen years old, my cousin and I spent time with a boy. He was cool, twenty-three years old, and drove a motorcycle. So we hung out with him. He died suddenly. The minister told the congregation that I should have spent the time telling him about Christ and reading the Bible to him. He said that we only have this one time

in life to make it right. We have no second chances. I ran out of the church crying. I knew that it was my fault that this friend of mine was not going to heaven, because I did not take the time to tell him about Jesus.

At home, Amy's mother supported their minister's viewpoint and reinforced this debilitating burden of shame and guilt for causing the eternal damnation of another soul. There was no way for Amy to resolve or repair her mistake. She was told she only had one chance to do right, and she'd completely failed. She continued to explain to me that not only did she fail this man, but that she has failed every person she has ever met in her life because she has not led them to Jesus. This fourteen-year-old girl carried this responsibility for the next twelve years of her life.

After the session began, she arrived at her memory of being in her mother's womb. As Amy went deeper into hypnosis, she seemed hesitant and fearful. Her voice often seemed childlike. She had little awareness of body choice or life plan. "I don't like the feel of my body." When I questioned her about the compatibility of this body and brain, she replied, "I think it is angry too. It is fighting it." She was not aware of anything else in the womb.

Amy continued back into a past-life memory, but it was difficult for her to reexperience. At twelve years old, she found herself in a dress of brown rags, her hair filthy, starving to death alone in a swamp outside of a small American village. She had been banished:

> I just feel like I can't go back to the town. I starve out here. I am alone. This life is just hard and lonely, and there weren't any good people there. I do not like that town, there is nothing good there. I don't feel anything good. I don't feel like it did anything for me. I can leave it.

We moved on to her death experience. During the death transition, she continued, "I am in the sky, but I am looking at my body. I am still by myself, but I am looking down. I am in the trees. I am mad. I am still mad."

I asked her, "What do you think about your death?"

She replied, "Well, it makes me mad, too."

Amy became more uncertain and hesitant. Transitioning into the spirit realm seemed new to her. I encouraged her to notice anything that came into her awareness.

> As I moved away, everything went black. Something is white and flickering. It is real white. It is dancing around and it is coming to me. It is way up ahead and I can't make it out. It looks like it has wings. It feels like I am kind of being pulled. I could fight it but I don't know where to go. The white light engulfs me and then moves back. It is a person. I am being pulled to outer space. (long pause) I can't go any farther.

After long, long silences, Amy realized that she could not go any farther. She must go back and revisit her past life. She resisted and was angry. I helped guide her through her resistance. As she quietly hovered over her twelve-year-old body again, she finally stated, "I guess I need to forgive people. I don't know why. I didn't do anything. They were just cruel, ugly people. I can't forgive them. (long pause) This is a lesson. I'm learning how destructive cruelty and the lack of love can be. I don't need to look at my body anymore."

Amy immediately felt a sense of freedom and lifted quickly away from Earth and into the spirit world: "My guide surrounds me and fills me with love and contentment." Released from that painful time, she immediately discovered her soul group. Her current brother appeared as white light with some hints of blue. She never recognized the others, who remain white like herself. When asked about her group, she stated,

> We have the same problems with people and forgiveness. They are doing about the same. I think we have a ways to go in our advancement. I am feeling some contentment, but it seems like we have more to learn. They are fun. We clown around. My group just flies around space. We are not on Earth but we are in our woods. It is just like being alive again. There are four white lights, and they are laughing. I don't know who they are. (1)

I asked her if the group had any goals for themselves. She quickly replied, "The big one." She seemed to think that said it all. When asked to clarify, Amy said:

> It's all about love of people and liking them. We are not doing real
> well with that goal. I feel like I cannot go any further. I am not
> able to go any further with my guide because I am not ready for it.
> It feels like there is something bigger. Anytime I leave the lights
> of my group, I am just in space. I feel the pull to be back with the
> group. I am happy there. They are familiar people.

Amy's voice became clearer and more confident about issues regarding her current life:

AMY: I have to work at it. I have hardships but not more than I can
  handle. I do not like humans. I would be content to stay where I am.
  No, I don't remember choices. I don't remember wanting this hardship on Earth either. I am trying to accept females, trying for fairness
  and to get it right. I have always been female.

TINA: Are you living this life according to your goals?

A: I am not doing enough with people. I need to involve myself with
  people. I isolate myself.

T: What are you to do?

A: What I dread the most. I am supposed to open my arms to people and
  embrace them and get in with them. I must learn to love and understand people.

T: What is the purpose of this particular life you are currently living?

A: To learn to love all. I am very loving but narrow. I need to be more
  accepting and loving of all.

T: Check with your guide to see how to attend to this.

A: The heart ... just the heart.

T: How does the church or religion fit in with this life purpose—or
  does it?

A: Yes, it does. Not religion, but God's church. God fits in. The creator... all for the reasons I do not understand. The creator of the earth and human beings so... it's just about love, that is all I can get.

T: I want you to check into the existence of hell. (2)

A: (long pause) Hmmm... I got a chill and flashes of faces. (long pause) Hmmm... But I think they are souls in torment. (even a longer pause) Hmmm... But I think now it is their own doing, their own creation. He (Amy's guide) was showing me it is dark and cold. (3)

T: What are you to know about this?

A: (long pause) Hmmm... It is their own creation. Just like me. I am not stuck. It is their own creation. It is a lack of understanding. They just don't get the simplicity! They just don't get it! They just are supposed to seek answers!

T: At what stage is your advancement compared to this?

A: I am far away from them.

T: How do you feel about all that you have learned?

A: I feel good. I can't explain it. I say stuck, but I am not stuck. It is about understanding, but I can't see it. It is perfect, and there is more. I can't explain it.

T: Is there anything else that your guide wants you to know?

A: Love, love, love—that's all there is...

It is now five years later. Amy is thirty-one years old. In a conversation with me, she recollects her past-life experience in the late 1700s where she died of starvation as a young girl.

A: It was bad. I was tormented by everyone. Similar things are still happening in this life.

T: What did you like most about the LBL experience?

A: What I liked most was seeing the other people there. I saw enough to make me a believer. There is a reason we are here. I now have peace of mind. The ideas of heaven and hell are messing people up. It is a relief to know that there is more than one chance to get it right.

T: What thoughts did you have as you listened to the recording of your LBL?

A: I had forgotten that much of this experience was between the lives here on Earth and also seeing the people between the lives. For example, I was with my little brother during the LBL. He is still alive with me in this life, but I remember reading in Dr. Newton's book *Journey of Souls* that only part of our energy is here in this life and some of our energy remains in the spirit world. I am closer to him than anyone. He is the only person that I even recognized during the LBL. It bothers me that I did not even see my own husband.

T: What impact, if any, did your LBL have on your current life?

A: It took a load off and it made sense. I liked it, and it gave a reason for us all to be here.

T: What would you say about hell now?

A: I saw people in pain and anguish. They were in a dark place, and it was cold. Faces kept coming up to me. I did not know anyone. I got the impression that they could have followed the light. Nothing was tormenting them. They just did not follow the light. They seemed more lost than anything. They just weren't trying to see the light. They just did not know. I saw a dark, cold, black place. When I realized that I was in the midst of this dark place, I stepped back. I did not recognize the faces. I just moved forward, and I moved out of it, into the brightness and warmth. Now I realize that the expressions on the faces were not in agony or pain. They were just confused and lost. They just didn't know where they were or what to do. (4)

T: When people read your story here, what do you really want them to understand from your experience?

A: I just got the impression that it is so much simpler. There is so much fighting and killing and guilty feelings for those who have died. You make the choice. It is all so simple. I feel better about everything.

T: Do you have anything else to tell me about your LBL experience?

A: It was so positive. It took away guilt and relieved my conscience. I still believe in Jesus Christ, but not in hell. I now believe we have more than one time to learn and improve. We have more than one chance.

This young woman had been conditioned her entire life to expect the inevitable: a horrifying, hellish life after death. In spite of her lifelong programming, Amy found something else. She was comforted by a loving guide and supported by her fun-seeking soul group. She experienced forgiveness and then freedom from anguish. She did not find hell where souls are condemned to agony and punishment for eternity, but rather a place where confused souls were making their own choices. Not only did she discover fun, simplicity, and understanding, Amy found more than one chance to learn and improve.

---

(1) Recognition of soul group colors, LBLH 125–127. Also see an analysis of white light energy and beginner souls, LBLH 96–97 and 143.

(2) In the thousands of LBL cases I have conducted, added to many thousands more by facilitators in TNI, we have found no evidence of the existence of a purgatory or hell in the afterlife. These are outdated human conceptions designed to frighten susceptible people into religious interpretations of proper conduct in life. In Amy's case, her initial visions of the spiritual gateway being cluttered with "tormented souls" was a preconditioned carryover that hell must exist on the other side. This indicates that she was not hypnotically deep enough in the theta state as well.

   On the larger issue of the human fear of punishment associated with the concept of hell, we have learned many things in this regard through hypnosis. If a soul has been in a host body engaged in evil acts that have caused suffering to others, there are opportunities for solitary reflection and counseling by our soul companions, guides, and masters after such a life. No human being is born evil, but souls can become contaminated by imperfections and mental damage to their host bodies, especially to the less- advanced soul. There are means for spiritual contrition for people who have severely hurt others during a lifetime, but going to purgatory or hell is not one of them. Karmic adjustments for past behavior will occur in our future lives, usually chosen by the offending souls themselves who, with help, will select certain bodies to learn specific lessons.

   For additional interpretations about the existence of purgatory, hell, evil, etc., see JS 49 and DS 3, 67, and 75.

(3) Darkness and cold are relative terms humans associate with their precon-ceptions about hell. In the early stages of their LBL sessions, some clients exhibit conscious interference with their belief systems concerning religious dogma. These beliefs may be confused with actual visualizations when they describe zones of self-imposed separation and seclusion from other souls in the spirit world for reasons other than punishment from a vengeful god.

(4) For more explanations about the rare phenomenon of disoriented spirits, see LBLH 70–71. There are no truly "lost" souls but rather spirits who won't go into the light right after a life because of unfinished business on Earth. For more explanations about the rare phenomenon of disoriented spirits, see DS 72–73 and LBLH 70–71.

30

I HAVE
just a
COUPLE QUESTIONS ...

Teoh Hooi-Meng
(KUALA LUMPUR, MALAYSIA)
HYPNOSIS TRAINER AND LBL PRACTITIONER
WITH THE NEWTON INSTITUTE.

Quite often, the preparatory work for a life-between-lives session can be lengthy. Clients often have many questions; rapport between client and facilitator is all-important, and the LBL practitioner will want to be as certain as possible that each client is absolutely ready to make the between-lives journey. The life-changing benefits derived from the following session clearly demonstrate the importance of such preparation.

ELSIE IS IN her late forties and is happily married with two children. She is a highly paid executive in a multinational organization located in a small town about two hours' drive from my office in Kuala Lumpur, and she appeared to have much in her life that others would envy. She had read all of Dr. Newton's books and had "just a couple questions" about spiritual regression that she hoped I could answer.

When we spoke, she told me she had been feeling rather down of late; furthermore, she had always felt a part of her was missing. Her job creates opportunities for extensive travel, and she'd had the privilege of securing the services of a couple of past-life-regression therapists while traveling abroad. Unfortunately, the sessions did not seem to have helped her much, so she was turning to me and the process of LBL spiritual regression.

Initially, our correspondence spanned a few months of emailing back and forth. One morning in September, after a final pre-session telephone conversation, I met up with Elsie at last. On first impression, she appeared to be a demanding, confident, and outspoken executive who would not leave any stone unturned in order to find her answers. The first thirty minutes proved to be more of an interrogation of me, where I thoroughly explained the concept of life between lives and the work of Dr. Michael Newton. Elsie clarified all her doubts and queries, and as I described some of my other clients' discoveries, I reassured her of my experience as a life-between-lives therapist.

A number of questions had been constantly bothering her, and she hoped to find answers through the LBL process. She sought clarification of her current life mission. Thoughts of death had been uppermost in her mind, and she wondered if this could mean that she would soon be meeting her own death. Elsie was also intrigued to find out why she had been so attracted to metaphysical subjects in recent years; she'd been buying and reading a lot of books about energy healing, Reiki, and past-life regression, and she did not understand the reason for such a shift in her interest.

Although happily married, she had become aware of uncharacteristic and seemingly unorthodox feelings toward one of her metaphysical teachers, and she yearned to discover the source of these feelings. And every now and then, since the demise of her beloved mother when she was ten years old, she'd had a sense of her mother's advisory, protective presence. At times, this awareness had extended to her dreams. Elsie was confused; did these experiences really signify the presence of her mother, or were they just her own wishful thinking? She wondered how she could become more closely attuned to her spiritual self and was keen to discover the identities of her soul mate and spirit guide.

The session was conducted in the manner suggested by Dr. Newton, commencing with the recovery of happy or neutral childhood memories and flowing naturally into regression to Elsie's earliest current-life experiences before returning to her mother's womb. Nothing spectacular happened during these times, but it was encouraging that Elsie displayed a great ability to recall her earlier memories.

The passage to her most recent past life was reported as "bumpy," which seemed to signify a lifetime full of challenges. True enough, she saw herself as a lonely traveler going by the name of Kamal and living in a Middle Eastern country. Kamal found himself walking around the countryside in search of medicinal herbs. He was robbed, beaten, and even tortured during this particular lifetime, and at certain junctures, this soul seemed to be attracted to reexperiencing traumatic events. Aside from the karmic lessons here, a key aspect of our work is to enter the spirit world from a death scene in a former life. This provides a natural transition to our ultimate destination in LBL. On the last day of the life, just before Kamal's death, he reported the presence of three loyal "disciples" at his bedside. Not blood relations, these three people had admired his devotion to herbal medicines and had patiently studied with him for a long time. He died of old age with no regrets; he felt he had accomplished his mission in this life and was now ready to "go home."

MENG: Kamal, how do you know that this is the day you are going to die?

ELSIE: I feel my body is aching, and mentally, I am so tired. The three of them are standing by my side. They do not utter any words, but their facial expressions tell me I must be very sick.

M: What happens next?

E: Ooh, why I am floating in the air? Why are they crying so loud? Ah, I am dead! But I feel so light ... floating. I feel free ...

M: Is there anything you wish to accomplish as yet? Are you able to communicate with any one of them?

E: No, I know I have done what I am supposed to do in this life. I have no regrets whatsoever. Yeah, I forgot to tell them there is a little book that I have written containing my lifetime research. I think that the youngest guy amongst them should be given this book to spread my teaching after I am gone. I trust him most.

M: How do you intend to do that?

E: I think I will go into his dream tonight and tell him so. He will be so sad and tired after my passing on, and I know that would be the most appropriate time to contact him. (1)

I encourage my client to do this and to let me know when her effort has been accomplished. She was silent for a minute or two and, as I waited for her signal to proceed, she shifted her body and said, "I am done now!"

The session continued:

M: Do you notice any sensations now?

E: (hesitates for a while) Oh, I am floating higher and higher now. I am floating out of my house, higher; I can see my house below, my town, my state, my country ... the earth seems to be below me, and I am ascending higher into the sky now. I am within the galaxy, with stars around me. Wait, I am been guided by some energy, this feels really good ... I have never felt so good before in my life ... it is just like going home now. I do not seem to have a physical body, but light describes my body shape. I am transparent and I feel light.

At this point, Elsie appeared to be very emotional, with tears flowing from her eyes.

M: What do you notice now?

E: I seem to stop. All around me are stars—beautiful, flickering, colorful stars dancing everywhere. Strange; I have a feeling that I have been here before. Now the dancing stops, and six—no, five—stars, which appear to be brighter than the rest, start to come toward me. They all feel very welcoming and encouraging. Now, the one on the right-hand side (3 o'clock) comes forward and greets me. (2) No words can be heard, but I know the star is telling me *Welcome home, my friend.* It is just like a message running through my mind.

M: To continue with our exploration together, can you or are you able to tell me what name you are called in this place?

E: Wait—I think it is a sound. Sounds like Hummee. Yes, my soul name is Hummee. (3)

M: Good, Hummee. I am glad you know that. Now, may I ask whether you can help me to assist Elsie to receive the answers to a number of questions that have been bugging her all this time? (4)

E (AS HUMMEE): Sure, I am glad to!

M: What is happening now?

E/H: The brightest star is leading me through the gateway now. Ha, I feel like I'm floating or flying in the air. This journey feels so light and easy. The journey is simply awesome, as I am weightless.

M: How do you look in this state? Do you have a body, color, or race?

E/H: No, I have no body, everything I sense about myself is just light and energy.

M: Where are you headed now?

E/H: I do not know.

M: Please report to me what is in front of you right now.

E/H: I am being led to a space by the light. This space looks like a huge room with no boundary, just a wall that seems to be expanding whenever I approach it. I feel warmth and a sense of belonging here. I notice a strong light coming toward me while the light that is guiding me retreats to my back. I am now surrounded by different colored lights. They are welcoming me back. We are of the same category—it is my own group. (5)

M: Do you feel or sense anyone you know here?

E/H: Wait, let me think. Well, the light located at 11 o'clock is so full of love, unselfish love. It is coming toward me now and encompasses me with its color. It feels so familiar.

M: Look right through and beyond the light; does it remind you of anyone?

E/H: Oh, she is my mom! (with emotion) I missed you so much! Why did you leave me so suddenly when I was still unable to fully appreciate your love? (Client then reports her mother's reply: *It was simply time for me to go home. You need to learn to be on your own, it is all in the plan. However, all this time I have been beside you and protecting you from where I am. In fact, to prove that to you, have you noticed me stroking your hair at night?*)

E: And I thought I was having hallucinations all this time. … So, you never left me, Mom. I feel so much more at ease knowing that you are always with me.

M: Hummee, can you help Elsie to understand why she has such a tendency toward unusual feelings about her religious teacher?

Here, my client's voice changes noticeably, assuming a calmer, steadier pace. Hummee replies:

E/H: Elsie must be aware that this man is actually from her soul group. His role is to help her achieve greater insight into her spiritual development. It is no coincidence that, after first encountering this religious teacher, Elsie has been more in tune with New Age teachings. Elsie should concentrate on synergizing their energies. They will complement each other in their mutual quest for higher understanding.

Here, Elsie murmurs to herself, "Thank goodness! Now I know he is actually my soul mate."

M: Elsie also wishes to know who her spirit guide is. Hummee, could this be the very first light that came to welcome you just now?

E/H: Elsie's spirit guide is not in physical form. Her spirit guide is represented by the gut feeling and instincts that she has been experiencing
all this time.

M: Very good. Let's continue.

E: I am beginning to leave this space, and I am zooming off in another
direction. The light is guiding me. We are stopping now in front of
a strange structure with a green-colored door and a large, high arch
above the doorway. I am being ushered in by my guiding light.

M: What happens next? Please report to me.

E: I can see a round-shaped table with some patches of translucent light
behind it.

M: How many of these patches of translucent light do you notice?

E: Let me count. There are five ... mostly blue and purple lights.

Hummee, as Elsie's soul, describes to me the individual color tones of what
is clearly her Council of Elders sitting in a semi-circle around her. Because
of their advisory, guiding nature, I continue to ask questions in order to
encourage Hummee/Elsie and derive maximum benefit from this meeting.

M: Hummee, may I know why you have been led to this place? Is this a
day of great learning or some kind of judgment?

E: I am here to communicate with these five souls who are responsible for
guiding my own evolution as a soul. They are here to provide answers
but not to pass judgment—I know that. I have been through this same
process many times before, and I do not feel any anxiety as I face
them; in fact, I feel totally calm.

M: That is good, Hummee. Elsie has asked me to find out the answers to
the following questions:

    1) What is her mission in this current life?

    2) How can she be more attuned to her spiritual self?

    3) She has been feeling the presence of death recently.
       Does it mean that her time is near?

Can you ask the council about this?

E: To answer the first question, an elder is standing up and sending the
following message to my mind:

"With love, assistance, and humility in learning, you will become a
healer. Take care in whatever you are doing right now. We are always
here to provide whatever resources you need in order to accomplish
your goal in life."

To address question two, the teacher assumes the role of providing
the answer: "Be humble, and seek your learning as if you were a little
girl. Trust that the little girl, or the little voice within you, will guide
you toward a deeper attunement to the spiritual realm."

A third elder who appears as an imposing goddesslike figure
answers the third question. She states that "there is no death, except
on the conscious level. The transition between the conscious and
unconscious level marks the concept of death. As souls, we do not die
but merely shed the bodily form. The thoughts of death are actually
one's own perception from earthly energy. Be at peace with your surroundings, Elsie, and you will be happy."

Two months after the LBL session, a very different-sounding Elsie phoned
me and thanked me for the assistance I had provided. This is what she
reported to me:

She is now very happy and at peace with herself. She has taken up a
course in energy medicine and has vowed to use her learning to help others.
She even comments that it feels as if she was always destined to learn, for
she understands the energy work much better than anyone else in her study
group.

She can now face her metaphysical teacher with clearer understanding.
She knows he is her soul mate and that they need each other to see the
greater light.

Perhaps most importantly, she no longer experiences any dreams about
her mother. Her LBL experience has comforted her and clarified her understanding. She remembers clearly the messages from the soul that was her

mother, and also from the council member who entreated her to understand that death is a conscious perception and that the nature of the soul is eternal indeed.

---

(1) Some souls are more skillful than others with implanting messages for people in a dream state. See dreams and Dreammasters, DS 22–31, 288–289.

(2) I developed the "clock technique" as a useful means for both client and facilitator to sort out and identify circular soul positions in a group upon re-entry of the soul to the spirit world in LBL therapy. For descriptive methodology of this technique, see DS 143, 279–280.

(3) The language of sound in the afterlife is complex, and nowhere is this more evident in LBL therapy than in the pronunciation of spiritual names. Some subjects have an easier time than others, but asking clients to spell out their soul name seems most effective. See DS 188–190 and LBLH 102, 128.

(4) LBL facilitators may use a therapeutic approach utilizing our soul/brain duality. Here, the soul self is asked to assist the temporary human ego in problem-solving. The use of an immortal soul name helps ground the subject in the spirit world. See JS 93 and LBLH 183–184.

(5) During the initial welcome of a returning soul, our guides often retreat to the background to sustain privacy; see homecoming, JS 27. The same practice by our guides is also used when souls first return to their spirit group after a life; see DScase 47, 280. For soul group colors, see DS 170–176.

31

A Soul Mate
relationship
Back on Track

Celia Kakoschke
(Bendigo, Australia)
Specializes in clients releasing
the past to live in the now
through spiritual integration.

Cassie is a married thirty-six-year-old woman with no children. The reason she came for a life-between-lives session was to gain more clarity and understanding of her life, both professionally and personally. Cassie explained that she had been married to her soul mate, James, for three and a half years, and although she knew he was the right person for her, their relationship had issues. The following history contains a lot of personal details that the author feels are necessary to highlight the impact Cassie's LBL session had on her life.

CASSIE TOLD ME that several months after meeting, she and James had moved away from the city to a large country town, where a year later they married. Initially out of work and with no local friends, issues arose around James's loneliness. In the beginning, he would spend hours each day on the computer, exchanging emails in chat rooms, which, while Cassie was out of town studying, eventually escalated to his meeting an online female friend. Cassie found out about this meeting when, five months after their move, she retrieved a document from the trash on the computer and found a record of an online conversation. The conversation implied that not only had they met, but that it had been a sexual encounter. When James was confronted, Cassie could see guilt in his eyes, but he denied anything had happened.

Cassie's prior relationships had included a man who cheated on her, and as a strong, intelligent woman, she vowed this would never happen again. Reinforced by a close relative telling her several times when she was a young girl that men could not be trusted, she found this to be a challenging situation. She honestly felt that James was her soul mate, yet this deep-seated fear that she was being cheated on and being made a fool of would not subside.

It was around this time that Cassie and James's sexual relationship became very intermittent. As both were now busy working, this aspect of their marriage was ignored, as they were still an affectionate couple, always kissing, hugging, and laughing, and Cassie felt this was more important than intercourse itself.

Cassie also told me that once a month, James would go to a friend's house and get drunk. She didn't like this, but she felt that she was being demanding by putting conditions on his drinking. Following some of these binges, she would ask whether he was unhappy with his life in any aspect, as she felt that drinking in this way often meant the drinker was escaping reality. He said that he was happy and nothing was worrying him.

Cassie had worked on most of her own childhood issues, but James had not. His childhood was very traumatic and challenging, and when issues arose, he avoided dealing with them through fear of what would be uncovered. He had said before that if Cassie were not in his life, it would not be worth living, and had threatened suicide, which Cassie took seriously.

James had been the first man she had ever truly loved. It was love at first sight; she literally took a step back when she first looked in his eyes. No one had ever opened her heart the way he did, made her laugh until she cried the way he did, or gave her the freedom to really express herself. But in the quiet times, her life was in turmoil. She found herself doubting who she was, what she thought she knew, their relationship, everything. Her shame at "not being enough" for him, guilt of not believing James when he said he would change, mistrusting anything he said, and the embarrassment of being "made the fool" were all too real for her. Many times, she thought it would be a lot easier to leave and find someone else, but then she would hear that counteractive voice saying, "But you know he's the one for you."

It was now time for Cassie's LBL session. Cassie is a highly kinesthetic person who is sensitive and emotional. She arrived for her session excited and looking forward to what we would uncover. Her journey back to her most recent past life was a short, emotional experience—her soul consciousness experienced its incarnation as a male fetus, Tom, who had miscarried at twenty-six weeks' gestation. The mother was Joy, Cassie's maternal grandmother in her current life. Tom joined the fetus in Cassie's most recent past life to help Joy's growth as a young woman then. Tom explained: "This was something Joy's soul had asked me to do in order to give her the escalated learning she had requested from losing a child." Even though he knew this was what Joy wanted, it was a very sad experience; he expressed the depth of his love for his mother, and he needed a few moments to comfort her because Tom and Cassie are the same soul. Then, after that brief past life in a fetus, his soul, who I will now call CS for "Cassie's soul," flew up into the spiritual realm.

CS was greeted by her guide, and the emotions were overwhelming. Cassie sat there with her hand on her heart, rivers of tears flowing down her cheeks with the love she felt while being embraced by her guide. Several times she told me to wait or shushed me when I tried to ask what was happening. It was obvious that Cassie just wanted to enjoy being in the moment, so I allowed her that freedom. (1) At times, I put my hand on her arm to reassure her and was able to feel those strong feelings of love myself.

After she was greeted by her guide, James's soul came forward. He is her primary soul mate, and she described their current life as their "celebration life," in which all four members of her soul group are coming together in the same family. One of the souls was that of Joy—Tom's mother, Cassie's maternal grandmother—and the other was Cassie's nephew Chas, with whom she has a strong affinity. Joy had died when Cassie was a child, and CS received confirmation that Joy's soul would return, this time as a daughter to Cassie and James. Part of CS's "reward" for coming as Tom was that they would eventually incarnate as a family group. The last time they all incarnated together in a close family group was far back in time. Although soul mates, the souls of Cassie and James had not been together in life recently, because their growth required working in separate areas. Their shared spiritual love, however, remained constant.

This was a very emotional reunion with her three soul group members. CS reiterated that James and Cassie's current incarnation is a celebration of their past lifetimes of individual hard work. She explained that both Cassie and James had difficult starts in their current lives to give them the skills and experiences they needed, but once that learning was in place, it would all be good.

We experienced several stops in the spirit realm, including a place like a laboratory in which CS works with energy. The energy work involves combining emotional energy for healing in an equation of sorts—"The combination of love and laughter heals most people, but different types of love and different qualities of humor provide different healing results." This suited Cassie's current personality perfectly—that, and the fact that her group was all about fun, laughter, and having pleasure while working in the lab on different projects.

During this period in the spirit realm, CS experienced the place of body and life selection and two visits to her Council of Elders. Each council visit allowed us to explore the reasons behind many developments in her current life. Cassie was reassured by her council during now-time therapy that she is doing well, that everything is as it should be, and that love and trust are all she needs. When I asked if any of the council displayed an item of any significance, she said that one wore a medallion showing a cougar baring its claws and roaring. When I asked what that meant, she replied: "It stands for courage... I need to be tough, to be strong and ready to fight if I need to; to fight for who I am." This cougar symbol has inspired and represented CS during a number of incarnations in which a tough fight and the need to stand up for herself and her beliefs has been necessary. (2)

In the place of body and life selection, CS said that she chose Cassie's body, with its high intellect and a high emotional state, to help her learn balance between mind and body. This was the heaviest body she had ever chosen in terms of size, and the choice was made to help her remain physically grounded while learning emotional and intellectual balance. Cassie finally understood the reason she was experiencing these extremes of calmness and overexcitement.

Cassie came out of the session highly charged, full of life, love, positivity, and that wonderful knowing that accompanies the soul truth that is LBL. As I looked into her eyes, I saw that about her she had a real sense of peace and calm, an experience she said she has never felt before.

CS had obviously decided that, once Cassie had experienced her LBL, it was time for a fast-track life change, mainly on a personal level, which Cassie reported to me four months after her session. Since confirming that James was her soul mate, that their relationship was "supposed to be," and that this was a "celebration life," she relaxed and began to trust more. She let go of the past, of the things he had done, and began to look forward to the future. It all seemed perfect... but there was more learning in store, all of which was made possible from experiencing her soul perspective.

Two and a half months after her LBL session, Cassie discovered yet more apparent infidelities on James's part and again had to deal with his overindulgence with alcohol. Her reaction this time was to calmly remove herself from the situation and the environment they shared. Although the concern remained that he would try to kill himself, she felt a strong, overwhelming sense of calm and comfort, reassured that "all was as it was." Despite repeated fears over the following days that she was being too cruel, these thoughts were always instantly replaced by an inner sense of calm and a deep-seated trust and confidence in the process. This came with a sense of being grounded, and Cassie was constantly reminded that she had chosen this particular body to perform exactly that role. She refused an initial attempt by James at reconciliation, and this surprised her because she found she could do this with love and peace, no anger or hurt feelings at all. It felt like direct input from her soul.

However, Cassie did feel a sense of confusion based on the fact that she had been told in her LBL that this was supposed to be a celebration life for them...and it didn't seem very celebratory at this time! Cassie had taken off her wedding ring, and for all intents and purposes was looking at a life without James as her partner.

After a while, Cassie felt strong enough to write James a detailed letter, encouraging him to explore his own childhood experiences and outlining her own strict boundaries for their relationship. She expressed that if he didn't want to face his issues and wanted to stay the same, that was okay, but then he could not be in a relationship with her.

They met up and talked about Cassie's relationship boundaries, and James added some of his own. He wanted to face up to the fact that he had been sexually molested as a child, and also to stop binge drinking. When Cassie expressed her fear that he would try to kill himself when she had left, he described how he had actually almost died. The night he had attempted reconciliation, he was in the city staying with his family, who have substance dependency issues. He didn't want to stay there, as that was a part of the life he no longer wanted, so he left without anywhere to go. It was a stormy night, and he parked under a tree. A short time later, he looked up, and the tree was wobbling. His instincts told him to move the car, which he did, and as he looked in his rear mirror, the tree fell where his car had been.

With the enhanced understanding given by her visit to the spirit realm, Cassie felt this demonstrated that both James and his soul were making a choice: he had the choice to stay there and die, or to move and go on with life. He had made the choice to live, and with that was the choice to go back into the trauma of his past and work through it. Cassie felt that suicide was no longer an option for him—if he had wanted an out, he would have taken it. She expressed her belief that this was the choice he had made, and that if he didn't work through his issues now, she believed he would come back in another life and have suicide issues again.

Cassie also came to the realization that even though this was supposed to be their celebration life, free will always plays a part. James had a choice whether or not he would deal with his past issues. If he chose to not do the work necessary to get him to their celebration time, Cassie knew she would find someone else to share her life with. Cassie also intuitively knew that if they were not together, their daughter (soul group companion Joy) would not be born to either of them—that she was only coming because it was their celebration life together. Cassie's soul gave her the reassurance and courage to know that it would all be okay, and that ultimately they would both be fine, no matter what choices they made. The cougar medallion became a wonderful reminder for Cassie to be tough and strong and true to herself.

Cassie spent time meditating, connecting with her soul, and trusting the answers she received. She recognized that the timing for everything had been perfect—they were looking at starting a family, and this was an issue that would have to be resolved before they brought a child into the world. Also, she knew that it was because James felt safe and secure with her that these issues had come up now. Until they met, he did not have security or love, and this relationship with her had given him the opportunity to look into his confusion about his sexuality. The feelings that came up when they were intimate (the pleasure of orgasm linked with guilt and shame from when he was molested) would have subconsciously led him to avoid intimacy.

Cassie's direct access to her soul gave her not only a deep sense of calm and comfort but also a deep knowing that all was as it was for a reason, and she was at peace. It helped her as she was almost able to dissociate from her human pain and float above it while still looking at the world through her own eyes and staying grounded. She was surprised at the inner strength and confidence she'd felt at a time that for most people would have been devastating. Prior to experiencing her LBL, Cassie believes that she would have left James, run away, and started afresh—definitely an easier option. The doubt, mistrust, and hurt would have surpassed any hope they had for the future. However, she found that the knowledge she received through her LBL session that this was their celebration life, as well as the direct access to her soul, gave Cassie the strength to overcome her fragile human emotions with such love and calmness. It truly was a blessing.

James moved back with Cassie while undergoing counseling with specialists in sexual assault. Their relationship continues to slowly grow, and Cassie sees more and more of the man that is James emerging. Their celebration life has begun ...

---

(1) When working with hypnosis subjects who are visualizing spiritual events in the afterlife, LBL facilitators must proceed with caution. Pacing, tempo, and cadence are important for many reasons, including allowing the client time to finish reporting on what they are seeing before moving on to the next question. New students of LBL facilitation do not realize that often, clients see more than they report about the spirit world. For many in the trance state, the afterlife is a sacred existence for their soul. See LBLH 42–43, 68, 74–78.

(2) Spiritual signs, symbols, and emblems that are displayed by Council of Elders to the souls who appear before them carry very special meanings and messages; see DS 224–242.

32

FINDING LAURA:
recovering a
LOST IDENTITY

Georgina Cannon
(TORONTO, CANADA)
INTERNATIONAL TRAINER, AUTHOR,
SCHOOL CLINIC DIRECTOR, AND MIND/
BODY/SPIRIT CLINICIAN USING HYPNOSIS
AND REGRESSION THERAPIES.

For most of us, memories of prior lives are hidden away deep within the subconscious. Yet, with a skilled facilitator using hypnotic trance, they can emerge so that previously diffuse and hidden memories may crystallize and resurface, bringing wisdom and understanding to this current lifetime.

Many folks journey from life to life with no conscious knowledge of the previous life or the person they used to be. And yet we live full, mostly complete lives without that knowledge.

Imagine, though, what it would be like to be in this lifetime having shifted from one identity to the next without the conscious memory of who you are and how you lived the first part of your life. This chapter describes just such an incredible experience, and how past-life and between-lives regressions truly helped one particular young woman.

THIS IS THE extraordinary story of Laura, who at age seventeen found herself wandering the streets of Toronto with no knowledge of who she was or how she had come to be there. Fortunately, a young woman from Quebec who was waiting at a bus stop saw Laura crying and alone. The woman asked if she could help, and on hearing the story, she took Laura home for some tea, something to eat, and a phone call to the police, to see if there had been any accidents or people reported missing.

Nothing, no one.

This wonderful young woman gifted Laura with a temporary home in which she stayed for a few months, living under an assumed identity and frightened about her past. She wondered who she had been and what terrible thing she had done that needed to be totally blocked from her consciousness. She scanned the papers daily for reports of missing persons, but none matched her description. From that time until she came to see me more than forty years later, Laura remained in complete ignorance of her true identity.

A few months into her new, mysterious life, Laura met her future husband, Don. She had become a ballroom dancing teacher, and he was a new student. They felt an instant connection, as though they had known one another in a previous life.

Through decades of their marriage, Don was a rock, supportive and determined to help his wife discover her true identity. They explored all avenues for identification discovery, including fingerprinting, Interpol, the police, the Royal Canadian Mounted Police, detectives, lawyers, and the Internet. "At least I knew I didn't have a criminal record," she joked. They couldn't travel beyond Canadian borders, though, as Laura had no citizenship documentation or health history.

They bought a house in the suburbs, danced their way through the evenings at the local nightclubs, and spent weekends and holidays on canoe trips, camping out deep in the wilderness to the sounds of howling wolves.

For more than a decade, they lived the Grizzly Adams lifestyle, building their own house in heavily forested crown land three miles away from the nearest trapper neighbor, canning vegetables on a wood-burning stove, fish-ing for bass and snaring rabbits. Often they would ski home with a couple of rabbits for the stew pot. They lived a happy, fulfilling life together for thirty-five years.

Finally, Don confided the secret to a lawyer friend, who suggested hypnotic regression. Out of fear for what she might find, Laura waited another nine years before considering hypnotherapy. Around that time, a chiropractor friend told them about a lecture I had given on past-life-regression therapy. Don called me immediately.

Laura was sixty when she first came to see me. Laura and Don came into the clinic for their first meeting and hypnosis session. In her own words, she wanted to know "Who am I, and where am I from?"

She was concerned about what she might have done and wanted to know whether she had a family or whether she'd hurt someone. She also considered that it might be significant that she was terrified of riding in cars.

I said I couldn't promise anything, but that I had success in the past helping people to recover lost memories. However, we couldn't get started right away. She was prone to occasional epileptic seizures and high blood pressure, so I asked that we have a letter from her medical doctor before doing any hypnosis. Although there was no formal hypnosis at that first meeting, I gave her a hypertension release CD because I felt it might allow her to practice relaxing to the sound of my voice.

Two weeks later, Laura came to the clinic with the doctor's letter, ready to experience past-life regression. Maybe she would find out more about herself that way and whether she had known Don in a previous lifetime. It seemed a good idea, as on the "way back" we could explore the re-entry into this life and maybe get some childhood clues. But although she experienced two very detailed lives, there was no information about her current lifetime.

A month later, Laura came into the office worried and scared. Scheduled for an angiogram and echocardiogram, she was frightened she might die without knowing who she was. We talked about it being much too soon for her to die—"you have lots of dance teaching left to do"—and she agreed. I facilitated a regular hypnosis session using mind/body healing techniques and future pacing so that she could see and experience herself celebrating Christmas. I connected her again with her guides and asked them to stay with her during the procedures.

It was almost a year later before Laura returned to the clinic. It turned out that she had needed open heart surgery. She told me: "I'm ready to find out now."

I asked and received permission to "do something different." I facilitated her back directly into the womb and then beyond into the interlife, where she literally zoomed up to the gates: "It looks like white mist, but friendly, not frightening, and there's people moving around in the mist...moving toward me. I feel this overwhelming love, and it's strange how light and free I feel."

There were four beings—"I can feel them as well as see them, they're surrounding me with a feeling that it's hard to explain. Beautiful blue colors, and gold and pink. There's a color I haven't seen before, I don't know what to call it...I feel like I'm buzzing, like I'm vibrating, and I realize I'm like they are. I'm free!" Laura started to laugh and became very animated. I was concerned she would bring herself out of hypnosis, but the laughter turned to gentle tears as she kept repeating, "It's all so beautiful...so gentle and beautiful."

This was a profound and emotional time for Laura. Released from her physical body, she realized she was more than just that. Reluctant to move away from that space and from this group, she lingered for a long time at the gateway with her greeters, who appeared to be both her soul circle and her "wisdom elders," as she called them. As we asked the purpose of this life struggle, she discovered she had chosen this lifetime to learn patience and forgiveness and was strongly urged to join parents who were frightened when they knew they were pregnant.

As we probed more, it became very clear that her group was intent on giving her the peaceful soul connection she had lost over the years, and considered everything else secondary or not important at that time. Every time we tried to move forward, we were told "not yet." We couldn't get any more information from the group about her current life; they were more interested in letting her reconnect with her true self. So much so, that when we asked after a while if it was time to move forward to another station in the interlife, we were told that "your learning for now is complete."

I was concerned that although Laura had this powerful experience, it still hadn't given her the information she needed. As we slowly journeyed back from the interlife to reenter the womb, there was a sudden jolt as her vibration lowered, and she encountered her moment of conception. She heard voices fighting and felt the energy of discord from that moment. The beauty and peace in her face and aura had disappeared, and her energy became fractured as she watched and felt herself growing toward birthing—and remembering her current early life.

Those first years were uneventful; herself and her mother, and at age two she recalled a baby sister. "I'm the big girl. I have a new baby sister." By the age of ten, Laura recalled a baby brother, and "We live in a place called Georgia. My dad's name is Barry Watson (not his real name) ... I don't know him."

At this point, Laura became excited and brought herself out of hypnosis. I suggested that she relax back into hypnosis and continue the journey so that we could find out more—which she did.

At fourteen years old, Laura abreacted, sobbing and shaking: "I don't like being fourteen, I don't want to be fourteen." We regressed back a year.

Thirteen-year-old Laura talked about moving to Detroit, Michigan, and being "in a house with mom, sister, and brother. We have to move. She has to find a job ... so tired ... so tired. Mom is worried. We need more money. I wish I was old enough to help. All we eat are beans and potatoes. I'm so tired."

Again, I tried to move forward but was rejected. Fourteen-year-old Laura didn't want to remember. (1)

After a gentle healing from her guides, Laura emerged from hypnosis, full of excitement, and jumped up from the chair and ran out into reception: "Don, I know my father's name!" They were both so excited. After a quick hug, they rushed out of the door to go home and get on the Internet.

In the past, Don had regularly searched the Internet for clues to Laura's identity. Weekly, he looked through all the missing persons websites for newly posted photographs and descriptions in the hope of finding something about Laura as a child. Now that he had names, he could start searching genealogy websites.

On Gencircles, he found a Barry Harold Watson born in a small town in Georgia. This Barry Harold Watson listed children with the same first names! Don kept checking. He found Barry Watson's obituary, which listed the same names for his children. Excited but cautious, he wanted to be sure it was the right family.

Concentrating on the brother, as he guessed that the sisters would be married and have different surnames, he worked through phone numbers of listed Barry Watsons across the United States and started making phone calls, but no luck. Finally, he tried a long shot and posted a notice on the Cousin Connect website.

Unexpectedly and to Laura and Don's elation, a month later, a response was posted: "Hi, I am the sister who Laura is seeking. My home phone number is..."

It was deeply moving to them to know that a family member had been searching for Laura. After many years of wondering, worrying, and speculating, Laura would at last be reunited with her lost self and lost family. It was an exhilarating, wonderful moment.

After the initial exciting phone calls, DNA tests proved that Laura had indeed found her sister and family.

Laura is adamant about staying in the now. She doesn't want to delve into the time of the lost years but rather relish what she has discovered for today and tomorrow. Mystery is not an issue for Laura. Her life has been positively transformed. She now has a passport, a family, and an identity, with dual citizenship in the United States and Canada. She has traveled to the United States to meet her family (she is one of six!). She now travels to Europe and literally anywhere she wants to! She is so grateful that every time she obtains another piece of documentation, like her United States' citizenship,

Canadian immigrant's papers, or a travel visa, she phones me in excitement to say thank you.

Although I regularly facilitate past lives and interlife or life-between-lives sessions, this one will always have a special place in my heart. It is a testimony to the power of love—from the kind stranger who originally gave lost seventeen-year-old Laura a home, to the dedication and support of Laura's husband, Don, and the never-flinching loyalty of her sister, who in over forty years never gave up the search to find her big sister. (2)

---

(1) Under normal circumstances, it might seem that Laura would be a perfect candidate for desensitization of the traumatic event that occurred to her between ages 14 to 17. After all, this evidently induced her amnesia. Assumptions could be made that this client suffered severe physical and emotional pain during this period, causing her mind to shut down to all memories of her past as a means of self-preservation. Some psychotherapists might argue that Laura will never be whole until she cognitively comes to terms with this damaging four-year period in her life. However, Laura had a perfect right to refuse such specific therapy. The author of this story has told me that Laura felt her future happiness depended on her not unblocking these teenage years. Certainly, she learned a great deal about her current identity by the skillful application of hypnosis, but what is more important here is that through additional spiritual regression, Laura discovered and then connected with her true soul self. It should be noted that all the karmic implications of the trauma she has suffered in this life will be revealed to her in the afterlife. LBLH 66–67.

(2) On a conscious level, there are a limited number of people who may overcome amnesia of their past-life existence without hypnosis. This ability is known as spontaneous recall, and while someone might be able to accomplish certain remembrances of their past lives, it is far more difficult with life-between-lives memories. For this sort of soul recovery, one needs a skilled LBL facilitator. That being said, Laura's case was a more classic form of amnesia with complete blockage of all memories of her current life. For that reason, this heart-warming story is quite unusual in terms of both the broad therapeutic approach used to uncover the core of her existence and then the final benefits Laura received in recovering much of her current identity.

The use of hypnotherapy is a commanding tool in overcoming many forms of amnesic blocks by reaching into the unconscious mind. However, this does open up a larger philosophical issue about recovering our spiritual memories as a soul. Our work has been challenged by some people with the following question: if amnesia exists at birth to block our soul life on a conscious level, are we not tampering with a divine ethical plan by using hypnosis to break these blocks? My answer is that if hypnosis can open up the beauty of our afterlife (or innerlife) experiences, then doesn't this give us an incentive to search for the truth about who we really are and where we came from? If we were not supposed to know about these truths, no amount of hypnosis, meditation, channeling, etc., could remove these blocks.

In my view, each person in a deep altered state of consciousness sees what they are supposed to see as determined by their personal guides. Some people are more blocked than others, depending on such factors as age, state of development, karmic challenges in this life, and so forth. Finally, I believe there is another factor at work here. Why are amnesic blocks about our afterlife lessening in the twenty-first century from the use of advanced methodological discoveries in hypnosis? We live in a world more overpopulated today than ever before, resulting in a diminished identity of the individual. Add to this the greatest prevalence of chemical dependency of all time. Drugs cloud the progress of the soul. Perhaps this is the reason our guides and spiritual masters are allowing more information to be released about our spiritual past than ever before in human history. See JS 66–68, 213, 248, 276.

LLEWELLYN ORDERING INFORMATION

Order Online:
Visit our website at www.llewellyn.com, select your books, and order them on our secure server.

Order by Phone:
- Call toll-free within the U.S. at 1-877-NEW-WRLD (1-877-639-9753). Call toll-free within Canada at 1-866-NEW-WRLD (1-866-639-9753)
- We accept VISA, MasterCard, and American Express

Order by Mail:
Send the full price of your order (MN residents add 6.875% sales tax) in U.S. funds, plus postage & handling to:

> **Llewellyn Worldwide**
> **2143 Wooddale Drive, Dept. 978-0-7387-1527-8**
> **Woodbury, MN 55125-2989**

Postage & Handling:

Standard (U.S., Mexico & Canada). If your order is:
> $24.99 and under, add $4.00
> $25.00 and over, FREE STANDARD SHIPPING

AK, HI, PR: $16.00 for one book plus $2.00 for each additional book

International Orders (airmail only):
> $16.00 for one book plus $3.00 for each additional book

Orders are processed within 2 business days. Please allow for normal shipping time. Postage and handling rates subject to change.

Journey of Souls
Case Studies of Life Between Lives

Michael Newton, Ph.D.

This remarkable book uncovers—for the first time—the mystery of life in the spirit world after death on earth. Dr. Michael Newton, a hypnotherapist in private practice, has developed his own hypnosis technique to reach his subjects' hidden memories of the hereafter. The narrative is woven as a progressive travelogue around the accounts of twenty-nine people who were placed in a state of superconsciousness. While in deep hypnosis, these subjects describe what has happened to them between their former reincarnations on Earth. They reveal graphic details about how it feels to die, who meets us right after death, what the spirit world is really like, where we go and what we do as souls, and why we choose to come back in certain bodies.

After reading *Journey of Souls*, you will acquire a better understanding of the immortality of the human soul. Plus, you will meet day-to-day personal challenges with a greater sense of purpose as you begin to understand the reasons behind events in your own life.

978-1-56718-485-3
288 PP., 6 X 9 $16.95

DESTINY OF SOULS
New Case Studies of Life Between Lives

Michael Newton, Ph.D.

A pioneer in uncovering the secrets of life, internationally recognized spiritual hypnotherapist Dr. Michael Newton takes you once again into the heart of the spirit world. His groundbreaking research was first published in the best-selling *Journey of Souls*, the definitive study on the afterlife. Now, in *Destiny of Souls*, the saga continues with seventy case histories of real people who were regressed into their lives between lives. Dr. Newton answers the requests of the thousands of readers of the first book who wanted more details about various aspects of life on the other side.

Destiny of Souls is also designed for the enjoyment of first-time readers who haven't read *Journey of Souls*.

978-1-56718-499-0
432 PP., 6 X 9 $16.95

LIFE BETWEEN LIVES
Hypnotherapy for Spiritual Regression

Michael Newton, Ph.D.

Dr. Michael Newton is world-famous for his spiritual regression techniques that take subjects back to their time in the spirit world. His two bestselling books of client case studies have left thousands of readers eager to discover their own afterlife adventures, their soul companions, their guides, and their purpose in this lifetime.

Now, for the first time in print, Dr. Newton reveals his step-by-step methods. His experiential approach to the spiritual realms sheds light on the age-old questions of who we are, where we came from, and why we are here.

978-0-7387-0465-4
240 PP., 6 X 9 $15.95

To Write to the Author

If you wish to contact the author or would like more information about this book, please write to the author in care of Llewellyn Worldwide and we will forward your request. Both the author and publisher appreciate hearing from you and learning of your enjoyment of this book and how it has helped you. Llewellyn Worldwide cannot guarantee that every letter written to the author can be answered, but all will be forwarded. Please write to:

Michael Newton
℅ Llewellyn Worldwide
2143 Wooddale Drive, Dept. 978-07387-1527-8
Woodbury, MN 55125-2989

Please enclose a self-addressed stamped envelope for reply, or $1.00 to cover costs. If outside U.S.A., enclose international postal reply coupon.

Many of Llewellyn's authors have websites with additional information and resources. For more information, please visit our website at

HTTP://WWW.LLEWELLYN.COM

If readers have questions about any of the cases in this book, they may contact the author/therapist directly from the referral directory located at

HTTP://WWW.NEWTONINSTITUTE.ORG